UPDATES & CORRECTIONS THROUGH MAY 1992

Please note the following changes, not reflected in the trail reports, which have occurred since the first printing.

Virtually all State Park fees have increased and other rises are pending. Expect at least the following:

> Developed (car) campsites: $12-16/night.
> Environmental campsites: $7/night.
> Day use: $5/vehicle.

UPDATES BY TRAIL (T) & PAGE (P)

T1 & T2: Car camping: $12/night($10 for county residents). Hike & bike camping: $3/person.

T5, P31: New ramp makes Walk-on Beach wheelchair accessible.

T12, P55, FEES: Car camping: $12/night ($10 for county residents).

T17,P75: Black Ranch trails delayed until 1993.

T24, P99, FURTHER INFO: 524-7175.

T30, P125, FURTHER INFO: 524-7175.

T31, P128, FURTHER INFO: 524-7175.

T32, P129: Shiloh Park expanded to 830 acres.

T32, P131, FURTHER INFO: 524-7175. Open to mountain bikes.

T37, P151, FEES: Day use $2/vehicle.

T39, P159, FURTHER INFO: 524-7175. Open to mountain bikes.

T42, P170, OTHER SUGGESTION: The new RIDGE TRAIL, Sonoma County's first section of the BAY AREA RIDGE TRAIL, links with Trail #42.

The spirit of the place . . . was a spirit of peace . . . of smooth-pulsing life, of quietude that was not silence, of movement that was not action, of repose that was quick with existence without being violent with struggle and travail. The spirit of the place was the spirit of the peace of the living, somnolent with the easement and contents of prosperity, and undisturbed by rumors of far wars.

—*Jack London,*
All Gold Canyon

The
HIKER'S
hip pocket
GUIDE
to
Sonoma
County

by
Bob Lorentzen

BORED FEET PUBLICATIONS
MENDOCINO, CALIFORNIA
1990

©1990, 1992 by Robert S. Lorentzen
Second printing, June 1992
Printed in the United States of America

Illustrations by Joshua Edelman
Symbols by Jann Patterson-Watters & Taylor Cranney
Maps by Bob Lorentzen and USGS
Design by Judy Detrick and Bob Lorentzen
Layout and Production by Elizabeth Petersen
Edited by Anne Fox

Published by
Bored Feet Publications
Post Office Box 1832
Mendocino, California 95460
(707) 964-6629

Library of Congress Cataloging-in-Publication Data
Lorentzen, Bob, 1949-
    The hiker's hip pocket guide to Sonoma county / by Bob Lorentzen.
    208pp.
    Includes bibliographical references and index.
    ISBN 0-939431-07-6: $12.95
    1. Hiking—California—Sonoma County—Guide-books. 2. Sonoma
County (Calif.)—Description and travel—Guide-books. I. Title.
GV199.42.C22S655 1990   90-44136
796.5'1'0979418—dc20   CIP

ISBN 0-939431-07-6

10 9 8 7 6 5 4 3 2

Dedicated to the Edelman family, Joshua, our incandescent illustrator, May, China and Leilani for being my family away from home and providing love, enthusiasm, humor and reality checks while I worked on this book.

This book is also dedicated to California Ocean Sanctuary, the movement to prevent the degradation and destruction that would result if oil exploration and development were allowed on the Northern California Coast. Save the coast for future generations, whether of people, fish, birds, whales or other life.

NO OFFSHORE OIL!
OCEAN SANCTUARY NOW!

For more information, write:

OCEAN SANCTUARY COORDINATING COMMITTEE
  P.O. Box 498
  Mendocino, CA 95460

LET'S WIN THIS ONE! ACT TODAY!

In memoriam,
Sam Harman
Edward Abbey

ACKNOWLEDGMENTS

My thanks to all who helped create this book. In particular I wish to thank Anne Fox and Margaret S. Fox, the dynamic duo, Anne for her judicious red pen, Margaret for her magic with pots and promulgation; Jann Patterson–Watters for symbols and camaraderie; Judy Detrick for her formative design; Liz Petersen, production artist, for her pluck, joy and professionalism; Bev and Verl Lyons for being there for shipping and receiving; David Springer for his discerning geology; Coastwalkers Richard and Brenda Nichols and Tom and Vivian McFarling for sharing their invaluable knowledge of Sonoma County trails.

Thanks to my dedicated and proficient proofreaders Gina Salamone, Maureen Oliva, Carole Raye, Karin Faulkner, Marsha Green, Amanda Avery and Katy Tahja; and to Linda Pack, Lenora Shepard, Celeste Bautista, Anthony Miksak, Carol Goodwin Blick, Marcia Bonham, Taylor Cranney, Tom and Judy Nichols of North Coast News, and the Regional Occupational Program of Mendocino for their support.

For guidance and feedback on specific trails I thank Dan Winkelman and Ashford Wood of Salt Point State Park, Steve Edinger of Sonoma Coast State Beaches, Fred Lew of Sugarloaf Ridge State Park, Bill Krumbein of Annadel State Park, Douglas Kauffman and Bill Grummer of Bothe-Napa Valley State Park, Kasey Cook of Lake Sonoma, Bill Barnhart of Sonoma County Parks, William and Joan Roth and Tim Henke of The Nature Conservancy, Ben Crabb of San Pablo Bay National Wildlife Refuge, John DeWitt of Save-the-Redwoods League, Bill Walton of Ft. Ross State Historic Park and Matt Atkinson of Jack London State Historic Park.

With special thanks to COASTWALK and all the other groups that have worked to save the natural beauty of Sonoma County's coastal areas, when hope, reason and conservation were all that saved the coast from being built up and paved over during years of growth.

CONTENTS

INTRODUCTION

THIS BOOK IS FOR RECREATIONAL PURPOSES ONLY

Sonoma rolls across the green and golden hills north of San Francisco Bay. These hills shelter a promised land of rich botanical diversity, where a thousand miles of meandering back roads deliver you to new, unexpected views with each turn, and dozens of parks entice exploration on foot.

Once the untamed home of grizzly bears and mountain lions, Sonoma County's million acres now stand as a transition between the sophistication of the Bay Area and the rugged forests and mountains to the north. Premium vineyards and upscale subdivisions vie for its sheltered valleys, while a wilderness of deep woods, graceful grasslands and tangled chaparral climbs its high ridges and hunkers in its deep canyons. These wild lands provide shelter for an array of wildlife.

This book tells how to find and walk, hike, jog or ride over 200 miles of scenic trails through beautiful country. The trails range from easy walks to difficult backpacks, with choices to fit the taste of every nature lover. The trails lead to a variety of habitats: beaches, tidepools, lagoons, dunes, headlands, grasslands, forests, stream canyons, ridges and mountain tops. You may also hike to waterfalls, a wildlife refuge and ghost town sites and along old railways. Five trails explore the broken country around the San Andreas Fault, and others investigate the literary heritage of Jack London and Robert Louis Stevenson. In short, there is something for everyone. So get out of your car and use your feet, bicycle, horse or wheelchair to explore Sonoma County.

HOW TO USE THIS BOOK

This book has three sections, each organized from the north to the south. Highway 1 is the starting point for the directions to all trailheads in the first section, the Sonoma Coast. The next section covers trails inland from the coast but west of Highway 101. The third section details trails east of Highway 101, including two trails in Napa County. No trail is more than two hours from Santa Rosa. From San Francisco it will take you 40 minutes to three hours to drive to the trailheads.

In the directions to most trails, you will find milepost numbers listed like this: M.33.00. These numbers refer to white highway mileposts placed frequently (but at irregular intervals) along Highway 1 by CalTrans, the State Department of Transportation. You can quickly determine the location of a trail by referring to its milepost number and its position in the book.

You do not have to start at the beginning of the book. Simply turn to the trail nearest your location and you will be on your way. Neighboring trails are on adjacent pages.

For each trail in the book, you will find a map, specific directions to the trailhead, the best time to go, appropriate warnings, and a detailed description with some history and/ or natural history.

You will find a group of symbols below the access information for each trail. They tell you at a glance the level of difficulty, type of trail, available facilities, whether there is a fee, and whether dogs are allowed. The list of symbols follows.

At the end of the book are appendices listing the trails most suitable for a particular type of recreation: bicycles, mountain bikes, equestrians, backpacking and handicap access. You can then locate these trails in the text by referring to the trail number.

THE DANGERS
HIKER'S TEN COMMANDMENTS

When on the trail, *always* keep your senses wide open so that you can best appreciate nature's pleasures as well as

THE SYMBOLS

WALK:
Less than 2 miles
easy terrain

EASY HIKE:
2 to 10 miles
Easy terrain

MODERATE HIKE:
2 to 10 miles
Rougher terrain

DIFFICULT HIKE:
Strenuous terrain
Backpacking possible

**MOUNTAIN BIKE
TRAIL**

BIKE TRAIL

HANDICAP ACCESS

**DOGS ALLOWED
ON LEASH**

CAR CAMPING

**WALK-IN OR
BIKE-IN CAMPING:**
Environmental camps

TIDEPOOL ACCESS

PICNIC SPOT:
May be tables or just
a good blanket spot

RECOMMENDED
FOR FAMILIES

INTERPRETIVE
NATURE TRAIL

TRAIL FOR
EQUESTRIANS

RESTROOMS
AVAILABLE

WATER AVAILABLE

FEE AREA

FISHING ACCESS

NO OIL EXPLORATION
OR DRILLING

her dangers. Don't let nature lull you into complacency. Here are ten rules to keep you out of danger, so that you may safely enjoy the beauty of Sonoma County.

1. DON'T LITTER. Most of these places are unspoiled. Do your part to keep them that way. Always hike with a trash bag and use it, even for matches, cigarette butts and bottle caps. I always pick up any trash I see in a pristine spot, my way of saying thanks to Mother Nature.

2. NO TRESPASSING. Property owners have a right to privacy. Stay off private property. There are enough public places without walking through someone's front or back yard.

3. NEVER TURN YOU BACK ON THE OCEAN. Oversized rogue waves can strike the coast at any time. **Watch for them.** They are especially common in winter. They have killed people. More subtle are the changes of the tides: don't let rising tides strand you against steep cliffs or on a submerged tidal island. The ocean is icy and unforgiving, generally unsafe for swimming without a wetsuit.

4. STAY BACK FROM CLIFFS. Coastal soils are often unstable. You wouldn't want to fall 40 feet into the icy sea, would you? Don't get close to the cliff's edge, and never climb on cliffs unless there is a safe trail.

5. WILD THINGS: ANIMAL. All the animal pests of Sonoma County are small. Watch out for ticks (some carry Lyme Disease), wasps, mosquitoes, biting spiders, scorpions and rattlesnakes. Human animals are easily the most dangerous, particularly during hunting seasons. Always listen for gunfire, especially outside state parks. UNDERWATER ANIMALS: When tidepooling or at the beach, always watch for sea urchins and jellyfish. Both have painful stinging spines. Remember, too, that mussels are quarantined each year from May through October; at that time they contain deadly poison.

6. WILD THINGS: PLANT. These mean business too, especially poison oak and stinging nettles, which can get you with the slightest touch. Many other plants are poisonous. It is best to not touch any plants unless you know by positive identification that they are safe; this is most important with mushrooms.

7. TRAIL COURTESY. Equestrians always have the right of way on trails, because you can move aside for a horse much more easily than its rider can yield to you. Mountain bikers must yield to hikers and horses and slow to walking speed on blind corners. As wonderful as bikes are, metal machines (especially when moving fast) can cause serious injury when other trail users do not know you are

coming. Mountain bikes are the leading cause of trail accidents and injuries.

8. TRAFFIC. Country roads are difficult and often overcrowded. Drive carefully and courteously. Please turn out for faster traffic. You will enjoy the journey more if you do. If you stop, pull safely off the road.

9. CRIME. Be sure to lock you car when you park it at the trailhead. Leave valuables out of sight, or better yet, back at your lodging.

10. ALWAYS TAKE RESPONSIBILITY FOR YOURSELF AND YOUR PARTY. This is a trail guide, not a nursery school. The author cannot and will not be responsible for you in the wilds. Information contained in this book is correct to the best of the author's knowledge. Author and publisher assume no liability for damages arising from errors or omissions. **You must take the responsibility for you safety and health while on these trails.** The coast is still a wild place. Safety conditions of trails, beaches and tidepools vary with seasons and tides. Be cautious, heed the above warnings, and always check on local conditions. It is always better to hike with a friend. Know where you can get help in case of emergency.

THE HISTORY

Native Americans lived in relative peace and abundance in the wilderness that was to become Sonoma County. Evidence of habitation can be traced back 2000 years. Four tribes, the Kashaya Pomo, Southern Pomo, Coast Miwok and Wappo, shared the bounty of this hill country, developing sophisticated, diverse cultures that engaged in commerce and cultural exchange.

The local Indians had contact with Sir Francis Drake when he explored the coast in 1579, with the Spaniards as early as 1775, and with the Russians in the early 1800s. The Russians became the first non-natives to settle in Sonoma County when they established Fort Ross in 1812. They treated the Kashaya Pomo fairly by nineteenth-century mores, paying to rent their land, hiring them as hunters and guides, and studying and recording their culture. (A Moscow museum holds the world's largest collection of Kashaya ceremonial artifacts.)

The Spanish had laid claim to all of California in 1521 with the conquest of Mexico, although they had never settled and seldom explored the land north of San Francisco Bay. But they considered the Russian intrusion a challenge to their sovereignty. After the Mexican war for independence from Spain ended, the Mexicans wasted no time responding to the Russian threat, establishing the last and northernmost mission at Sonoma in 1823. The local Indians were baptized and forced to labor, making adobe bricks and planting vineyards. Meanwhile, the United States also warned against Russian imperialism, proclaiming the Monroe Doctrine in 1823.

In 1833 Lieutenant Mariano Vallejo was sent to Sonoma to establish a military presence. In 1834 the outpost changed from church to civil authority. The Mexican government ordered Vallejo to divide the arable land of present-day Sonoma County into land grants. Vallejo gave them to people trusted not to join with the Russians. In 1836, when Vallejo's nephew became governor of Alta California, he promoted Mariano to General and encouraged further settlement north of the Golden Gate.

Meanwhile, the Russians had depleted the otter population and were losing money on Fort Ross. After their offer to buy land on San Francisco Bay was refused, the Russians sold out and abandoned the fort in 1841.

Americans had begun arriving in Sonoma in 1827, as word of the abundant land and mild climate spread east. Moses Carson, Kit's half-brother, settled in Sonoma before Mariano Vallejo. The first wagon train arrived in 1841. By 1846 ten percent of California's population was American.

On June 14, 1846, 33 American settlers seized the pueblo of Sonoma at daybreak, arresting General Vallejo, raising the Bear Flag and declaring independence. Less than a month later, the American war with Mexico began, as the American flag was raised over Monterey. The Californios, long isolated from Mexico, offered token resistance. Six months later the hostilities were over, although the formal treaty was not signed until 1848.

So the United States conquered California just in time for the Gold Rush. For the preceding twenty years, the town of Sonoma had rivaled San Francisco as the leading settlement in the north. But the Gold Rush changed that in a hurry. As a deep-water port, San Francisco was the debarkation point and the gateway to the gold fields. Sonoma, not located on the golden road, became a provincial town.

Sonoma County boomed, however, as it took on the business of supplying food and lumber to prospering San Francisco and the miners in the Sierra foothills. Bodega and Sonoma grew. Petaluma began as a hunting camp to supply

San Francisco with meat. Valley Ford, Pine Grove (later Sebastopol), Bloomfield, Guerneville, Healdsburg and other towns were born and prospered. Settlers laid out Santa Rosa in 1853 and stole the county seat from Sonoma in 1854. By 1870 Sonoma was the sixth most populous county in the state, well ahead of Los Angeles.

In the 1870s and 1880s, railroads spread throughout Sonoma County, bringing a reliable way to transport goods to market, causing new waves of growth and more boom towns. The dairy and cattle industries grew. The invention of the artificial chicken incubator established Petaluma's poultry industry. Wines were produced in greater volume and quality increased. By 1900 the county population was nearly 40,000. and the growth had just begun. In 1990 the population approaches 400,000.

If Sonoma County still had the extensive rail network that covered the county in 1900, trains could transport the increasing crowds of commuters who threaten gridlock on the existing roads.

As you read about and hike the trails, many more details of Sonoma County's complex history will fall into place.

THE CLIMATE

The climate of Sonoma County differs considerably from one part of the county to another. The coast is cool and often foggy, mild enough for year-round hiking if you are prepared for varying conditions. Inland areas tend to be somewhat cooler in winter, much hotter in summer, with the hottest extremes in the north and east. In planning your excursions, keep in mind the following about the seasons in Sonoma County:

November to March are the rainy months, time to bring rain gear and waterproof boots. Still, there are often fine sunny days between storms.

April and May offer mild sunny days, often windy, with occasional rain storms. The wind may be gentle, or fierce and unrelenting. The landscape is at its most lush and beautiful. Bring layered clothing and hats.

June, July and August bring hot, sunny summer days inland, often too hot for comfortable hiking except perhaps in the early morning. Occasionally the fog will move inland to cool things off. On the coast it may be sunny, but thick, chilly fog can move in suddenly. You may be comfortable in shorts, but always bring layered clothing in case the fog comes in. Sometimes you can beat the fog by heading a few miles inland. (This is the most crowded season, especially

August.)

September and October are a beautiful time. Fog is less common. Though there may be rainstorms, most of the days are calm and warm. The land is dry, the hills golden, and the sunsets often spectacular.

GET READY, GET SET, HIKE!

You should be chomping at the bit to get out on the trail by now. Here are a few suggestions of what you might need to take on your hike: layered clothing—sweater, sweatshirt, hat, windbreaker or rain coat; insect repellent; suntan lotion; sunglasses; and small first aid kit (at least bring moleskin for blisters). Not essential, but highly recommended for all but the shortest walks: water container, extra food, pocket knife, flashlight and extra batteries, matches and fire starter, map, compass (helps if you know how to use it), and of course you would not want to be caught without your *Hiker's hip pocket Guide!*

Additional suggestions: camera; dry socks; binoculars; and field guide to birds, wildflowers and/or trees. If you are backpacking, you should consult an equipment list for that purpose.

When you are out on the trails, remember to slow down, open your senses and enjoy. Most people hike at a rate of 2 to 3 miles per hour. But beach sand or steep terrain may slow all but the most hardy to as little as one mile per hour. Leave ample time to do the hike you plan at a pleasant pace. Hike not to count the miles, but for the enjoyment and appreciation of nature. Happy trails to you!

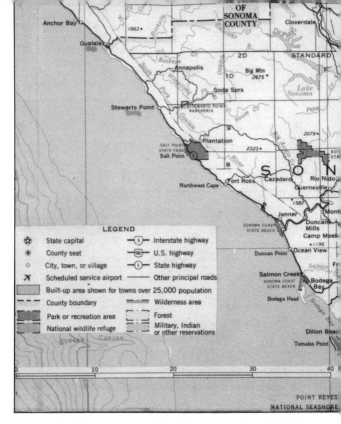

THE SONOMA COAST

Sonoma County's pristine 62-mile coastline has remained sparsely populated and mostly untamed despite having been first settled 180 years ago. The survival of its wild character owes much to its rugged, fractured and varied topography, but even more to the fact that the County's highest concentration of public lands is here.

Three tribes of Native Americans originally inhabited this coast and the adjacent ridges. The Coast Miwok lived from Wrights Beach south. The Kashaya Pomo, still present in the area, lived from Shell Beach north to Stewarts Point. The Southern Pomo controlled the short segment of coast in the area where Sea Ranch is today. These tribes lived an abundant, generally peaceful life thanks to the bounty of the sea, rivers, forests and grasslands.

White explorers came early and relatively often to visit this land. Sir Francis Drake landed somewhere (a point of much historical controversy) along this coast to make repairs to his ship, meeting some of the coast dwellers. Spaniard Sebastian Vizcaino named many coastal landmarks during his voyage in 1602. Other Spanish galleons sailed the coast before and after, during a period of intense

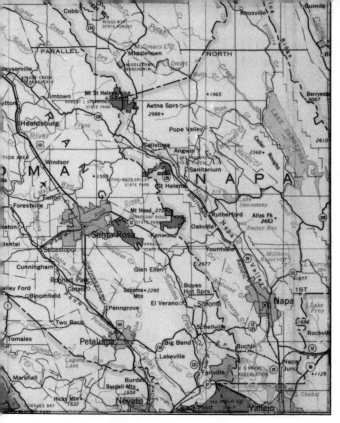

trade with the Phillippines. It was not until 1775 that Juan
Francisco de la Bodega y Quadra put ashore at the bay
that was to take his name, surveying the surrounding area.
But the Spaniards never made a permanent settlement on
the coast north of San Francisco.

The Russians established a colony at Fort Ross in 1812,
having camped at Bodega for eight months in 1809. They
quickly decimated the abundant population of sea otters
and seals, selling the valuable pelts primarily to the
Chinese. The Russians left in 1841.

In belated response to the threat of Russian colonization,
the Spaniards finally made a stab at settling the coast.
They made two land grants in the 1840s, the 35,000-acre
Rancho Bodega to Captain Stephen Smith of Boston, who
established the first sawmill on the coast, and the 20,000-
acre Rancho German to Captain Ernest Rufus, a German.

But the Americanization of California and the onslaught
of the gold rush quickly changed the character of settlement
along the coast. Lumber boom towns sprang up to supply
the huge demands of San Francisco. Stewarts Point and
Timber Cove began in the 1850s, followed by Gualala,
Black Point, Fisk Mill, Duncans Landing, Louisville and
several more. A stage was in operation around 1860, and

a railroad reached Duncans Mills on the Russian River in 1877. Before long the Russian River was a popular vacation spot for San Franciscans.

Today the ports, mills, railroads and most of the towns are long gone, but the vacationers come in hordes every summer. They come with good reason, for this coast offers some of the most spectacular, untamed beauty in all of California. South of the Russian Rvier the coastal terrain is fairly gentle, backed by grasslands. North of the river mouth a rugged, precipitous coast with few signs of human habitation meets the wild Pacific, offering solitude and breathtaking beauty.

GUALALA POINT REGIONAL PARK

The park is in a spectacular setting on the south shore of the normally placid Gualala River, extending upstream from its mouth for about 1½ miles. The land was the northernmost portion of the Rancho German land grant, donated to Sonoma County when Oceanic Properties created the extensive subdivision called Sea Ranch. The park covers the diverse habitats of beach, rugged sea cliffs, grassy headlands, tidal river and redwood and bay laurel forest. It is in the extreme northwest corner of Sonoma County.

1.

HEADLANDS to BEACH LOOP
WINDBREAKS AND WILDFLOWERS

The western portion of the park is covered by a fine network of trails offering several choices. Though the following trail report details the unpaved headlands-to-beach loop, a paved bicycle and wheelchair path can easily be followed out to the same beach and headlands area.

The modern Visitor Center fits nicely into the beautiful headlands landscape. The center has informative displays and provides a welcome refuge from the strong winds often blowing here.

From the Visitor Center, follow the paved path northwest for 200 feet. There you meet a grassy trail that continues northwest where the paved path swings west.

DISTANCE: 1¼-mile loop.

TIME: One hour.

TERRAIN: Grassy headlands between river and sea cliffs leading to broad beach at river mouth, then to rocky point.

BEST TIME: Spring for wildflowers. Whale watching is best December through March. Anytime is good.

WARNINGS: Watch for killer waves on beach: six people were swept into the sea here in February 1986; one of them drowned. Watch for poison oak tangled with other plants.

DIRECTIONS TO TRAILHEAD: Turn west off Highway 1 at M.58.2, about .25 mile south of the town of Gualala. Drive .5 mile to the Visitor Center.

FEES: Day Use: $2/vehicle. Car camping: $10/night. Hike/bike camping: $3/night.

FURTHER INFO: Gualala Point Regional Park (707)785-2377.

Take the grassy path leading gently downhill through lush headlands. In 300 feet a trail on your right heads downhill to a pleasant picnic area near the river.

Continuing northwest, in 100 feet you meet a trail on your left, which leads southwest on the leeward side of an old cypress windbreak to another picnic area. The main trail continues west-northwest around the windbreak, passing over headlands filled with wildflowers. On your right the Gualala River is a prime habitat for aquatic birds. Many species of grasslands birds live near the trail.

At ¼ mile your footpath joins the paved trail, continuing to the beach near the river mouth. In late summer or early fall, you can ford the river near its mouth, continuing north to the end of the beach. At medium to high water, however, the river is not safe to ford.

Our trail description turns southwest on a fork of the paved path, quickly coming to a restroom and to the end of the paved path in about 300 feet. The grassy path

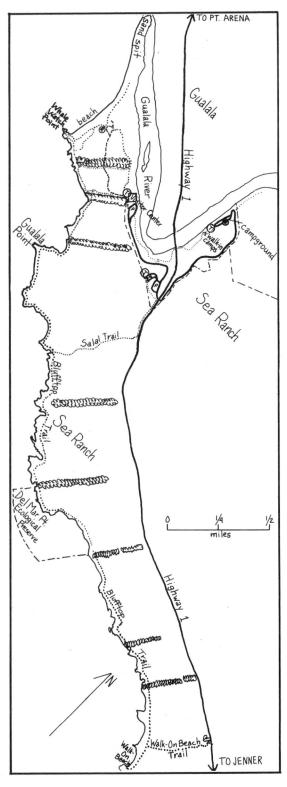

TO PT. ARENA

Sand spit

Gualala River

Gualala

Highway 1

Whale Watch Point

beach

Gualala Point

Center

walk-in camps

campground

Sea Ranch

Salal Trail

Blufftop Trail

Sea Ranch

Del Mar Pt. Ecological Preserve

Blufftop

Trail

Highway 1

N

Walk-On Beach

Walk-On Beach Trail

TO JENNER

0   1/4   1/2
miles

continues south from here, following the edge of the bluff overlooking the beach.

The trail forks again in another 200 feet. Here you can choose either the left path, protected behind a row of cypress, or the right fork, continuing along the spectacularly eroded sandstone bluffs above the beach.

Around ½ mile you bear right into a "tunnel" through the cypress trees. Your trail heads west onto a narrow rocky promontory known as Whale Watch Point. It soon comes to sandy bluffs on the leeward side of a cypress windbreak overlooking ocean cliffs on the south. You may continue 250 feet farther west to the windswept point beyond the windbreak. Look north from the point for a view of the beach and the town of Gualala. The wooded ridge beyond extends west to the point of Haven's Neck and the big sea stack called Fish Rock.

Returning to the sandy bluff east of the cypress trees, take the right fork southwest along the bluff's edge. You quickly come to a stairway on your right leading to a flat, rocky tidal shelf (fishing access). Continuing along the bluff, you soon plunge into a broad cypress windbreak, a home for many small birds. As you clear the cypress thicket, you meet the windbreak trail forking to the left. (You may return by that trail if you prefer.)

The trail continues southeast near the edge of the bluff. Two benches provide fine views of the coast. Just 300 feet after the second bench, you come to a fence and a sign indicating the park boundary. The start of the new Blufftop Trail leads through the fence here (see Trail #3). You turn northeast here, following the fence and windbreak along the Sea Ranch boundary. In another 300 feet you enter a "tunnel" through pines. Leaving the tunnel, you meet the paved path in 20 feet. Follow the bike path for 500 feet back to the Visitor Center and your car.

2.

RIVER TRAIL SOUTH
ALONG A QUIET STEELHEAD STREAM

The campground along the Gualala River lies at the western edge of a dense redwood forest on a quiet tidal stretch of the river. You can often hear the surf crashing just a mile to the west. The roar intrudes upon, but does not overcome, the quiet of the campground.

Though there are many large redwoods here, the many old stumps show evidence of pioneer logging. Most of these

have springboard cuts still showing on their eroded surfaces, indicating that the trees were cut before the introduction of chainsaws. (The sawyers would stand on these springboards five or ten feet above the ground to avoid cutting through the thicker, often scarred wood at the tree's base.) Many of these old stumps have new plants growing healthily from their tops. If you walk through the campground, you will see the following plants atop stumps: elderberry, huckleberry, sword fern and bay laurel.

Where the redwood trees stop near the southwest end of the campground, bay laurels grow very large, with gnarled trunks up to four feet in diameter.

The river trail leads south through this dense bay laurel forest from the south end of the campground. Seven walk- or bike-in campsites are located in this forest along the first 400 feet of trail. (They are a bargain at $3 per night.) Just beyond the last campsite, the trail comes to a grassy clearing; a dense tangle of brush grows on your right, between you and the river.

At ⅛ mile the trail swings right and follows the river bank. It continues through tall brush for the next 300 feet, crossing a small wooden bridge.

About ¼ mile from the trailhead, you pass under the highway bridge. Many cliff swallows nest under the bridge, especially on its west side. From March through September, the swallows will be chattering and feeding over the river. Your trail then leads uphill away from the river, following a fence. Then, passing an old snag, you leave the grassy river flat and climb the face of the bluff. The tangle of brush along the trail includes many species: willows, bay laurel, ceanothus, blackberries, wild rose, paintbrush and poison oak. The trail switchbacks twice, coming to a bench where you may rest and enjoy the view.

As you come to the top of the bluff, the flora changes to bluff grassland, scattered with low cypress. Another ⅛ mile along the bluff's edge brings you to a pleasant picnic area. A few hundred feet beyond, you come to the Visitor Center. At this point you may return to the campground or continue to the network of headlands and beach trails (see Trails #1 and 3).

RIVER TRAIL SOUTH:

DISTANCE: 1 mile round trip (connects with 1¼-mile headlands/beach trail).

TIME: One half hour.

TERRAIN: Down the river canyon, under the highway bridge, then climbing the bluff to headlands.

BEST TIME: Spring for wildflowers, but nice anytime.

WARNINGS: Watch for poison oak and stinging nettles.

DIRECTIONS TO TRAILHEAD: Turn east off Highway 1 at M.58.2, about .25 mile south of the town of Gualala. Go .7 mile to the campground, then .1 mile farther to its south end.

FEES: Day use: $2/vehicle. Car camping: $10/night. Hike/bike camping: $3/night.

FURTHER INFO: Gualala Point Regional Park (707)785-2377.

ENVIRONMENTAL CAMPS: 7 walk- or bike-in camps are located from 75 feet to 400 feet along the trail in a dense bay laurel forest by the river.

3

BLUFFTOP TRAIL
ALONG THE SEA RANCH COAST

State law mandated this trail in 1980, after years of litigation that went all the way to the U.S. Supreme Court. The trail was finally opened in 1987. Though the trail passes many houses in the Sea Ranch subdivision, it provides the only public access to a marvelously convoluted coast with headlands rich in wildflowers. On a recent spring visit, the author counted more than two dozen varieties of wildflowers in bloom.

This description starts at the north end of the trail, where it meets the trails of Gualala Point Regional Park. You can also reach the Blufftop Trail via the Salal Trail (see Trail #4) and the Walk-On Beach Trail (see Trail #5).

From the Visitor Center at Gualala Point Regional Park, follow the paved path northwest for 200 feet. Then walk the pavement southwest for another 250 feet. Where the pavement turns right, take the dirt path that continues southwest through the trees and along the fence that marks the Sea Ranch boundary.

At ¼ mile a break in the fence marks the start of the Blufftop Trail. Turn left, heading through the fence and the cypress windbreak. Then the Blufftop Trail turns south, following the edge of the bluff. For the next ¼ mile, the nearby shore is mostly hidden behind dense cypress. At ½ mile you reach a point with unobstructed views south to Gualala Point and northwest to Whale Watch Point.

Then your trail plunges through another windbreak. At ⅝ mile your trail jogs right, passing above a small, inaccessible pocket beach. You head southwest to Gualala Point, shrouded in bushy cypress. Gualala Point Island, just offshore, is a nesting ground for Brandt's cormorants and other seabirds.

At ¾ mile you leave the cypress trees for open headlands. Your trail continues southeast, hugging the edge of the bluff. Near one mile you cross two small gullies and follow the rugged shore. Large yellow bush lupine are scattered along the grassy headlands. You soon descend into a canyon where forest and soft chaparral plants mix. After crossing a creek at 1¼ miles, you meet the Salal Trail (Trail #4).

Climb the steps heading southeast up onto a headland with tall grasses, bush lupine, berry vines and Douglas iris.

BLUFFTOP TRAIL:

DISTANCE: 6½ miles round trip, 3½ miles one way to Walk-On Beach.

TIME: Three to four hours.

TERRAIN: Along headlands near the bluff's edge, crossing several creeks and passing through numerous cypress windbreaks.

BEST TIME: Spring and early summer for wildflowers.

WARNINGS: Do not trespass on adjacent private property. Watch for poison oak. Be careful along the bluff's crumbly edge. Stay on the trail and away from the edge.

DIRECTIONS TO TRAILHEAD: Turn west from Highway 1 at M.58.2 into the day-use area for Gualala Point Regional Park. Go ½ mile to parking area at end of road.

FEES: $2/vehicle, day use.

FURTHER INFO: Gualala Point Regional Park (707)785-2377.

You wind along the lupine-covered bluff near the shore. Beyond 1½ miles your trail winds onto a point, passing the wind-sculpted end of a cypress windrow.

At 1⅝ miles you come to a creek with still pools overlooking the shore. Cross a bridge over the creek and come to a view of the waterfall where the creek drops to the ocean. Then continue generally southeast along the bluff.

At 1⅞ miles you cut in around a tiny cove and wind through more bush lupine, then head south. At 2 miles you approach another windbreak, this one marking the boundary of the Del Mar Landing Ecological Reserve. The Reserve was created to protect the rocky intertidal zone, habitat to an abundance of marine invertebrates. No fishing or collecting is allowed here.

The trail soon forks. Follow the right fork along the edge of the bluff. At 2⅛ miles a wooden beam and an old rusty stake mark Del Mar Landing, where lumber schooners were loaded around the turn of the century. Some unusual rock

formations lie along the shore.

You soon come to the end of Del Mar Point. Your trail turns north briefly, then east. At 2¼ miles you pass a rock outcrop nearly buried in lush vegetation. Delicate star tulips, or cat's ears, grow among the grasses nearby. Parallel paths lead across the bluffs. You may take either one, because they rejoin not far ahead. You pass through an old redwood split-rail fence at 2⅜ miles. Near 2½ miles you head into a broad windrow, then wind to cross a bridge over another small creek.

Continue southeast through the wildflower-dappled headlands. You soon find that you are alongside a rocky cliff with fantastically eroded rocks. The rocks here are similar to the more extensive rock formations at Salt Point (see Trail #10), visible along the coast to the south. At 2¾ miles your path bends to the right and heads out to a small point, then turns east to cross a bridge. The small creek below is hidden in a dense tangle of vegetation. Beyond the creek grows a thicket of salal and cow parsnip. Soon your trail splits in two. The right fork is the most scenic, heading out to a small point, then quickly rejoining the other fork. At 3 miles you approach another old windrow, which you promptly pass through.

In ¼ mile you come to the junction with the Walk-On Beach Trail, 3¼ miles from your starting point. You can go another ¼ mile southeast and descend the stairway to the beach. Or you can head northeast to the Walk-On Beach Trailhead, which would be perfect if you arranged a shuttle vehicle ahead of time. Otherwise, return along the Blufftop Trail to Gualala Point Regional Park. (You may also turn right when you reach the Salal Trail, follow that back to the park, then walk another ½ mile along the road to the Visitor Center.)

4.

SALAL TRAIL
COASTAL CREEK HABITAT

The Salal Trail leads southeast from the restroom and parking area, then follows the south shoulder of the road to the park entrance on Highway 1. Your trail then parallels Highway 1 south for ⅛ mile.

A wooden post with the coastal access symbol marks where the trail heads away from Highway 1. Go through a dense berry patch, then down a stairway into the creek canyon at ¼ mile. This little creek canyon forms a habitat distinct from the coastal grasslands surrounding it. Many species thrive in the cool, damp, wind-protected environment, including fragrant wild azalea, madrone, salal, silktassel, alder, berries and oaks.

Your trail heads down the canyon, coming quickly to stands of redwoods, Bishop pines and droopy Douglas firs. You come to a small wooden bridge, then to a paved road beyond ⅜ mile.

Cross the road and continue southwest, passing a pumphouse before the trail comes back alongside the creek in an area lush with willows, alders, sword ferns, skunk cabbage and salmonberries. These are soon joined by Bishop pines and cypresses.

At ½ mile you cross a small bridge beside wild azaleas, then plunge into a dense tunnel of growth dominated by silktassel, alders and thimbleberries. In 300 feet you come to a more open portion of the trail where paintbrush thrives in a rocky spot. Then you drop into another tunnel of brush, mostly bay laurel.

Near ⅝ mile you come to a dense stand of redwoods on the creek. The trees are snapped off just above the level of the surrounding grasslands, attesting to the protection this little canyon provides from prevailing strong winds. This pretty spot has a small waterfall. You continue along the left side of the creek. In another 300 feet, you find a dense salmonberry thicket beside the trail. Salmonberries ripen

SALAL TRAIL:

DISTANCE: 1½ miles round trip (or 2½-mile loop with the north portion of Blufftop Trail).

TIME: One hour.

TERRAIN: Grassy headlands spotted with cypress, then down narrow, wooded coastal creek canyon to rocky beach.

BEST TIME: Spring for azaleas and other wildflowers, but anytime is nice.

WARNINGS: Do not trespass on adjacent private property. Watch for poison oak and nettles.

DIRECTIONS TO TRAILHEAD: Turn west from Highway 1 at M.58.2 into the day-use area for Gualala Point Regional Park. Take the first left inside the park, parking near the restrooms.

FEES: Day use: $2/vehicle.

FURTHER INFO: Gualala Point Regional Park (707)785-2377.

in May and June. Then you come to another paved path with miners lettuce growing beside it. The trail bends left and passes through a brushy area where you should watch for nettles.

Not quite ¾ mile from the trailhead, a small rocky beach comes into view at the mouth of the creek. The wooded habitat gives way to soft chaparral plants: skunk cabbage, cow parsnip, horsetail ferns, grasses and assorted wildflowers.

You come to a junction with the Blufftop Trail (see Trail #3), which goes north for one mile to meet the trails of Gualala Point Regional Park, and south for 2 miles to meet the Walk-On Beach Trail. You can prolong your hike by going either left or right. Or you can simply descend the stairway to the tiny beach, enjoy the shore, and return the way you came.

5

OTHER SEA RANCH TRAILS
SHORT AND SCENIC

THE WALK-ON BEACH TRAIL (.8 mile round trip) descends from the parking lot into coastal scrub forest of madrone, willow, grand fir, cypress and Bishop pine. As you head south, watch for poison oak in the understory. You cross a paved road after 500 feet, then head southwest through grasslands west of a large cypress windbreak. Beyond ¼ mile you come to a junction with the Blufftop Trail (see Trail #3). Go left here for ¼ mile to reach the stairway at the far end of Walk-On Beach.

THE SHELL BEACH TRAIL (1.2 miles round trip) heads southeast through pines to a wooden bridge. Just short of ⅛ mile, you cross a paved road, then continue over grasslands scattered with trees. At ¼ mile you walk between houses, then cross a second paved road. In 300 feet you reach a stairway to the pleasant beach, protected somewhat by the point to the north.

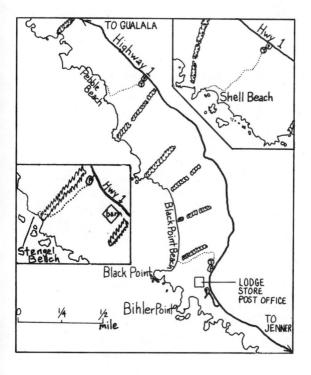

OTHER SEA RANCH TRAILS:

DISTANCE: ½ mile to 1¼ miles round trip.
TIME: One half to one hour (each trail).
TERRAIN: Coastal grasslands leading to small pocket beaches.
BEST TIME: Spring for wildflowers, low tide for best enjoyment of beaches and tidepools. Nice anytime.
WARNINGS: Respect adjacent private property—do not trespass. Watch for rogue waves when on the beach. Trails are open 6 a.m. to sunset.
DIRECTIONS TO TRAILHEADS: All on west side of Highway 1 at the following mileposts (just south of Gualala):
    Walk-On Beach Trail: M.56.50
    Shell Beach Trail: M.55.20
    Stengel Beach Trail: M.53.96
    Pebble Beach Trail: M.52.30
    Black Point Beach Trail: M.50.83
FEES: Day use: $2/vehicle.
FURTHER INFO: Gualala Point Regional Park (707)785-2377.
OTHER SUGGESTION: If you rent a house in the Sea Ranch subdivision, you will have access to all the private trails there as well as trails described in this book.

THE STENGEL BEACH TRAIL (.4 mile round trip) descends from the parking lot and heads southwest along a beautiful old cypress windbreak and a fence. In 500 feet you meet a private trail and a break in the fence. Your trail bends right and heads through the break to meet the stairway to broad, sandy Stengel Beach.

THE PEBBLE BEACH TRAIL (.6 mile round trip) heads south between shore pines. At 250 feet you cross a private path at a right angle. Your trail leads west through Bishop pine forest. A lush creek runs on your right, home to skunk cabbage, ferns and other water-loving plants. At ⅛ mile you leave the creek for grassy headlands. Before ¼ mile the trail follows a cypress windbreak. You soon meet another private path on the left. Go right, crossing a small wooden bridge. In 150 feet you meet the stairway to Pebble Beach. The beach is gray, pebbly sand with good tidepools at low tide.

THE BLACK POINT BEACH TRAIL (.6 mile round trip) goes north across lush, grassy headlands. After 300 feet you cross a private road. The trail turns west in 150 feet, heading directly toward the sea cliff. You cross a private Sea Ranch trail, then come to a sturdy stairway descending 86 steps to the south end of the beach. To the south is Black Point, a rock outcrop with windblown cypress, long a landmark to navigators on both land and sea. To the north the black sand and pebble beach extends about ½ mile.

SALT POINT STATE PARK
INCLUDES THE NEXT SIX TRAILS

Salt Point State Park is Sonoma's slice of coastal heaven. The park's 7000 acres sprawl along five miles of convoluted shore, extending inland to 1000-foot-high wooded ridges more than two miles inland. The adjoining Kruse Rhododendron State Reserve adds 317 acres of second-growth forest. Ten creeks dissect the uplifted marine terraces of the park.

The changing seasons bring a diversity of moods to the land here. In winter the surf roars and crashes and the creeks sing. In spring wildflowers sparkle in lush green grasslands. In summer grasslands fade to gold and brown, while the ocean takes on a glassy calm. Immense beds of giant bull kelp grow offshore. Great blue herons stand on the heads of the kelp, seeming to walk on the still waters as they pick their meals from the sea.

The Kashaya Pomo were the original human inhabitants of the land. They had villages on the ridges and descended to the shore to harvest sea food. The Pomos camped in the forest to stay out of the wind. They cooked their catch on the leeward side of rocks, where middens are found today. They salted the surplus, trading it and salt with inland tribes, mostly for obsidian to make tools and weapons.

When the Russians established Fort Ross in the early 1800s, their Aleut hunters camped at Gerstle Cove to hunt otters. The Russians left in the 1840s, soon replaced by Americans, who came to cut redwoods and low-grade

sandstone blocks. They loaded the lumber and stone on ships, hauling the materials to San Francisco to build the booming city.

Overland transportation improved when Wells Fargo established a stage line from the Russian River to Fisk Mill and Plantation about 1860 (later extended to Gualala), but the infamous gentleman bandit Black Bart often robbed the stage. The stage road was improved around 1870 with the help of the Sonoma County Board of Supervisors, but even then it took driver Lew Miller 12 hours to negotiate the wild ride from Jenner to Gualala. Today Highway 1 follows much of the original stage route.

Salt Point State Park offers an enchanting maze of trails that interconnect the ten biotic zones within the park. In one day of hiking you can start on windswept headlands overlooking the ocean, climb through tall forest to reach the stunted growth of the Pygmy Forest or the sag ponds and valleys along the San Andreas Fault, then return to your campground. Whatever season you visit Salt Point, the pristine land provides new and diverse treasures of wild-flowers and moods.

6

CHINESE GULCH/ PHILLIPS GULCH LOOP

KRUSE RHODODENDRON STATE RESERVE

The Kruse family started a sheep ranch in these coastal hills in 1880. The marginally productive land could not raise enough sheep to support the family, so they diversified into logging and tanbark harvesting. In 1933 the family donated these 317 acres to the state as a Rhododendron Reserve, preceding the establishment of adjacent Salt Point State Park by almost 40 years. In the 1970s another 1350 acres of the original Kruse Ranch were added to Salt Point State Park. They make up the extreme northern portion of the park.

This easy hike has three chances for early return, should you decide to shorten your hike. In May and June, the brilliant pink blossoms of native rhododendrons brighten the forest along your trail.

From the parking area, your trail climbs 50 feet east to a trail map and the posted start of the Rhododendron Loop. Continuing east between redwood split rail fences, you climb through mixed forest of redwood, Douglas fir, grand fir and Bishop pine, with scattered tanoak and madrone. The muffled roar of the surf filters through the forest, the ocean less than ½ mile away.

In 300 feet dense clusters of rhododendrons line the trail. Soon the short Rhododendron Loop goes left for a quick return to the parking area. You take the Chinese Gulch Trail, climbing gradually northeast into dense forest. The murmur of a stream rises from the east. You leave the split rail fences behind as your trail bends left, coming to a one-person seat on a twisted wax myrtle to your left. Other plants in the crowded understory include evergreen and red huckleberry, hairy manzanita, salal, sword fern and evergreen violet.

You climb into tall forest with a dense understory. You soon pass a circle of redwoods encompassing a large fragment of a charred stump. The notches in the stump, called springboard cuts, indicate that it was cut long ago, before the advent of chainsaws, as were most of the redwood stumps along this trail.

You climb east at ⅛ mile, passing second-growth redwoods to four feet in diameter. You meet and climb along

CHINESE GULCH/PHILLIPS GULCH LOOP:

DISTANCE: 2⅜-mile loop, with several shorter options.
TIME: One hour.
TERRAIN: Rolling, wooded hills cut by several canyons.
ELEVATION GAIN/LOSS: 360 feet+/360 feet-.
BEST TIME: May.
WARNINGS: Watch for poison oak.
DIRECTIONS TO TRAILHEAD: Turn east off Highway 1 at M.42.75 onto Kruse Ranch Road. Go .4 mile to trailhead parking area.
FURTHER INFO: (707)865-2391.

the rim of the steep canyon of Chinese Gulch. Passing a rest bench, you descend into the gulch at ¼ mile. A spur on the right descends quickly to the gravel road, your second chance for an early return.

You stay left to cross a bridge over the creek. Along the creek redwood sorrel blooms most anytime of year. Hedge nettle, deer and sword ferns and a dense carpet of moss also thrive here.

You climb steeply out of the canyon, crossing a small bridge over a tributary. You switchback left above two large stumps with springboard cuts, then switchback to the right. Cross a short boardwalk at the top of a steep slide, then contour through the forest.

Beyond ⅜ mile your trail swings left, climbing past a rest bench. Walking through an open understory, you soon switchback left. The trail levels at ½ mile as you pass through a redwood circle. You switchback steeply to the right, climbing to cross a gully at ⅝ mile. Your trail levels, then starts a gentle descent. Tanoaks dominate the forest here, providing a different, more luminous quality of light.

At ¾ mile your descending trail approaches a gulch where a bend of the road comes into view. You drop steeply to the gulch and a junction. You can go right, coming to the road in just a few feet for a shortcut to the trailhead.

The described hike goes left to climb southeast, then steeply east to ⅞ mile, where your trail levels. You dip through a small gully. Then the understory becomes dense again, jammed with rhododendron and huckleberry. Soon tall golden chinquapin and dense Labrador tea, with pungent white flowers in summer, crowd the trail.

At one mile you climb northeast as the forest thins. You promptly return to dense forest with a crowded understory. Start a gradual descent, crossing the road at 1⅛ miles, then descending south on the Phillips Gulch Trail.

You soon draw near Phillips Gulch Creek, below on your left. Follow the sound of rushing water to 1¼ miles. Then your trail bends gradually right, crosses a side gully and levels. Most of the next mile is descending or level. At 1⅜ miles you cross another bridge over a tributary, then continue a gradual descent through mixed forest.

After another small bridge the trail levels, following an old wagon road. Descending gradually at 1½ miles, you pass through a dense stand of young redwoods. Soon your path bends right, leaving the old road to cross a gully at 1⅝ miles. You climb gently through forest with an open understory. You pass a circle of redwoods on your left, descend briefly, then level.

At 1¾ miles you meet one more junction. The trail on the right climbs quickly to meet the road. Taking the right fork saves little time, although it eliminates considerable climbing. Take the left fork for some of the prettiest scenery on this hike.

The left fork descends west, then southwest. You descend six switchbacks into a canyon that feeds Chinese Gulch Creek. The sixth switchback, at 2 miles, overlooks the creek in the side canyon. You follow the creek downstream, crossing it on a bridge at 2⅛ miles, just above its confluence with Chinese Gulch. In another 75 feet you cross Chinese Gulch at a beautiful spot where a bench provides a resting spot. The murmur of the creek mingles with the distant roar of surf. Lush vegetation, dominated by salal and huckleberry, thrives in the moist environment.

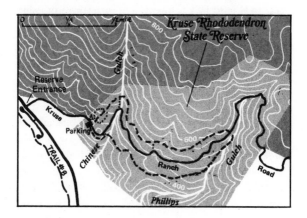

From here you have nowhere to go but up. The trail climbs switchbacks through a dense stand of redwoods. At 2¼ miles you overlook Chinese Gulch. You climb steeply by two more switchbacks, pass the toilets and come to the parking lot.

7.

FISK MILL COVE to HORSESHOE COVE

FOLLOWING THE PARK'S NORTHERN SHORE

From the parking area, your trail descends southwest through mature Bishop pine forest for 150 feet to an intersection. Go right, following steep, wooded bluffs above the shore. In ⅛ mile, look behind you to see jutting Salt Point. Continue northwest through the forest, climbing with a carpet of pine needles underfoot. Your path soon forks at a lichen-covered rock. Take the left fork, coming to another fork in 150 feet.

The short, 250-foot spur on the left climbs to an observation platform atop Sentinel Rock, offering a spectacular view. Broadleaf ceanothus and poison oak grow in the understory along the trail. From the wooden deck at the end of the spur you look northwest to the high headland of Horseshoe Point, west to open ocean and south toward Salt Point. Tiny Fisk Mill Cove lies 120 feet below. Coast silktassel, toyon, leather fern and sticky monkeyflower grow beside the deck.

Returning to the main trail, you descend northwest to a rough gully crossing overlooking the cove. Your trail climbs gradually north through the forest, then levels to wander back to the edge of the bluff. You make a winding descent into Cannon Gulch. At ⅜ mile you switchback left, descending to meet a vague spur on the left that descends steeply to the spectacular pocket beach of Fisk Mill Cove. The cove was called Tabatewi by the Kashaya Pomo, meaning "place of much gravel." You may see Pacific loons, great blue herons, grebes, murres and pelicans.

Going right on the main trail, you descend to a creek crossing with lush coastal scrub including red elderberry,

---

FISK MILL COVE to HORSESHOE COVE:

DISTANCE: 4¼ miles round trip to point, 6¼ miles round trip to north end of trail.

TIME: Two to four hours.

TERRAIN: Along the shore on gentle bluffs cut by stream canyons, then climbing to dramatic promontory of Horseshoe Point, with optional descent along the shore of Horseshoe Cove.

ELEVATION GAIN/LOSS: 360 feet+/360 feet- round trip to point, 560 feet+/560 feet- round trip to end of trail.

BEST TIME: Spring, summer for wildflowers.

WARNINGS: Watch for poison oak. Stay back from edge of crumbly bluffs.

DIRECTIONS TO TRAILHEAD: Turn west off Highway 1 at M.42.63 into Fisk Mill Cove parking area. Turn right and drive .1 mile to Bluff Trailhead (.1 mile before end of road).

FEES: Day use: $3/vehicle.

FURTHER INFO: Salt Point State Park (707)847-3221.

OTHER SUGGESTION: You can also walk to Horseshoe Point and Cove from parking areas at M.43.9 and M.44.54 (no day-use fee).

---

salmonberry and western coltsfoot beneath Bishop pines and stunted redwoods.

Climb steeply out of the gulch and through a broken fence to meet a trail that branches right, heading northeast to Highway 1. You turn left to continue along the headlands. As you turn away from Fisk Mill Cove, a spur trail branches left. Go 75 feet to a beautiful spot above the shore, a cemetery for the pioneer Fisk family, who moved to this coast in 1860.

Return to the main trail, a rutted double track heading northwest through tall grasslands toward a fence. As you join a broader trail from the highway, veer left toward bluff's edge to pass through the fence. You descend to cross a small creek at ⅝ mile, where a spur on the left descends to a rocky beach.

Your trail leaves the gulch and forest to head west along the shore. You dip through another small gully where wax myrtle, cypress and Bishop pine grow, then continue west over open headlands.

At ¾ mile you meet a broad trail. The right fork heads east to Highway 1 at M.43.22. Take the left fork to head southwest toward the south-facing point. You veer inland to cross a gully, then continue southwest to a fork. Take the faint left fork toward a rock outcrop.

At ⅞ mile the rock is right before you. Veer to the left of the rock, heading south to the bluff's edge, site of the loading chute for the Fisk lumber mill, where schooners were loaded in the boom days of the timber trade. You pass several posts and rings that were used to anchor and feed the cables to ships waiting offshore. The many offshore rocks made navigation difficult for the nineteenth-century sea captains. Ice plant grows along the bluffs.

Pick your way west along the shore, passing bush lupine, paintbrush and buttercups. At one mile you approach the point. Turn northwest, then north along the park's westernmost shore, heading toward the high headland of Horseshoe Point.

Around 1⅛ miles your trail veers right, rounding a small cove. Continue north along the convoluted coast. At 1¼ miles you have three trails to choose from. All of them merge not far ahead as you cut inland to wind around a mushroom-shaped cove, then head along the shore.

At 1⅜ miles you cross the small creek of scrub-filled Deadman Gulch, where mimulus, coltsfoot, yellow water iris, alder and willow tangle with other seaside plants. You stay near the sea's edge, passing to the left of a scrub-draped rock outcrop sheltered by a stand of pines at 1½ miles.

Continue along the shore, winding through fields of bush lupine where native blackberry intertwines with the introduced Himalaya species. Soon a spur on the left winds southwest to a small point with a fine view of the coast. Continuing northwest beside the shore, you pass several more small coves and points. Harbor seals and California sea lions haul out on offshore rocks. Red-shafted flickers live in the grasslands.

Around 1⅝ miles multiple paths provide a choice of routes along the shore. Continue northwest, hugging the edge of the bluff, heading toward the tree-shrouded rise of Horseshoe Point. Sea palms grow on the offshore rocks. You soon join a trail with better tread, heading northwest over gently sloping grasslands. A rocky, sparsely wooded ridge runs to the right of the trail.

From 1¾ miles you climb gradually along the shore. Around 1⅞ miles a prominent sandstone outcrop covered with a garden of succulents stands between you and the ocean. The outermost rocks shelter many shorebirds. You continue northwest, climbing gradually toward the rocky point, through grasslands with scattered cow parsnip, sea thrift, purple seaside daisy and coast buckwheat.

When you meet a sandstone shelf, turn right and climb steeply up a grassy chute into the pines. The pines shelter iris, buttercup, sticky monkeyflower and coast silktassel. The trail becomes vague here, but you promptly meet a better path. Turn left and climb northwest, paralleling the ridge on your right. At 2 miles you climb steeply but briefly. Dense, low-growing ceanothus and salal shelter delicate star tulips in spring.

You top the ridge at 2⅛ miles. Follow it briefly northwest to the 186-foot-high summit of Horseshoe Point. Hen and chicks and other succulents thrive on the moisture-catching rock outcrop, along with poison oak. The large boulder just west of the summit makes a fine viewpoint and picnic spot if it is not too windy. You have a grand view up and down the rugged, winding coast. Gualala Point sprawls seaward 13 miles northwest.To the northeast of Horseshoe Point, the protected waters of Horseshoe Cove jog east to only 300 feet from Highway 1.

You can retrace your steps to the trailhead for a 4¼- mile round trip. If you wish to continue east, then north around the shore of Horseshoe Cove, the trail gets rougher and less traveled. To continue, double back along the ridge for a few hundred feet to a low saddle where a rough, winding footpath descends steeply east, then passes through an old fence in a sea of beach grass. The rough trail continues east along the bluff. Lush vegetation grows along the path, including blue Mendocino gentian, poppy, paintbrush, hedge nettle, beach morning glory, purple seaside daisy, Douglas iris, coffeeberry, yarrow, bush lupine and beach strawberry. You turn north to descend to a low spot on the headlands at 2⅜ miles, then climb to another high point at 2½ miles. From this vantage you look north to the main arm of Horseshoe Cove and south to another arm. Descend along the bluffs to 2⅝ miles, where you cross a gulch.

Continue another 300 feet to a fork. Take the left fork to a high, short promontory at the bluff's edge. You overlook a steep cliff face where cormorants and pigeon guillemots can be seen nesting on the cliff and fishing in the churning surf below.

You can continue north to 3⅛ miles, where your trail winds east to meet Highway 1 at M.44.54 at the northern park boundary. From here, unless you have shuttled a second vehicle, you must return to Horseshoe Point, then return the way you came, winding along the shore. Or you can take the broad path that winds east from the southern summit. It returns to Highway 1 at M.43.9, but you can veer right on a path ⅛ mile before the highway and return to the shore to retrace your steps southeast along the headlands to the Fisk Mill parking area.

8.

FISK MILL to
STUMP BEACH OVERLOOK

OUTCROPS, COVES, GULCHES AND SURGE CHANNELS

Your trail south along the coast from the Fisk Mill Cove parking area starts at the same trailhead as the trail north, Trail #7. At the junction 150 feet down the trail, take the left fork. The sign says South Cove .3 mile. You head southeast through pine forest, where coffeeberry grows densely in the understory.

You soon descend through a small clearing. Go left at a fork, winding through the forest rather than heading out to the bluff's edge. Beyond ⅛ mile descend to cross a bridge over a gully, then meet the shore at the top of eroded cliffs.

Continuing southeast, you wind along the seaward base of a wooded rock outcrop. Beyond ¼ mile you cross a bridge over a gully with lush salal, ferns and berry vines. Climb steps, pass through a clearing, then return to the forest.

At ⅜ mile you walk along the base of another rock

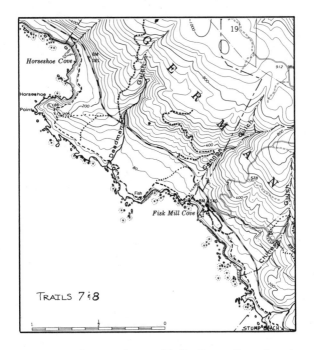

TRAILS 7 & 8

outcrop at the top of steep bluffs. Bay, silktassel, coffeeberry and poison oak grow beside your trail. You descend to a picnic table with a magnificent view south along the coast. A trail descends from the left (from the Fisk Mill South parking area).

Follow the wooded bluff southeast, passing a rock with an egg-shaped hollow. You cross a bridge at ½ mile, then leave the forest for open, grassy headlands. A rough trail on your right descends steeply to tiny South Cove.

Continue south along the shore to a point overlooking offshore rocks, a popular haul-out for harbor seals. Your trail turns south-southeast, following the bluffs over open headlands. You cross grassy Chinese Gulch just above where its stream plunges to the surf line in a waterfall.

Your vague trail heads southeast, passing to the left of a patch of bush lupine. At ¾ mile the path bends right, heading south toward the coast. A spur on the left leads to Highway 1 at M.42.14 in just 150 feet.

As you return to the bluff's edge, follow it southeast along the shore, passing seaside daisies, irises and buttercups. At ⅞ mile a flat rock shelf lies along the tide line. Notice the magnificently eroded shore, with surge channels where the surf pulses through shoreline rocks on the right.

At one mile you ford the creek of Phillips Gulch, where mimulus and beach silverweed grow. On your right the creek plunges 30 feet to the surf. You climb a steep incline

DISTANCE: 2¼ miles round trip to Stump Beach
overlook, 2¾ miles round trip to blanket picnic spot.
TIME: One hour.
TERRAIN: Along rolling headlands cut by several
creeks above the shore.
ELEVATION GAIN/LOSS: 280 feet+/280 feet-, round
trip.
BEST TIME: Spring, early summer for wildflowers.
WARNINGS: Stay back from edge of bluffs. Watch for
poison oak in coastal scrub.
DIRECTIONS TO TRAILHEAD: Turn west off Highway
1 at M.42.63 into Fisk Mill Cove parking area. Turn
right and drive .1 mile to Bluff Trailhead (.1 mile
before end of road).
FEES: Day use: $3/vehicle.
FURTHER INFO: Salt Point State Park (707)847-3221.

along the bluff's edge. After 200 feet your trail veers left,
climbing to the east side of the rocky top ahead. You reach
the top at 1⅛ miles, then continue southeast, soon coming
to an overlook of the huge cove of Stump Beach.

You cannot walk safely down to the cove from this trail.
High cliffs block your passage. You can reach Stump Beach
from the end of Trail #10, or you may park at M.41.2 for
a short walk to the beach. If you want to prolong this hike,
you can head east along the high bluff for about ¼ mile.
At 1¼ miles you come to a stand of Bishop pines. Continue
through grasslands, paralleling the highway, to a rough
gully crossing. Then head southeast through the forest to
another clearing at 1⅜ miles, where seaside daisies and
asters grow. Sheltered by the trees, this small clearing is a
pleasant spot for a blanket picnic, with a fine view of Stump
Beach Cove.

When ready to return, retrace your steps along the
bluff's edge or follow the upper headlands back to South
Cove, then follow the trail back to your starting point.

9

PYGMY FOREST LOOP

CLIMB TO THE FOREST OF DWARFS

Your trail leaves from the parking area for the Hike/Bike Campground, where you may want to use the toilets, water faucet or phone. You climb north on an unmarked fire road, ascending through mixed forest with an understory of huckleberries, salal, ferns and redwood violets.

At ⅛ mile you reach a junction. The North Trail goes left, eventually leading to Stump Beach. You go straight, climbing along the Pygmy Trail. The steady climb encourages you to breathe deeply the fresh coastal air. Rhododendrons, clintonias and trilliums flower abundantly in spring.

By ¼ mile Labrador tea joins the understory plants. This pungent and poisonous relative of the rhododendron often occurs in pygmy forest, but covers a much broader range as well. Soon, tall woodwardia ferns grow on the left of your steadily climbing trail. Also known as giant chain ferns, they often occur with redwoods, as they do here.

At ⅜ mile, you climb to a junction beside two water tanks. Go left for the shortest route to the pygmy forest. Your fire road climbs gradually to reach the third terrace, where it levels briefly. Madrone, tanoak, wax myrtle and manzanita mix with grand and Douglas firs, redwoods and Bishop pines. Watch for cottontailed pygmy brush rabbits. You climb intermittently, then descend briefly to cross the headwaters of Warren Creek. You meet the upper end of

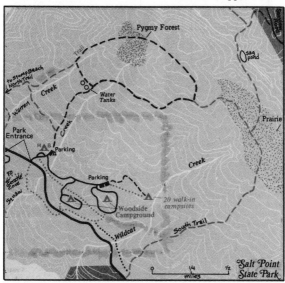

PYGMY FOREST:

DISTANCE: 2⅝-mile loop, 5-mile loop or longer.

TIME: One or two hours.

TERRAIN: Climb through redwood forest to pygmy forest at 900 feet elevation and return.

ELEVATION GAIN/LOSS: 650 feet+/650 feet-.

BEST TIME: Spring for wildflowers, anytime nice.

WARNINGS: No water along trail.

DIRECTIONS TO TRAILHEAD: Turn east off Highway 1 at M.39.78. Go straight to day-use parking, near Hike & Bike Campground.

FEES: Day use: $3/vehicle. Car camping:$10/night.

FURTHER INFO: Salt Point State Park (707)847-3221.

OTHER SUGGESTIONS: You can also reach the PYGMY FOREST by ascending NORTH TRAIL (M.40.74) or SOUTH TRAIL (M.38.73), or by descending PLANTA-TION TRAIL from Seaview Road, east of park.

the North Trail at ⅝ mile, turning right to continue a gradual climb. You climb steeply again beyond ¾ mile, ascending to the fourth terrace.

At ⅞ mile your trail levels. In 200 feet you suddenly enter pygmy forest, growing on level, nutrient-leached soil. Not far beneath the surface lies a dense hardpan that prevents most plants from breaking through to any nutrients in the soil below it. Along with stunted Bishop pines and redwoods grow two uncommon species that occur primarily on pygmy soils: Mendocino cypress and Fort Bragg manzanita. While Mendocino cypress occasionally grows more than 100 feet tall on nutrient-rich soils, the species is most prevalent on pygmy soils. A 100-year-old tree here may be only three feet tall. Fort Bragg manzanita has the smallest leaves of all the manzanitas.

On the Mendocino Coast, the fourth-terrace pygmy forest occurs around an elevation of 400 feet, with isolated pockets of fifth-terrace pygmy at about 600 feet elevation. Since the fourth-terrace pygmy forest at Salt Point occurs around 900 feet above sea level, one can surmise that this portion of the coast has been (and may still continue to be) uplifted at a faster rate than the coast sixty miles north.

The trail passes through true pygmy forest for about ¼ mile. At 1⅛ miles the road resumes a gradual climb. You quickly leave the most dwarfed area of the pygmy forest for an area of transitional vegetation. In the transitional zone, you have many of the pygmy associated species, but they tend to grow larger and be mixed with other species. Bear grass also grows here.

Your path curves right to climb gradually southeast through transitional pygmy. Soon a large hairy manzanita grows twenty feet tall on the right of the trail. Your path bends right and descends gradually.

At 1⅜ miles North Trail ends as it comes to another fire road. You can go left here for a longer loop of 5 miles, heading east to a large prairie with abundant wildflowers in spring. (In the prairie a spur forks left to descend ⅝ mile to a sag pond along the San Andreas Fault at Miller Creek, then climbs to Seaview Road at one mile.) From the prairie you can descend the South Trail to meet a power-line footpath that branches right (200 feet before the highway) to Woodside Campground and your trailhead.

Our described route goes right at the junction, descending west through mixed forest. At 1½ miles your trail steepens and bends left. Then your descent eases.

Beyond 1⅝ miles your path levels on the third terrace for nearly ¼ mile. You pass a spot where the road turns suddenly to loose sand. This is the top of an ancient dune that formed along the shore about 300,000 years ago, then was uplifted along with this entire coast.

Your descent steepens again as it bends left to cross Squaw Creek around 1⅞ miles. You may spot coffeeberry on the right, soon followed by corn lilies on the left. Descend alternately steeply and gradually through forest.

At 2¼ miles you return to the junction where the two water tanks stand. Retrace your steps downhill, returning to the parking lot at 2⅝ miles.

10.

SALT POINT to STUMP BEACH
ALONG TWISTING, HISTORY-RICH ROCKY SHORE

One of the earliest towns on the northern Sonoma Coast was Louisville, situated on Salt Point overlooking Gerstle Cove, where the parking area for this trail is today. Louis

Funcke and Louis Gerstle established Louisville in 1870, naming it after their Kentucky hometown. The founders planned to capitalize on San Francisco's booming growth by shipping timber and stone to the city to feed the building boom. Their town plan showed streets all over the Salt Point headlands.

By 1872 California's largest hotel stood on the bluff above Gerstle Cove. A big lumber operation was in full swing, with a horse-drawn railway up the coast to Stump Beach, where the canyon of Miller Creek was extensively logged. The sandstone rocks of Salt Point were quarried into building blocks, used mostly to build streets and retaining walls. Two ship-loading operations ran down to the cove, a wooden loading chute and a high-line cable operation. The quarried rock was loaded by the latter.

By the late 1870s, Louisville was declining. The most accessible trees had been cut, and only the quarry was productive. Neither the town nor the hotel had fulfilled the grandiose dreams of its founders. Today nature has reclaimed this wild coast.

From the parking area, a paved trail descends southwest over headlands covered with yellow bush lupine. Quarried blocks of sandstone lie beside the trailhead. The paved trail winds, descending gradually to the tip of Salt Point in ⅛ mile, where the pavement ends. Harbor seals haul out on the offshore rocks. If the sky is clear, you may see Bodega Head southeast along the coast near the Sonoma-Marin county line. You may even see the headlands of Point Reyes jutting seaward beyond the Head.

From the point, a dirt path heads northwest along the shore. Dense lupine grows beside the trail. Sea palms cling to the tidal rocks on your left. Your trail passes to the right of a rock outcrop where poppies and sea thrift grow. As you merge with a trail from the right, your path improves. Tidal rocks to the left of the trail have been eroded into intriguing shapes by the action of the waves.

Continue northwest paralleling the shore. At ⅜ miles you pass quarried rocks. Your trail soon veers right to wind around a cove. At ½ mile you ford seasonal Warren Creek, where calla and corn lilies grow upstream. The big rock to the east was one of the main quarry sites.

You wind west along the bluff's edge on a narrow path, paralleling the broad old road just inland. A dense tangle of coastal scrub covers the headlands. The plants include coyote brush, cow parsnip, angelica, broadleaf ceanothus, blackberry, salal, sword fern, coffeeberry, yarrow, beach

morning glory and beach strawberry.

The footpath fords a small stream where woodwardia fern, twinberry and wax myrtle grow with other soft scrub plants. You continue along the shore, passing many discarded quarry stones. Irises, hairy star tulips, coast goldfields and buttercups add color in spring and summer.

You merge with a broad path before ⅝ mile and head west toward a point, then turn northwest to parallel the convoluted shore. At ¾ mile your trail passes a grassy headland that extends west to a rocky point. Continue north on the broad path that soon returns to the shore, then veers right to round another cove.

You merge with another broad path at ⅞ mile, where you cross a tiny seasonal creek. Climb gradually on the broad path over headlands covered with bush lupine. At one mile the climb steepens, but your path levels in another 250 feet. Soon a side trail on your left heads west.

The side trail leads over grassy headlands for 400 feet to overlook tidal rocks sculpted into fantastic shapes. Do not go near the sea's edge here unless it is summer or the sea is calm and the tide is out. In winter, waves smash over these tidal rocks, sometimes sending spray 100 feet in the air. If conditions are right, you can go down to explore the tafoni, rocks carved into lace and honeycomb formations and other wondrous shapes by wave action. Notice the natural depressions in the rock that catch sea water during

---

SALT POINT TO STUMP BEACH:

DISTANCE: 3⅜ miles round trip to Stump Beach, 3miles
    for headlands loop, 6½ miles for Stump Beach-North
    Trail-Pygmy Forest loop.
TIME: One to three hours.
TERRAIN: Along open, convoluted shore with unusual
    rock formations, then descending to a large cove.
ELEVATION GAIN/LOSS: 120 feet+/120 feet-, round
    trip. 180 feet+/180 feet- for headlands loop.
    1040 feet+/1040 feet- for combined loop.
BEST TIME: Spring and summer for wildflowers.
    Moderately low tide for exploration of shoreline rock
    formations.
WARNINGS: Watch for oversize killer waves at
    shoreline, especially in winter.
DIRECTIONS TO TRAILHEAD: Turn west off Highway
    1 at M.39.90 (signed Gerstle Cove Campground). Go
    straight past campground for .5 mile, then take right
    fork to Salt Point parking area.
FEES: Day use: $3/vehicle. Car camping: $10/night.
FURTHER INFO: Salt Point State Park (707)847-3221.
OTHER SUGGESTIONS: STUMP BEACH can also be
    reached from parking lot at M.41.2 for a shorter, but
    less dramatic approach to the cove. NORTH TRAIL
    can also be reached from M.40.74.

---

winter and storm tides. When the water had evaporated
from these basins, the local Indians came to gather the pure
sea salt that remained. They used it to preserve fish and
game. The Kashaya Pomos had such a surplus of salt that
they traded with tribes as far away as Clear Lake. The salt
was a foundation of the Pomos' prosperous culture, traded
for obsidian and other goods from the inland tribes. The
Pomos name for Salt Point was Kabesilawina, meaning
flattop rock.

    Return to the main trail, and descend north. At 1¼ miles
you pass a rock outcrop to the right of the trail. At 1⅜ miles
your trail swings to the right and heads east along the rim

of Stump Beach Cove. In another ⅛ mile, when the two-wheel track bends right to climb southeast, you should veer left, continuing along the edge of the cove.

At 1⅝ miles you meet a steep old road that descends to Miller Creek and Stump Beach. The fine blond sand of the beach is well protected by the high walls of the deeply set cove, providing a fine rest or picnic spot with a superb view. Another trail climbs steps southeast to reach the parking area at M.41.2, where there are picnic tables and a toilet.

When you leave the beach, climb back up the steep road to the headlands. From there you can retrace your steps along the bluff trail for a round trip of about 3⅜ miles.

Or you can turn left and climb southeast on the two-wheel track for ⅛ mile. As the trail descends slightly, you come to a fork. Take the right fork, heading south across the grassy headlands. You parallel the highway on a faint trail with grand views of the rolling headlands of Salt Point. About ¼ mile from the junction, you will see two trail signs on your left. If you want to prolong your hike, turn east past the signs to cautiously cross Highway 1. You can climb east into the forest on the North Trail (at M.40.7). As the sign says, it is 1.8 miles to the Pygmy Forest, where you join Trail #9, which you follow back to Woodside Campground.

If you would rather take the shortest route back, continue south across the rolling headlands to the Salt Point parking lot at the southern tip of the point for a loop of 3 miles.

11.

SALT POINT'S SOUTHERN COAST
SPARKLING COVES SHROUDED IN PINE FORESTS

While this trail is described from the southernmost picnic area near Gerstle Cove, you can start your hike from any of the campgrounds in the park. It is 3⅜ mile from Gerstle Cove Campground, 7⅞ mile from Woodside Campground to the trailhead. You can also link this hike with Trail #10 for a grand tour of the coast from the southern boundary to Stump Beach.

The park map does not show the trail running south from the South Gerstle Picnic Area. But when you reach the end of the road, a well-trod path starts at a gate and descends to cross Squaw Creek, where Bishop pines, alders, bay laurels and silktassel grow right to shoreline. South Gerstle

51

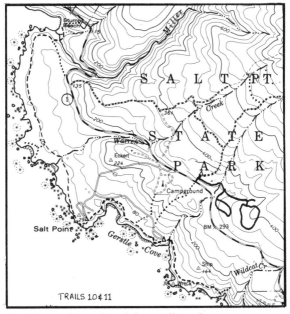

TRAILS 10 & 11

Cove lies at the outlet of the small creek.

In 300 feet from the trailhead, branch right onto a narrower track along the bluff's edge. Grass nut, or Ithuriel's spear, sends clusters of violet flowers skyward from the grasslands beside the trail. Before ⅛ mile you come to a point that looks north to the cove. Veer left and climb inland to cross a small creek, then bear right at a fork (the left fork leads to pleasant Environmental Camps) to walk the level, rocky grasslands of the open bluff above small coves. Pink shades of owl's clover and the purple of aster and seaside daisy sparkle in the grass.

Your trail heads south paralleling the shore. At ¼ mile the view opens to the southeast. Ocean Cove and Timber Point are in the foreground. The high ridge behind Sonoma Coast State Beach lies beyond. On a clear day you can see Bodega Head and the headlands of Point Reyes jutting seaward. Nearby offshore rocks are a favorite haul-out for harbor seals. Continue along the shore, passing a convoluted, rocky point between you and the blue Pacific.

Trail and shoreline turn east at ⅜ mile. You enter a forest of Bishop pine growing right to seaside. The violet flowers of elegant brodiaea grow along the trail in the forest. Your trail crosses rough ground, fords a seasonal creek and leaves the forest to climb over the top of a picturesquely eroded rock. You wind around a small cove and steep gully at ½ mile, passing Indian potato.

Your trail improves, following the shore for another 300 feet to overlook a deep cove just short of the wooded ridge marking the southern park boundary. Bishop pine forest grows down to the sea's edge in this spectacular, protected spot. Offshore from the ridge, a sea stack has a triangular window. The park boundary also marks the southern boundary of the original Rancho German, granted by the Spaniards to Captain Ernest Rufus in 1841. Rancho German extended north along the shore all the way to the current Mendocino County Line.

Retrace your steps, returning to the trailhead at 1⅛ miles. If you feel lazy today, you can end your hike here. But you have barely begun to tap the treasures of this shore. You can extend the hike by going northwest along the blufftop below the road.

The trail heads northwest over grasslands towards North Gerstle Cove (hidden), beyond which Salt Point juts west into the ocean. At 1¼ miles you pass pines and a windblown wax myrtle. Soon you dip into a small gully, passing through a stand of Bishop pines to a rough creek crossing.

SALT POINT'S SOUTHERN COAST:

DISTANCE: 1⅛ miles round trip to south boundary, 2¼ miles round trip to Gerstle Cove.

TIME: One half hour to south boundary, one hour to Gerstle Cove.

TERRAIN: Along a convoluted shore with alternating grasslands and pine forests.

BEST TIME: Spring, early summer for wildflowers.

WARNINGS: Watch for poison oak. Stay back from crumbly bluff edge.

DIRECTIONS TO TRAILHEAD: Turn west off Highway 1 at M.39.90. Go straight for .5 mile, then turn left and drive .5 mile to parking lot for picnic area.

FEES: Day use: $3/vehicle. Car camping: $10/night.

FURTHER INFO: Salt Point State Park (707)847-3221.

ENVIRONMENTAL CAMPS: Salt Point offers several excellent walk-in camps in two locations; ask the ranger.

Returning to the grassy blufftop, you continue west along the shore. At 1⅜ miles a spur on the right climbs to Gerstle Cove Campground. You soon overlook Gerstle Cove Reserve. Your trail winds to the right around the cove, crossing two small wooden bridges at 1½ miles.

Then you come to an A-frame overlooking North Gerstle Cove. The building will serve as a Visitor Center (expected to open in 1991). It will have exhibits of the park's ten biotic zones and a fine view of the cove from the deck.

To visit the cove or continue to Salt Point, you can go west from the Visitor Center to parallel a paved road. Then turn left and descend south on a dirt road to meet the paved Gerstle Cove access path (a short ⅛ mile side trip to the cove's shore).

You can continue south toward Salt Point. At 1⅝ miles a modern restroom, fish cleaning station and cold-water diver's shower lie on the right. Just 100 feet ahead is the start of Trail #10. You can continue along the shore or return to the trailhead to complete a 2⅛-mile hike.

12.

STOCKHOFF CREEK
REDWOOD CANYON AT STILLWATER COVE

Your trail begins at the lower end of the day-use parking lot. You descend northeast into a dense forest of grand fir and redwood. Huckleberry, redwood sorrel, salal, forget-me-not, and sword and bracken ferns grace the lush understory. As you approach Stockhoff Creek, large red huckleberry bushes and a red elderberry grow on the left.

At ⅛ mile turn right on the Loop Trail. Trillium, evergreen violet and five-finger fern join the understory plants. Stay on the right, passing a bridge over the creek. Continue up the creek, climbing along the sidewall of the canyon, then descend to cross a small bridge over a tributary.

You climb again, then descend to a rest bench at ¼ mile. You soon return to the level flood plain of the creek. In 200 feet corn lilies grow beside the trail. They bloom in late summer, although the blossoms may linger well into winter. Some redwood stumps along the trail have springboard cuts still showing. Early-day loggers wedged a platform into these cuts, providing a place to stand to make the saw cuts above the tree's swollen base.

You approach the park's eastern boundary, then cross a bridge over the creek to head downstream briefly. Your

STOCKHOFF CREEK:

DISTANCE: ⅞-mile loop, 1⅛ miles including trip to cove.

TIME: One hour.

TERRAIN: Up a wooded creek canyon to an old one-room schoolhouse.

ELEVATION GAIN/LOSS: 140 feet+/140 feet-.

BEST TIME: Spring for wildflowers.

WARNINGS: Watch for poison oak and stinging nettles.

DIRECTIONS TO TRAILHEAD: Turn east off Highway 1 at M.37.02 and follow signs to day-use parking.

FEES: Day use: $2/vehicle. Car camping: $10/night (hot showers for campers!).

FURTHER INFO: Stillwater Cove County Park (707)847-3245.

OTHER SUGGESTION: A long stairway leads to STILL-WATER COVE, protected by steep bluffs. At M.37.28 a WHEELCHAIR-ACCESSIBLE PATH descends to the beach at the cove. At M.37.57 a trail explores the park's NORTH HEADLANDS.

trail switchbacks to the right, climbing up and away from Stockhoff Creek. Clintonia grows beside the trail (red flowers in spring, blue berries in summer and fall). You climb gradually above the west side of the creek.

At ½ mile you switchback steeply left and climb southwest. Two uncommon riparian plants, both with small white flowers, grow here. Bedstraw is a spreading or climbing vine, while redwood inside-out flower grows close to the ground. You climb 150 feet to drier habitat where the rare rattlesnake plantain is found. This member of the orchid family has green leaves with a white center stripe, spikes of tiny white flowers in summer.

Your trail climbs through the forest, then levels beside a glade. At ⅝ mile you approach a red schoolhouse in a clearing surrounded by redwoods. The Fort Ross District School has led a charmed, well-traveled life. Established at Fort Ross in 1885, it was moved board by board to Seaview

Ridge in 1924. The school was moved again in 1938, then to its present site in 1970. Peering in the windows, one might guess the students had just left for vacation.

Your return loop heads into the forest from the front of the school. In 200 feet you meet an old road where you turn right and descend through an enchanting forest. By ¾ mile you return alongside the creek, then cross it on a sturdy bridge. Along the creek grow fat solomon's seal, western coltsfoot, thimbleberry, hedge nettle, elk clover, stream violet, and other riparian plants mentioned earlier.

Just 20 feet from the bridge, your trail forks. Take the left fork for a quick return to the starting point at ⅞ mile. Or take the right fork down the creek to Stillwater Cove at one mile. From there you can turn left and climb 127 steps to your starting point. Or you can cautiously cross Highway 1 and explore the spectacular shoreline of the cove before returning up steps or trail to your car.

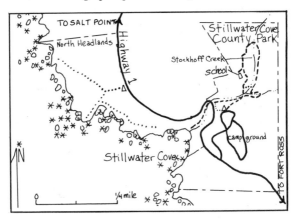

FORT ROSS
STATE HISTORIC PARK
INCLUDES THE NEXT FOUR TRAILS

Fort Ross Park comprises over 3000 acres of steep, wild country in one of the most rugged areas of the California coast. The next four trails explore different facets of this isolated land: gentle headlands atop surf-pounded cliffs, rolling forest and grasslands cut by deep stream canyons, protected coves and beaches, and the remote tidal beaches and rocks of the Lost Coast, hidden at the base of towering cliffs. Three of the trails explore the San Andreas Fault, which has had a big role in shaping these awesome slopes.

In your rush to explore these natural wonders, do not

forget to explore Fort Ross itself, the imperial nineteenth-century outpost of czarist Russia. It provides the only physical link with one of California's strangest and most amazing historical epics.

In March 1812, 25 Russians and 80 native Alaskans led by the peg-legged adventurer Ivan Kuskov landed here with the intention of establishing a permanent colony for the czar and his Russian American Company. They paid the Kashaya Pomo blankets, pants, tools and horses to use the Pomo village of May-tee-nee. The Russians quickly built a sturdy fort of redwood and several houses, naming it Rossiya to honor their homeland.

The Russians and Alaskans were no strangers to the California coast even then. In fact the presence of Russian fur hunters on the coast had provoked the Spanish to settle San Francisco forty years before Fort Ross began. A Russian trading party had visited the Presidio of San Francisco in 1806. In 1808 Kuskov had led a hunting expedition that camped at Bodega for eight months, sneaking their baidarkas (fur-covered kayaks) into San Francisco Bay to hunt otters under the noses of the Spaniards. That expedition returned to Russia with over 2000 pelts. At around $100 a pelt, the Russians could not afford to stay home.

Aside from the valuable furs, the Russians hoped to establish trade with Spanish California and produce enough food to supply their struggling colonies in Alaska. If they were able to gain any territory through the escapade, so much the better. By the time the Spaniards learned of the fort, it was already built and well-armed. Kuskov had chosen the high bluffs for Fort Ross because he knew they could be defended from attack.

The Russians hurried to solidify their anchor on the coast, establishing farms at Bodega, Freestone and Willow Creek and paying the Pomos to build, hunt and farm for the colony. The native Alaskan hunters traveled hard in their quest for otter pelts, ranging as far as Baja California. One report states that they gathered 200,000 pelts in their years of residence in California. Fort Ross soon had nine buildings inside the stockade and 40 or 50 outside, defended by 41 cannons.

The outpost reached a maximum population of 300 or 400. It served as a meeting place for European explorers, scientists and scholars visiting the West Coast. They explored most of present-day Sonoma County, becoming the first to accurately map the area and investigate its biology and ethnology. The most famous visitor may have been David Douglas, the Scottish botanist who lent his name to fir trees, irises and other plants of the area.

The systematic hunting of the Alaskans quickly depleted the sea otter population. Meanwhile, poor soil, gophers, insects and fog combined to cause crop failures, and grizzlies marauded the large herds of horses and cattle. Within twenty years of its founding, the colony was losing money and in serious decline. In 1839 it was put up for sale.

As the last commandant, Alexander Rotchev brought a brief renaissance. A renowned writer and scholar, he was married to Princess Elena Gagarina, who had given up high society for love. They both agreed that their years at Ross were the happiest of their lives. When French diplomat de Mofras visited in 1841, he was charmed by the Rotchev's choice library, French wines and the piano on which Elena played Mozart. Even the Mexicans dared to visit in these last years. A group of 30 rode all day from Sonoma, then danced all night.

The Mexicans declined to buy the colony and in December 1841 John Sutter offered 30,000 pesos for it. Sutter did not want the land, only the supplies, equipment and livestock for his Sacramento Valley ranch. Within a few months the Russians were gone.

The Pomo took over the fort, reclaiming their land for three decades. In 1873 the Call family acquired the fort and 15,000 acres. They ranched and logged the area into the twentieth century; some still live nearby today.

The state of California bought the fort and three acres in 1906 and began to preserve and restore it. The 1906 earthquake collapsed the chapel, which has now been rebuilt three times. The commandant's house to the right of the fort's main entrance is the only building that survives *in original form, making it one of the oldest wooden buildings west of the Mississippi River. But the other buildings have been meticulously restored, providing a marvelous feeling of the Russian settlement that nearly changed the history of California.*

13.

FORT ROSS NORTH HEADLANDS
TO NORTHWEST CAPE AND BEYOND

The trail to Northwest Cape leaves from the southwest corner of the main parking area. You head southwest on a gravel road. When the road bends left, you meet a grassy path on your right. Follow the path southwest to cross a hiker's ladder over a fence at ⅛ mile.

Descend a long-used path toward the tip of Northwest Cape, passing between rock outcrops, then crossing a sheep path. As you leave most of the rocks behind, your trail becomes vague and forks. Take the left fork, descending south to approach the steep bluff edge where sticky monkeyflower and coast buckwheat grow. Follow a trail southwest along the bluff, coming to Northwest Cape at ⅜ mile.

On your left the very tip of the point juts south. Be careful and stay back from the edge of the cliff. You have a grand view east to the fort and southeast to Fort Ross Cove, with Sonoma's Lost Coast to its right. On a clear day you can see Point Reyes nearly 40 miles down the coast.

Head northwest, following the bluff's edge. The eroding shelf on your left has exposed layers of topsoil, sand and sandstone. You may see killdeer darting over the grass.

At ⅝ mile you reach the western tip of the cape, where angelica and iris grow. Follow the shore northeast, passing rocks covered with bright orange lichen on their north sides. Sword ferns cling to the base of the rocks. Pass a steep, dangerous path to the beach; a better one lies ahead.

At ¾ mile you pass a gully where the rough trail on the left descends to the rocky shore and tidepools. You continue north along the bluff's edge, climbing gradually to pass to the left of a low rocky hill. You can turn east here, heading toward the tall trees that shelter the fort for a short hike of 1¼ miles.

The described route goes left past a dry rocky gully to cross a seasonal creek at ⅞ mile. You head northwest through grasslands. The headlands are more lush here, providing shelter for great blue herons, northern harriers,

DISTANCE: 2¾-mile loop or 3¼ miles round trip.

TIME: One or two hours.

TERRAIN: Gentle headlands descending to Northwest Cape, then northwest on headlands to overlook of Kolmer Gulch Cove and Beach.

ELEVATION GAIN/LOSS: 120 feet+/120 feet-.

BEST TIME: Spring, early summer for wildflowers.

WARNINGS: Stay back from steep, crumbly bluffs. Watch for poison oak.

DIRECTIONS TO TRAILHEAD: Turn west off Highway 1 at M.33.00 into main parking area for Fort Ross State Historic Park.

FEES: Day use: $3/vehicle.

FURTHER INFO: Fort Ross State Historic Park (707)847-3286.

black-shouldered kites and other birds. You pass another small gully as your trail returns to the edge of the bluff.

At one mile you cross a small creek where it tumbles off the bluff. The stream shelters windblown Bishop pine and wax myrtle, mimulus, coast buckwheat, lupine, beach morning glory and iris. You pick up a sheep trail to continue northwest over open grasslands, nearing the bluff's edge again at 1⅛ miles.

Before 1¼ miles you cross a creek at its mouth, where yarrow grows beneath wind-sheared pines and wax myrtle. A dilapidated wooden bridge served as a crossing for the logging railway that ran along these bluffs during the heyday of the Call Ranch.

Continue northwest along the heavily grazed level headlands, where many Douglas iris bloom in spring. An alternate track forks left to meander along the bluff's edge to a point, but the described trail goes straight. Around 1⅜ miles the paths merge. You veer right to circumvent a pocket cove where the surf crashes 80 feet below. Pelagic cormorants nest on the cliffs below you and Brandt's cormorants are often seen here. Double-breasted cormorants nest to the south on offshore rocks near the mouth of the Russian River.

As you continue northwest, the blufftop narrows and steepens. Highway 1 draws nearer your path. You pass coyote mint, purple seaside daisy, poppy and aster. By 1½ miles you return to the bluff's edge.

You meet a faint trail before 1⅝ miles. It climbs for 250 feet to meet Highway 1 at M.34.08. You can walk northwest only 100 feet, coming to an overlook of Kolmer Gulch Beach and Cove 80 feet below. The beach is a mixture of light sand from west of the San Andreas Fault (where you are) and dark, gravelly sand that has washed down the creek from east of the fault, about a mile upstream. (To explore the fault east of here, see Trail #14.) Do not descend to the beach from the overlook. You can walk to the beach on a rough ¼-mile trail from the other side of the gulch. It leaves Highway 1 at M.34.53, descending southwest.

Retrace your steps southeast across the headlands toward Fort Ross. After the creek with the old railroad bridge, you can shorten the return trip by veering left toward a rock outcrop. After you cross another creek, turn east, then southeast to meet an abandoned stretch of Highway 1. Then walk the old highway southeast back to the trailhead.

14.

KOLMER GULCH

FOLLOWING THE SAN ANDREAS RIFT ZONE

NOTICE: This trail will not open to the public until the end of 1990. Please call first.

In 1990 Fort Ross State Park tripled in size, adding a magnificent area of steep, open hillsides and wooded canyons extending east to 1500-foot elevation Seaview/Meyers Ridge, where tremendous vistas encompass the precipitous coastline and the fort. The Save-the-Redwoods League purchased 2157 wild acres surrounding the old park on three sides, then sold the land to the state for half the price.

The expanded park includes some shaky ground. About two miles of the San Andreas Rift Zone bisect the new acreage from northwest to southeast. Several old logging roads provide access to the fascinating rift zone. On this hike, you will see fault trenches and sag ponds amidst rolling country torn by the fault. Try not to visit on the day of the big one!

Your trail is an old logging road behind a locked gate, where the rift zone crosses Fort Ross Road.In 1906 the road and fence here were offset 7½ feet by the big quake. To the left of the trailhead stands an immense bay laurel. Its many-branched trunk is nearly 40 feet in circumference. As you descend gradually northwest, you pass a pioneer rose bush and a huge Douglas fir snag.

In 250 feet a depression on your left shelters redwoods up to ten feet in diameter. Many old redwoods here were snapped off during the 1906 quake. This gully is a fault trench, a surface manifestation of the tear in the earth's crust that lies below. The rift zone crosses the road ahead. Then a fault trench follows the road on the right, where several sag ponds lay hidden in young redwood forest. Sag ponds are seasonal or year-round pools where water does not drain from the fault trench.

As you leave the forest for open meadows, notice the gently rolling terrain around you. This gradual country, so unlike the steep, convoluted hills that dominate this stretch of coast, contains several parallel fault trenches with many sag ponds.

At ⅛ mile your road forks. Take the right fork, signed Upper Kolmer Gulch. You immediately cross a tributary of Kolmer Gulch where it flows northwest following the rift zone. Your road bends left, climbing along the fault.

At ¼ mile the path levels. On your left you overlook a deeply eroded gulch along the rift zone. As you descend gradually, Steer Field Road forks right to climb steeply.

You cross a tiny stream where giant horsetail ferns grow, then resume the climb northwest, passing redwoods, huckleberries and woodwardia ferns. Soon your trail levels again, as Tan Oak Trail forks right to climb steeply north. Between the forks Oregon grape and Douglas iris grow beneath redwoods.

Take the left fork, descending gradually. At ½ mile coast silktassel grows on the right. Continue a gradual descent, passing many stumps beside much healthy regeneration. On your left the terrain still drops steeply into the gulch. Bush lupine and coyote brush grow on the right.

At ⅝ mile another fault trench lies on the left. You descend along the lip of the trench to overlook a year-round sag pond where red and green duckweed covers the surface of the pond. You come to a large logging landing. The main road bends right to descend northeast, then north. At ¾ mile the road bends right to descend steeply toward the sound of rushing water.

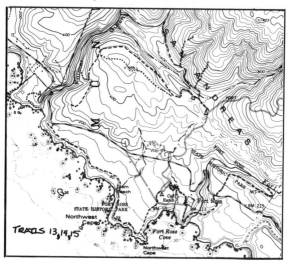

TRAILS 13,14,15

Before ⅞ mile you come to Kolmer Gulch Camp, along the creek in an area much disturbed by logging. The camp has picnic tables, barbecue pits and water piped from a spring, a great picnic spot (no camping allowed). From here you can explore up or down the creek. Descending along the creek, it is less than ⅛ mile to the junction of creek and fault line where the terrain gets rough. Downstream the creek turns northwest to follow the fault line for about ¼ mile before resuming its southwest-flowing course.

Retrace your steps up the road, returning to the first fork at 1⅝ miles. You can return from here to reach the trailhead at 1¾ miles. Or you can go right to explore more of this fractured country. The west fork climbs northwest, soon passing a large sag pond on the left. The ocean forms the horizon to the southwest. Your road levels, with the deep gulch now on your right.

Your route bends sharply left at 1¾ miles, starting a long, backward-S curve that descends gradually through heavily grazed meadows. As your route turns northwest to approach a forest of young Douglas fir, a spur on the left heads west through a fence, climbing gently through grasslands. You may return on the spur, but stay on the main fork now, following the rim of the gulch northwest through the forest. An old plow rusts on a rise to your left. You pass through a mixed forest of Bishop pine, redwood, Douglas fir, bay laurel and wax myrtle. Spearmint grows in moist spots along the road.

You crest a small rise at 2 miles, level briefly, then climb gradually to 2⅛ miles, where you level before climbing again. The deepening canyon that drops away on the right marks the rift zone. Beyond it the terrain rises steeply to

63

KOLMER GULCH:

DISTANCE: 1¾ miles round trip to Kolmer Gulch
  Camp, 4¾ miles round trip for full hike.

TIME: One to three hours.

TERRAIN: Through forests and meadows along San
  Andreas Rift Zone, passing slough trenches and sag
  ponds, then descending into heavily wooded Kolmer
  Gulch.

ELEVATION GAIN/LOSS: 340 feet+/340 feet- to camp.
  780 feet+/780 feet- for full hike.

BEST TIME: Spring for wildflowers and sag ponds,
  summer to see old orchard in its glory.

WARNINGS: **Call before going.** Watch for poison oak.

DIRECTIONS TO TRAILHEAD: Turn east off Highway 1
  at M.33.00 onto Fort Ross Road, opposite main
  entrance to Fort Ross. After .5 mile, the fort's old
  fenced orchard is on the right. Your trail is a fire
  road, just beyond on left. Do not block the gate.

FURTHER INFO: Fort Ross State Historic Park
  (707)847-3286.

OTHER SUGGESTION: THE OLD FORT ROSS
  ORCHARD is across the road from the trailhead. It
  contains some of the oldest cultivated trees in the
  West, including original Gravenstein apple stock.

the headwaters of Kolmer Gulch.

You crest another rise at 2¼ miles, where you can look
northeast to the steep glades at the precipitous head of the
gulch. Tiny evergreen violets grow on the road shoulder.
The road winds, beginning a gradual descent at 2⅜ miles.

At 2½ miles you reach a broad, barren landing to the
right of the road. The road turns west, then southwest from
here, paralleling deep and wooded Kolmer Gulch on your
right. I spotted a wild sow in early spring, trailing her litter
of multicolored piglets on this little traveled path. (Stay
away from wild pigs; they can be viscious!)

Around 2⅝ miles your descent gradually increases. You
may hear the rumble of traffic rising from Highway 1 about
¾ mile away. As you turn south, you can see the ocean
through the trees. Make a winding descent to 2¾ miles,
where an osprey nest perches atop a broken-top redwood
overlooking the gulch. Many tree stumps line the road, but

the forest along the bottom of the gulch is undisturbed.

You descend southwest, then south. As the dark green foliage of grand firs begins to mix with the redwoods and Douglas firs, you come to a fork. The main road drops steeply on the right, descending north into Kolmer Gulch. Take the left fork here, climbing south into moderately large mixed forest at 2⅞ miles, where calypso orchids, trilliums and evergreen violets thrive in spring.

The road soon levels, leaving the mature forest for young forest mixed with grasslands. Iris grow in large patches. At 3 miles you reach a large meadow. In 300 feet your path splits again. If you take either fork to 3⅛ miles, the forest comprises exclusively Bishop pine amidst grasslands.

You can see Highway 1 winding about ¼ mile below. Beyond it is the rugged coast north of Fort Ross (see Trail #13). (You could easily descend to the highway from here and walk the headlands southeast to the fort, but you had better have arranged a car shuttle beforehand.)

Retrace your steps up the road. You can return on the same route you came or veer right on a footpath at the grassy landing ⅛ mile beyond the barren landing. The path crosses a fence in 75 feet, then heads southeast through an immense grassland. It climbs gently to a rise, then descends gradually with wonderful views of Bodega Head, Tomales Bay and Point Reyes Peninsula. You rejoin the dirt road near the old plow, then retrace your steps to the trailhead.

15.

FORT ROSS CREEK

CLIMB TO SAN ANDREAS FAULT

The rugged, wooded canyon of Fort Ross Creek cuts deeply through steep, rolling grasslands east of the fort. About ½ mile upstream from its mouth, the creek meets the San Andreas Fault. Over many millennia, lateral ground movement along the fault has caused the creek to turn northwest along the fault for ½ mile, running perpendicular to its general northeast to southwest course. This wondrous manifestation of plate tectonics is most easily seen on a map. This intriguing hike explores the creek along the fault line, beautiful country with grand views of the fort and its surroundings.

From the parking area, take the trail to the right of the Visitor Center. You head south into cypress forest, then turn southeast, passing a spur on the right to the picnic area. Then your trail swings left, following a split redwood fence to the Visitor Center's back door, where a deck offers a fine view of Fort Ross through the trees. You briefly follow a seasonal creek, then veer right to cross it on a sturdy bridge.

You descend gradually at ⅛ mile, then veer left toward the fort. On your right are buildings of the Call Ranch, established in 1873. Soon your path bends right to follow the rough-hewn redwood walls of the fort, coming to the entrance at ¼ mile. If the fort is open, you can explore the exceptional historic buildings of the compound (be sure you do before leaving the area). The trail to Fort Ross Cove and Creek continues south to a paved road in 250 feet.

Go left on the road briefly, coming to the fort's south door. You turn right on the gravel road that descends south for ⅛ mile to the bluff's edge, then makes a big bend left to descend northeast into Fort Ross Cove.

The cove was the site of California's first shipyard. The Russians constructed at least four sea-going (but not very seaworthy) ships here during the heyday of the fort between 1818 and 1824. Although the Russians had considerable ship-building skills, they knew virtually nothing about working native California woods. Only the last of the ships demonstrated much seaworthiness. Archaeologists have excavated in the cove recently. The fort's bathhouse, cooperage, tannery and blacksmith shop were also at the cove.

Beyond ½ mile from the trailhead, you come to picnic tables and a chemical toilet along Fort Ross Creek at the head of the cove. From here a trail heads east, crossing the creek on a small bridge, then climbs along a gulch. The dense vegetation includes willows, hazel, coyote brush, elk clover, sticky monkeyflower, paintbrush, coastal manroot and poison oak.

FORT ROSS CREEK:

DISTANCE: 3¼ miles round trip.

TIME: Two hours.

TERRAIN: Easy descent to Fort Ross Cove and mouth of creek, then climb to old Russian cemetery. Cross Highway 1 and climb dirt road to ridge overlooking wooded creek canyon. Optional descent to creek along San Andreas Fault.

ELEVATION GAIN/LOSS: 440 feet+/440 feet- round trip to ridge, 520 feet+/520 feet- round trip to creek.

BEST TIME: Spring, early summer for wildflowers.

WARNINGS: Watch for poison oak. Steep uneven terrain beyond end of road descending to creek.

DIRECTIONS TO TRAILHEAD: Turn west off Highway 1 at M.33.00.

FEES: Day use: $3/vehicle. Car camping: $10/night.

FURTHER INFO: Fort Ross State Historic Park (707)847-3286.

At ¾ mile your trail switchbacks left and climbs through grasslands where baby blue eyes grow. At ⅞ mile you come to the old Russian cemetery. On this grassy knoll lie the Russian adventurers who were not lucky enough to return to their fatherland. During the early days of the Call Ranch, the several dozen graves were still marked by a few wooden Russian Orthodox crosses. The crosses, long ago returned to the soil, have now been replaced with one large Russian cross.

Go southeast, then east through a gate to cautiously cross busy Highway 1. Then climb northeast on the dirt fire road behind another gate. As you climb look southwest for a view of the fort. Notice the deep, wooded canyon of Fort Ross Creek as it climbs north on your left, then bends sharply right to cut through the headlands in front of you.

At 1⅛ miles your road bends right and climbs east, following the rim of the forested canyon of Fort Ross Creek on your left. You can hear the murmur of the creek rising through the forest. Your road bends southeast and climbs steeply at 1¼ miles, then levels atop a 320-foot hill, where you have a bird's eye view of the fort and the rugged coast. Start a gradual descent, passing a pump house and three water tanks. At 1⅜ miles you enter the forest. The road bends left and comes to a semicircle of old tourist cabins, now housing for archaeologists doing research in the park.

At 1½ miles the road ends. Go north between the last two cabins to find a hole in the fence; you are overlooking Fort Ross Creek where it intersects with the San Andreas Fault.

There is no real trail beyond this point, so you might want to retrace your steps from here. But if you are game to explore, it is not far down to the cool, gurgling creek. Just upstream a sturdy fence marks the park boundary. When the 1906 earthquake occurred, the fence that was here at the time was torn and offset 12 feet. It is this same displacement, occurring in smaller and perhaps larger increments over eons, that has caused the half mile jog in the direction of the creek.

Pick your way downstream, following the flat-bottomed, steep-walled canyon. Large redwoods grow with bay laurels along the flat; Douglas firs and tanoaks favor the slopes. Calypso orchids, trilliums, redwood sorrel and other plants of the deep forest grow in the understory. You can go about ⅛ mile downstream before a couple of massive log jams make further passage difficult. Find your way back to the fire road and retrace your steps to the trailhead.

16.

SONOMA'S LOST COAST

WALKING THE SAN ANDREAS FAULT AT ABALONE HOTEL

The primarily gentle terrain of the rest of the Sonoma Coast does not prepare one for the rugged and wild grandeur of the Lost Coast between Fort Ross and Russian Gulch. The area is relatively small, only six miles of coast, but inch for inch it matches the craggy beauty of Big Sur or the King Range, the more famous Lost Coast. If you are fit and check your tide tables scrupulously, you can walk the secluded beach at the base of dizzying cliffs, a place that belongs to the wild Pacific Ocean more than to Sonoma County. You will see magnificent tidepools, walk through the San Andreas Fault and visit a land that is usually seen only from sea. For this hike I recommend sturdy boots for the uneven, sometimes loose footing, and hiking with a friend. You must not attempt the hike in winter, when a high tide is rising or during storms.

From the end of the dirt road, you head south to dip through a gully that shelters willows, horsetail ferns, mimulus and sun cups. Follow the fence southwest onto a narrow promontory, crossing the fence beyond ⅛ mile. You then carefully descend a steep, winding path southeast over loose soil to the shoreline at ¼ mile. (If this descent feels unsafe, the Lost Coast is NOT for you.)

You head southeast along a beach of large rocks. Fort Ross Reef lies offshore just below the water's surface. It teems with sea life, including abundant abalone that gives this area the nickname "Abalone Hotel."

At ⅜ mile offshore rocks provide nesting grounds for cormorants and other sea birds. Beyond ½ mile massive piles of driftwood lie along the beach. Soon the rocks on the beach are smaller. You round a shelf of sandstone at ⅝ mile, then reach the mouth of Mill Gulch.

Beyond ¾ mile you approach the narrowest point on the beach so far on the hike. At +5 feet tide, you must climb the rocks above the surf to proceed. **Do not pass this point in winter or during storm seas, or if the tide is rising.** If tide and seas are low enough you can continue south.

You soon have a view of rugged cliffs rising on your left, with Highway 1 rounding a big curve 400 feet above. At one mile you pass old cast iron wheels still mounted on their axle at the base of the cliff. Harbor seals frequent the offshore rocks. You round another point where you need to watch for waves at high tide. Then the beach turns east to meet the San Andreas Fault.

At 1⅛ miles you come to the base of a slide of gray clay. As you look at the slide and the cliffs above, you are looking into the San Andreas Fault. The rocks here are fractured down to their molecular structure. The gray clay is actually mylonite, pulverized rock with a structure just like ground glass. The fault is about ¼ mile wide here. In other places it gets as wide as one mile.

Much seaweed and driftwood lie along the beach, now composed of small stones that provide easier walking. At 1¼ miles the beach narrows at the base of another slide. The small creek of Timber Gulch empties onto dark sand at 1⅜ miles. The dark sand indicates that you are now on the North American Plate rather than the Pacific Plate, where you began the hike.

Enjoy walking the fine, dark sand, the Riviera of the Lost Coast. You pass more seeps at the base of slides. You pass a narrow spot after 1⅝ miles that is safe to pass at a tide

SONOMA'S LOST COAST:

DISTANCE: 5½ miles one way, 10 miles round trip.

TIME: All day to do full hike.

TERRAIN: Rugged beach walking punctuated by scrambles over rock outcrops.

ELEVATION GAIN/LOSS: 370 feet+/370 feet-, one way; 340 feet+/340 feet-, round trip.

BEST TIME: Moderate to low tide.

WARNINGS: Watch for killer waves along beach. Stay off this beach during storms and in winter. You need a tide lower than 3.0 feet during your hike. Inquire about conditions before you go. Use extreme caution on slippery tidal rocks. Hike with a friend and wear sturdy boots.

DIRECTIONS TO TRAILHEAD: Turn west off Highway 1 at M.31.36 to entrance for Fort Ross Reef Campground. Go left immediately, open gate, then close it behind you. Then drive .4 mile to end of road and the trailhead.

FEES: Day use: $3/vehicle. Car camping: $10/night.

FURTHER INFO: Fort Ross State Historic Park (707)847-3286.

OTHER SUGGESTIONS: You can also start this hike from FORT ROSS, adding 1½ miles in each direction, but this is considerably more difficult to do in a day. Or you can start from RUSSIAN GULCH or BLACK RANCH at the south end (see Trail #17).

lower than +4.5 feet. By 1¾ miles the lower beach is composed of small rocks, but the upper beach is fine, dark sand. This leads into a beach of all sand, more relief for your rock-weary soles.

At 1⅞ miles you pass another small creek, where the cliffs on your left rise abruptly. You are now east of the fault line. The rocks here are not fractured. The cliffs stand tall without continuous crumbling, rising 1600 feet in less than a mile. Another small seep at 2 miles is jammed with monkeyflowers and other moisture-loving plants. Continue along the broad, sandy beach, passing more seeps on the cliff-face above the beach.

At 2¼ miles the broad beach ends at a rock outcrop. Walk southeast over intermittent rock and sand. The narrow beach becomes broader at 2⅜ miles, where a large seep has formed algae-covered mineral terraces. You pass a pyramid-shaped rock at the sea's edge at 2½ miles. Another offshore rock is a popular perch for pelicans and cormorants. Between the two rocks, an emergency exit trail climbs steeply to Highway 1.

Continue along the beach of mixed rock and sand. You pass the remains of cars along the base of the steep cliff, then another small creek. At 2⅝ miles you climb up and over a jumble of rocks where purple seaside daisies grow, then descend to a rocky beach at the base of a slide-torn cliff. The beach provides moderately easy walking for ⅜ mile. At 2⅞ miles, sea fig and seaside daisy grow on the cliff above the rocky beach.

At 3 miles the beach narrows. You reach another spot where you need a moderately low tide to proceed. Then the beach becomes broader, with scattered patches of fine sand. Pass several more seeps on the cliff-face. Beyond 3⅛ miles a steep gulch cuts through the cliff. Sheep graze on the steep bluffs above. You soon pass another narrow spot.

Then the beach broadens to its widest and sandiest so far on the hike, offering easy walking at the base of steep cliffs. At 3⅜ miles you approach a rocky point over which you must scramble. It is easier than it looks. Pick your way to the top for good views up and down the Lost Coast. Then scramble down the south side and continue over large rocks on the beach. The easiest path is at the base of the cliff.

At 3⅝ miles walking on fine sand provides a respite. Pampas grass grows on the steep bluffs. Harbor seals often fish offshore here. At 3¾ miles you pass rich tidepools where many sea vegetables grow. Anemones, sea stars, bat stars, turban snails and hermit crabs abound. You pass a small cove, then meet a narrow passage at 3⅞ miles where the best route climbs over a rock shelf.

Then you walk a gravelly beach. At 4 miles a 50-foot-tall sea stack stands at tideline, with more sea stacks ahead. Pick your way over uneven terrain. You soon pass the base of a taller sea stack, a pointed landmark that can be seen for miles up and down the coast. It stands above the tideline. Scramble between massive rocks. Sea rocket grows in the shelter at their base. You pass more rocky tidepools where mussels, gooseneck barnacles and sea palms thrive.

At 4⅛ miles you walk a rocky beach with gradual bluffs on the left. Before 4¼ miles the beach turns to gravel as you approach a huge, domed rock outcrop that juts seaward. You reach the base of the huge rock at 4⅜ miles.

If you are hiking back the same way you came in, this is a good place to turn back. Russian Gulch lies 1⅛ miles southeast over rugged terrain. The immense rock presents cliffs to the ocean, precluding any chance of walking around the west face.

To continue, you must scramble up the steep chute between the outcrop and the steep, grassy headland to which it is attached. Use extreme caution as you climb the loose, crumbly rock along the chute. In just 200 feet, you top the notch, about 75 feet above sea level. Be careful as your path plunges steeply down to a small, rocky beach on the other side of the big rock. In 250 feet the beach ends. You must scramble over a jumble of rocks for 250 feet.

At 4½ miles you return to beach sand briefly, then hop a few more boulders to a large sandy beach. The dark sand provides easy walking to 4¾ miles, where you pass a seep along the cliff. The beach narrows at a point where you might have to scramble over rocks at high tide.

Beyond the narrow spot, you return to sandy beach, passing a big sea stack at 4⅞ miles. You approach one last cove, nestled between two giant rock outcrops and the bluffs. The beautiful emerald pool looks as if it might be a haven for mermaids. In fact it provides great tidepooling at a minus tide.

At 5 miles you can go no farther along the beach. To return to the trailhead, retrace your steps from here for a

10-mile round trip.

If you are hiking through to Russian Gulch, you have nowhere to go but up. A narrow, steep and rocky path climbs southeast to the low-point on the ridge to the left of the rock outcrop. Use caution on the steep climb. At the top you have a magnificent view of the coast southeast. Russian Gulch, your destination, is the larger of the two sandy coves. Bodega Head juts seaward 12 miles away.

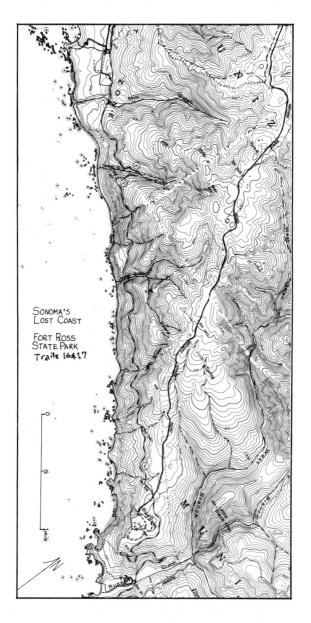

Sonoma's
Lost Coast

Fort Ross
State Park
Trails 16 & 17

A well-trod trail heads east over rolling grasslands for ⅛ mile. Then the trail turns southeast, following the bluff's edge for 400 feet. At 5¼ miles your trail turns left and descends northeast toward the parking lot at Russian Gulch, passing through grasslands and coastal scrub. Watch carefully for poison oak in the scrub. You climb over a fence and come to the parking area at 5½ miles. Welcome back to civilization!

SONOMA COAST STATE BEACH
INCLUDES THE NEXT SEVEN TRAILS

Actually a string of many beaches separated by rocky bluffs, this state park unit offers more than 5000 beautiful acres along a diverse, mostly gentle 18 miles of coastline from the new Black Ranch unit in the north to Bodega Head in the south. The beaches become crowded during summer and holiday weekends, but you can always find some solitude if you look in the most remote corners. A marvelous array of wildflowers brighten the creeks and headlands in spring and early summer.

In winter you will often have this expansive coast nearly to yourself. Ferocious surf and wild seas indicate the rugged, untamed nature of these gentle lands. You must always use caution along North Coast beaches and head-lands, watching for oversized waves and keeping in mind your route of escape. But especially in winter keep the wild ocean at safe distance. In 35 years, these beaches had 73 known drownings and 80 reported rescues. Winter also brings the greatest abundance of bird species. More than 200 species have been counted in the Audubon Society's Christmas count, of a total of more than 300 species found during the year.

In addition to the developed trails described in the next seven hikes, many beaches and headlands offer short, easy access where you can just sit or picnic, contemplating the majestic meeting of shore and sea. Some offer fishing, tidepooling and diving as well. Here are the mileposts of places otherwise not covered in the text.

M.15.94: Rock Point
M.15.22: Gleason Beach
M.14.68: Portuguese Beach
M.14.40: Schoolhouse Beach
M.14.20: Carmet Beach
M.14.05: Marshall Gulch

17.

NORTH OF JENNER

SHORT TRAILS EXPLORE STEEP, WILD COAST

Between Jenner, at the mouth of the Russian River, and Fort Ross, 13 miles up the coast, Highway 1 tortuously twists and climbs over one of the most spectacular sections of its entire length, along the faces and folds of rugged cliffs that rise up 1300 feet from the sea. The San Andreas Fault dissects the shore here. The collision of the North American and Pacific tectonic Plates causes these towering cliffs. It is worthwhile to take your time on this tangle of highway, pulling out for the hurried local traffic, stopping to admire the sweeping views, taking a walk or two to admire the details of wildflowers and the cliffs plunging to the sea.

Several short, easy trails investigate these awesome headlands, each one exploring a different aspect of the varied, rugged terrain. The northernmost of these trails begins 600 feet above the Pacific, where Highway 1 reaches its dizzy summit at the junction with Meyers Grade. The 275 acres of the Black Ranch have just been acquired for public access through the efforts of COASTWALK and the Coastal Conservancy. The new trail (to be completed July 1991) offers wheelchair access to this plunging, view-rich headland and a link to the Lost Coast hike (see previous trail) far below. The second trail is a level beach walk at Russian Gulch. The third hike surveys rolling headlands where a lumber loading chute once was and where pere-grine falcons sometimes nest in summer. The fourth trail descends from the rolling, wildflower-rich headlands to the secluded north end of the beach where the Russian River meets the Pacific.

THE BLACK RANCH TRAILS (one mile paved, handicap-accessible loop; 2¾ miles steep round trip to beach; 3½ miles round trip to Russian Gulch) head east on asphalt from the gravel parking lot, offering grand views south along the coast. At ¼ mile you turn south and descend along

DISTANCE: ½ mile to 3½ miles round trip.

TIME: One half hour to two hours (each trail).

TERRAIN: Black Ranch: High bluffs overlooking steep headlands.

    Russian Gulch: Easy walk to beach.

    North Jenner Headlands: Descend rolling, headlands to follow convoluted bluff's edge.

    Descent to Russian River mouth: Over headlands to point, then steep descent from bluff to beach.

ELEVATION GAIN/LOSS: Black Ranch: minimal on paved loop; 600 feet- to beach. Russian Gulch: negligible. North Jenner Headlands: 160 feet+/160 feet- round trip. Descent to Russian River mouth: 180 feet+/ 180 feet- round trip.

BEST TIME: Spring, early summer for wildflowers.

WARNINGS: Stay back from steep, unstable cliffs. Watch for poison oak.

DIRECTIONS TO TRAILHEAD: All on west side of Highway 1 north of Jenner at the following mileposts:

    Black Ranch: M.26.3

    Russian Gulch: M.24.55

    North Jenner Headlands: M.23.83

    Descent to river mouth: M.23.21

FURTHER INFO: Sonoma Coast State Beach (707)875-3483.

the top of steep rolling grasslands. Beyond ⅜ mile the paved trail comes to an observation platform atop a knoll with a 270 degree view. Sonoma's Lost Coast sprawls below you. If the day is clear, you can see Fort Ross Reef to the northwest and Point Reyes 35 miles south. Your paved path climbs to another view area by ⅝ mile. The pavement climbs from there to the trailhead.

For hikers able to navigate steeper terrain, a dirt footpath descends south, then southeast, following the old coast wagon road to ⅞ mile. The trail switchbacks right, descending steep headlands, then left to traverse the top of 200-foot cliffs plunging to the isolated Lost Coast. At 1¼ miles you meet the trail climbing out of the Lost Coast. The right fork descends steeply to the isolated low-tide beach. The left fork follows the bluffs east to 1½ miles, then descends through coastal scrub and poison oak to the Russian Gulch parking lot at 1¾ miles.

THE RUSSIAN GULCH TRAIL (¾ mile round trip) parallels the creek from the parking lot through willows and red alders to reach the surf in ⅜ mile. The ⅛-mile-wide beach is sheltered by 120-foot cliffs.

THE NORTH JENNER HEADLANDS TRAIL (1½ miles round trip) descends southwest across rolling grassy headlands where coyote brush, lupine and purple aster grow. You reach the bluff's edge before ⅛ mile, then turn left to follow it southeast. Douglas iris, yarrow, pennyroyal, paintbrush, seaside daisy and pearly everlasting grow in the grass, while coast buckwheat, bush lupine, angelica and hen and chicks hug the cliffs above the ocean. Beyond ¼ mile your path bends right to follow the bluff's edge out to a point, where you have views up and down the ragged coast. The promontory ¼ mile west is sometimes home to nesting peregrine falcons in summer.

Your trail climbs north, then turns east, climbing gradually to meet a steep spur on the right at ⅜ mile that descends steeply south to a cove. You continue along the bluff's edge, veering right on a spur as the well-trod path forks left to return to the road. You follow the vague trail along the top of the cliff through low coastal scrub with paintbrush and sticky monkeyflower. At ½ mile you climb east to wind around several eroded gullies, then descend south to bluff's edge. At ⅝ mile you reach a point overlooking a cove where harbor seals haul out on the rocks. Side trails descend steeply to the small beach.

The main trail winds east to Highway 1 to get around a big gully. You can return northwest to the trailhead from

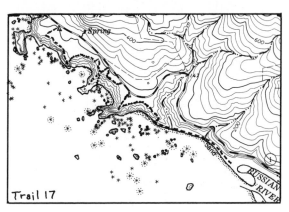

Trail 17

here or descend southwest to return to the bluff's edge at ¾ mile, then follow it southeast for another 250 feet before another big gully forces a return to the road at M.23.34. Retrace your steps, more or less, to the trailhead.

TRAIL TO NORTH SIDE OF RUSSIAN RIVER MOUTH (1¾ miles round trip): Descend southwest across the grassy headlands. The trail descends ⅛ mile to a point where you have a view of the river mouth and surrounding coast. A spur heads to the tip of the point, but follow the trail that turns east along the blufftop, nearly returning to the road at ¼ mile. Black sage, paintbrush, coast buckwheat and other plants grow on the bluff face. Walk a wood plank across a tiny creek, then head southeast toward the river mouth, passing bush lupine and poppies. At ⅜ mile your trail starts a gradual descent as the trail becomes vague. You soon veer right amidst shoulder-high lupine and begin a steep, winding descent south down the cliff face. You reach the beach by ½ mile, just 300 feet from its north end. Walk southeast along the beach. Walk ⅜ mile down the beach to the river mouth.

18.

POMO CANYON to SHELL BEACH
FROM REDWOOD FOREST TO COASTAL VIEWS

Willow Creek has carved a broad, deep canyon similar to that of the nearby Russian River. The creek's grasslands, rimmed by dense forest, are a favorite hunting ground for red-tailed hawks and black-shouldered kites. If the road is closed to Pomo Campground, you must walk the level 1½ miles to the trailhead, adding one mile to total hike.

From the parking lot at the end of the road, a trail heads southwest toward the Environmental Camps and into the redwood forest. In 50 feet, turn right on the unmarked Pomo Canyon Trail, passing to the right of two toilets beside a bay laurel. The trail climbs gradually, heading north through redwood forest. You quickly pass two trails branching left, but stay on the main trail, passing picnic tables overlooking the meadow along Willow Creek.

Soon your trail veers left, starting a steady climb up a ridge forested with young redwoods, tanoaks and gracefully arched bay laurels. Shift into low gear for the steady climb ahead. At ⅛ mile a trail sign confirms that you are on the right path. Soon your climb eases briefly in a clearing where huckleberries thrive. You quickly return to the forest, continuing to climb the ridge.

Your ascent slackens around ¼ mile. In 250 feet you leave the broad skid road you have been following for a footpath that veers right. You pass a Douglas fir eight feet in diameter. California hazel grows nearby. This native relative of the filbert has velvety oval leaves. Its nuts are a favorite of squirrels.

Your trail narrows at ⅜ mile, passing ancient Douglas firs, bent and forked by the powerful coastal winds they have endured over their several-hundred-year lives. A break in the forest offers views north to the grassy ridges near the Russian River. You leave the forest for a brushy clearing where gooseberry bushes tangle with hazels and ferns. The brush here occasionally obscures the trail.

Before ½ mile you are again under a forest canopy of arching bays and wind-topped firs. The trail ducks under a horizontal bay trunk and resumes a steady climb.

At ⅝ mile you leave the forest, breaking into grasslands. Your trail turns left and climbs south along the grassy ridge. In spring and summer these meadows are filled with poppies, lupines and other wildflowers. Even in fall the pink to purple blooms of godetias and the yellow flowers of tarweed grace the trail. Look northwest for a vista of the mouth of the Russian River.

Your trail levels at the top of a small gully. At ¾ mile you approach a saddle between two rock outcrops. Your path soon veers right and wraps around the rock outcrop on your right. You might detour for an easy scramble to its rocky top, where the fine view extends up the coast beyond the river mouth all the way to Northwest Cape at Fort Ross. You will find coast buckwheat, hen and chicks, poppy, sticky monkeyflower and leather ferns growing on the rock's north and west faces.

Returning to the trail, duck under a bushy bay tree and begin a gradual descent. An old, single-line telephone pole marks the ⅞-mile-point. Join an old road and descend through grasslands scattered with coyote brush. A spring

DISTANCE: 5½ miles round trip (6½ miles if road to
Pomo Campground is closed).

TIME: Three or four hours.

TERRAIN: From creek canyon climb through forest,
over a ridge and through grasslands, then descend to
marine terraces and the beach.

ELEVATION GAIN/LOSS: 720 feet+/720 feet-, each way.

BEST TIME: Spring for wildflowers.

WARNINGS: Do not block gate at trailhead. Watch for
poison oak. Carry water on this arduous hike.

DIRECTIONS TO TRAILHEAD: Turn east off Highway 1
at M.19.79 onto Willow Creek Road. Go 2.6 miles to
where Pomo Campground Road forks right. From
November to March, park here (do not block gate).
From April to October, the campground is open, so
you can drive ½ mile to the trailhead. Western
trailhead is at M.18.22 on Highway 1.

FEES: Day use: $3/vehicle when campground open.
Environmental camps: $6/night.

FURTHER INFO: Sonoma Coast State Beach
(707)875-3483.

ENVIRONMENTAL CAMPS: POMO CAMPGROUND
offers walk-in camping in a beautiful spot near the
trailhead. WILLOW CREEK offers more walk-in sites
near the Russian River. Both open April-October.

on the left is a favorite animal watering spot.

At one mile you descend gradually, heading west with
forest on your left and vintage Sonoma coast and hills
everywhere else. Coffeeberry mingles with the coyote
brush. You swing left and climb a short hill into redwood
forest to cross a murmuring stream. Another short climb
tops out at 1⅛ miles. Then you descend, redwood/fir forest
on your left, dense scrub of coffeeberry and California
blackberry on your right.

You cross another brook at the edge of a beautiful forest,
then descend north, then west around a big bend. You
climb a small hill and pass under the old phone line. At 1¼
miles the town of Jenner appears to the northwest. You
cross two more creeks in the next ⅛ mile as you head west
through grasslands. Then descend along a fence line where
poison oak grows.

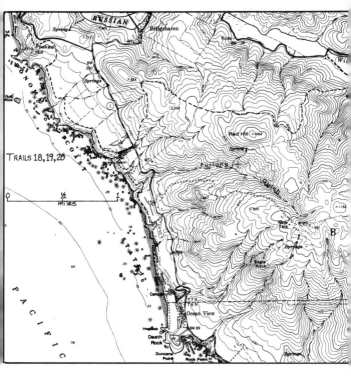

At 1½ miles the view west opens up to the ocean and horizon. Soon you can see Highway 1 winding far below. Continue along the fence on a gradual descent nearly to 1¾ miles. You finally turn left to climb a hiker's ladder over the fence. Now you wind south, descending to cross a small creek at the top of its canyon, then joining another road to climb the ridge to your south. At 1⅞ miles you pass a side trail on the right and continue your climb.

Beyond 2 miles you tend southwest on a series of short ups and downs through wildflower-studded meadows with views north to Jenner and the Russian River. At 2⅛ miles you ascend the last hill between you and Shell Beach. Another old road enters from the left at 2¼ miles. Then you climb quickly to the summit. From this ridge you overlook the entire southern Sonoma Coast. On a clear day you see Bodega Head to the south, with Point Reyes jutting seaward beyond it.

If you want a shorter, easier round trip hike than the full excursion described here, this is your ideal turnaround point. By turning back now, you will save one mile and nearly 1000 feet in elevation gain *and* loss. (Or you may have a shuttle car waiting at the west end.) If you have most of the day left, you can make it to Shell Beach, rest, then trudge back over the ridge to Pomo Canyon.

Near the summit you pick up an old paved road and follow it on a steepening descent. As the road swings gradually left, you have views of large on- and offshore sea stacks below. At 2½ miles a large boulder stands on your left. You pass under a power line.

At 2⅝ miles you switchback left as your descent eases. You quickly come to a gate and the western trailhead at 2¾ miles. Just across Highway 1 (at M.18.2), the road to the Shell Beach parking area descends west. Use caution crossing the highway. It is ⅛ mile from the trailhead to the parking area, another ⅛ mile to the beach (The Coastal Trail heads *north* from the northwest corner of Shell Beach parking lot. It heads *south* from the southwest corner.)

If you plan to return to the Pomo Canyon Trailhead today, be sure to leave at least two hours of daylight and carry a flashlight.

19.

BLIND BEACH to SHELL BEACH
THE KORTUM TRAIL

About 100,000 years ago, all but the start of this hike was below sea level, being carved by waves into the gently sloping terrace you see today. This portion of the California coast has been uplifting since then, pushed upward from sea level by the collision of the offshore Pacific tectonic Plate and the onshore North American Plate. Despite the major earthquakes that this region is subject to, most of the uplifting has been extremely gradual. On the average this shore rises one inch every 100 years.

In recent history, since white settlers arrived in the 1800s, ranchers have grazed their cattle and sheep here. Cattle still graze the headlands from Blind Beach to Shell Beach. The headlands south of Shell Beach were closed to grazing in the 1980s.

The difference in policy between the two areas has produced striking results that will be evident if you hike all 4 miles of trail. The recently grazed land is largely devoid of native vegetation, overrun with introduced species. The southern segment of trail has recovered many native species in a short time. The northern 2 miles are recommended for the views and the marine terrace geology; the southern 2 miles merit attention more for the native plants.

The disruption of the environment here could have been

much worse. In 1972 a subdivision was planned for these coastal terraces. Some streets were installed and a few houses built before coastal preservationists managed to halt construction. After that battle was won, former county Supervisor Bill Kortum and the group COAAST fought to acquire the land for a state park. They went on to build the trail you will hike today. In 1990 it was designated as the Kortum Trail.

If you have two cars in your party, you can park one at each end of the trail and not have to retrace your steps.

From the Blind Beach parking lot, follow the road south for 300 feet to find the trailhead. From there the trail angles south to cross a hiker's ladder over a fence. Head southeast across grasslands with scattered Douglas iris and coast buckwheat. Cylindrical green posts mark the trail.

After ⅛ mile the trail climbs toward Peaked Hill. Remaining native vegetation includes coyote brush, yarrow and buttercup. At ¼ mile you approach rock outcrops along the ridge. Hedge nettle and miners lettuce grow in protected pockets beside the rocks.

If the day is clear as you top the ridge, take a faint trail on the right that climbs quickly to the windswept 377-foot summit of Peaked Hill. At the rocky top an inspiring view of this rugged coast stretches to the horizon, with Bodega Head pointing seaward 10 miles south.

Beyond the ridge your trail turns east and descends. At ⅜ mile you parallel the road, then cross another hiker's ladder. As you continue east along the fence, notice the natural (ungrazed) vegetation to the left of the fence.

You turn south and descend to a small rock outcrop at ½ mile. At the rocks your path bends left to descend southeast. After a small gully, your descent eases as you approach a large onshore sea stack. You come to the imposing sea stack at ⅝ mile. It shelters leather ferns, hen and chicks and other coastal scrub plants. The trail goes to the right of the rock outcrop and descends to bluff's edge.

Head south-southeast along the bluff, where many Douglas irises and buttercups grow. A tall sea stack offshore called Gull Rock provides nesting for Brandt's cormorants, western gulls and pigeon guillemots. Beyond ¾ mile you cross a creek with still pools. Your trail traverses level headlands just inland from steep cliffs. Pass another immense onshore sea stack, with six large stacks offshore.

At one mile you descend into a scrub-choked gulch to cross a small bridge. As you climb out of the gulch, notice the eroded wall of the canyon. You can see layers of

BLIND BEACH to SHELL BEACH:

DISTANCE: 3¾ miles round trip to Shell Beach; 8 miles round trip to Wrights Beach (including Trail #20).

TIME: Two hours round trip to Shell Beach, four hours round trip to Wrights Beach.

TERRAIN: Over the ridge of Peaked Hill, then down to gently sloping, grass-covered marine terrace overlooking the shore.

ELEVATION GAIN/LOSS: 360 feet+/360 feet- round trip to Shell Beach Trailhead; 140 feet+/220 feet-, one way.

BEST TIME: Spring, early summer for wildflowers.

WARNINGS: Stay off Goat Rock: every year people fall or are swept into the sea from this spectacular but dangerous sea stack. Stay back from the very edge of the crumbly, unstable bluffs. Watch for poison oak, especially on the last part of the trail.

DIRECTIONS TO TRAILHEAD: Less than one mile south of the Russian River mouth, turn west off Highway 1 at M.19.15 onto Goat Rock Road. Go .75 mile to the Blind Beach parking area.

FURTHER INFO: Sonoma Coast State Beach (707)875-3483.

OTHER SUGGESTIONS: GOAT ROCK BEACH lies at the end of the road, providing a mile of broad sand to wander. A SHORT TRAIL descends from Blind Beach parking lot to the beach in ⅝ mile. TRAIL #20 can be combined with #19 for a long ramble on coastal bluffs. TRAIL #18 can also be linked with this trail for a spectacularly varied, but arduous 10½-mile hike.

rounded, ocean-polished pebbles laid down when this was the ocean floor.

Your trail continues across level headlands. Around 1⅛ miles a rough trail provides access to a small, rocky, low-tide beach (be careful!). The main trail continues across the overgrazed headlands. Beyond 1¼ miles you cross another hiker's ladder at the head of a gully. Your trail jogs east around a big ravine that cuts the headlands ahead.

At 1½ miles you cross a bridge over another unnamed creek. Follow the creek back to the bluff's edge and follow it south. You swerve inland again to cross another hiker's ladder at 1¾ miles.

The headlands south of the fence have not been grazed.

They are covered with a thick layer of natural vegetation including coyote brush, cow parsnip, paintbrush, yarrow, purple miniature and bush lupine, flowering currant, twinberry, star solomon's seal and poison oak. Red hot poker, an introduced species with showy orange and yellow flower spikes, also grows here.

You reach the Shell Beach parking lot at 1⅞ miles from the trailhead. You can 1) retrace your steps, 2) descend a trail on the right to Shell Beach (⅛ mile, great tidepools at low tide), 3) climb east over the ridge on Trail #18, or 4) continue south on the Kortum Trail to Wrights Beach (see Trail #20).

20.

SHELL BEACH to WRIGHTS BEACH

NATIVE PLANTS ON THE KORTUM TRAIL

Your trail starts at the southwest corner of the Shell Beach parking lot. You head east, paralleling the lot for the first 200 feet, then turn south to cross a bridge over the first of five creeks between here and Wrights Beach.

The creek canyon shelters a dense tangle of plants, including sticky monkeyflower, cow parsnip, purple bush lupine, twinberry, paintbrush, flowering currant and salmonberry. From the creek you climb to headlands cov-

SHELL BEACH TO WRIGHTS BEACH:

DISTANCE: up to 4¾ miles round trip.

TIME: Two or three hours.

TERRAIN: Over headlands with native vegetation, crossing several creeks, then descending to the black sand of Wrights Beach.

ELEVATION GAIN/LOSS: 100 feet+/200 feet- to Wrights Beach; 300 feet+/300 feet-, round trip.

BEST TIME: Spring, early summer for wildflowers.

WARNINGS: Stay back from crumbly bluff edge. Watch for poison oak in coastal scrub. Watch for killer waves, stay back from tide line when walking on the beach.

DIRECTIONS TO TRAILHEAD: Turn west off Highway 1 at M.18.22 into Shell Beach parking area.

FURTHER INFO: Sonoma Coast State Beaches (707)875-3483.

OTHER SUGGESTIONS: You can camp at WRIGHTS BEACH CAMPGROUND at M.16.8 and do the hike in reverse. WRIGHTS BEACH also has a WHEELCHAIR-ACCESSIBLE PATH to the beach.

ered with coastal scrub. Your trail follows the creek west. If you look at the cutbank across the creek, you can see a cross-section of the ocean sediments laid down long ago on this ancient marine terrace.

At ⅛ mile your trail reaches the bluff's edge, where beach strawberry and narrow-leaved mule ears grow. You can see Shell Beach below. As you follow the bluff southeast through tufts of native grasses, the diversity of plants in the coastal scrub vegetation diminishes. Still, buttercups, lupine, blue-eyed grass and paintbrush brighten the way.

You soon turn east, following the green posts away from the ocean, climbing gradually. At ¼ mile your trail bends right and climbs past mugwort and purple bush lupine. You soon descend into a second gulch, where the coastal scrub includes many of the same plants you saw at the previous creek, plus other species: thimbleberry, sword fern, coastal manroot and nettle.

You cross a bridge and climb back onto the marine terrace. The modern house on your right is now owned by state parks. You cross the driveway of the house at ⅜ mile, then traverse the headlands. You soon turn right and descend to bluff's edge, following it briefly.

At ½ mile you approach Furlong Gulch, the deepest canyon along the Kortum Trail. Your trail bends left, descending east to the bottom of the canyon. You switchback three times, descending toward the beach and a rough creek crossing at ⅝ mile. Purple seaside daisy and coast buckwheat grow on the canyon floor. A dark sand beach lies at the mouth of the canyon.

Climb back onto the headlands and follow the edge of the bluff south. Sea thrift grows profusely along the trail. Before ¾ mile you pass a small promontory on your right, a pleasant rest spot with great views up and down the beach. The trail winds inland to pass houses at ⅞ mile, then meanders back to the bluff edge.

Before one mile your trail turns left and heads inland again. You cross the pavement of a cul-de-sac, part of a subdivision planned for these headlands before coastal access advocates stopped the development and established a park instead.

From the pavement your trail descends into a scrub-filled gully, crosses a bridge and climbs back to the headlands. You follow the edge of the gully west.

At 1⅛ miles your trail begins to descend to the beach. By 1¼ miles the trail ends, depositing you on the long, dark sand strand of Wrights Beach. Steep, varied bluffs rise above the beach, dense coastal scrub alternating with bare, jagged rock.

At 1⅜ miles you pass a gully jammed with dense, lush vegetation. Then you walk the fine sand at the base of layered rock formations. Stay back from the water line on the steep beach; dangerous rip currents and rogue "killer" waves can occur here.

Around 1½ miles the beach is composed of wave-polished pebbles, a good spot for beachcombing. At 1⅝ miles the beach broadens. You begin to see more people on this broad playground of a beach. At 1⅞ miles the first sites of Wrights Beach Campground are nestled at the base of bluffs to the east.

At 2 miles from Shell Beach Trailhead, the day-use parking and picnic area lies at the mouth of the canyon east of the beach. You can continue along the beach for almost ⅜ mile to the base of Duncans Point, where the beached sea stack called the Hogback and the small island of Death

Rock lie. But if you do, stay back from these outcrops, no matter how low the tide or calm the ocean. Death Rock is closed to hikers, being one of the most dangerous, deadly spots on the entire California Coast.

If you did not plan a car shuttle to Wrights Beach, retrace your steps to the Shell Beach Trailhead.

21.

BODEGA DUNES LOOP
SHIFTING SANDS ON THE SAN ANDREAS

The Bodega Dunes sprawl over 900 acres of coast, from the mouth of Salmon Creek (source of much of the sand) to Bodega Harbor. The shifting sands reach inland for up to one mile, bordering the west shore of the harbor. The live-stock of early settlers overgrazed the dunes, decimating the native vegetation. This caused the dunes to shift, threatening homes, farms and Bodega Harbor. In the 1930s European beach grass was planted to stabilize the dunes. Women rode wagons pulled by tractors up and down the dunes, planting grass shoots by hand.

The dunes are home to many mammals, including deer, jack rabbits, mice, voles, foxes, raccoons, weasels and badgers. Birds that inhabit the dunes include red-tailed hawks, northern harriers, short-eared owls, California quail and ring-necked pheasants. Many sea birds frequent the beach and the mud flats of the harbor. Monarch butterflies winter in eucalyptus trees in the campground.

From the parking lot, a paved trail passes restrooms and picnic tables, then heads southwest into dunes covered with European beach grass. The pavement ends as a boardwalk begins. The boardwalk bends right, passing through an area closed to foot traffic to protect and restore dune vegetation.

In 400 feet you reach an observation deck (wheelchair access to this point) overlooking long, dune-backed South Salmon Creek Beach. Descend to the fine blond sand of the beach, reaching the shore before ⅛ mile.

Always keep an eye on the surf, being aware that oversized rogue waves can strike any time, but especially in winter. It is best to hike at least 50 feet above the high-water line, unless it is a calm summer day.

Head south along the beach toward Mussel Point, which juts seaward 1½ miles south. As you walk the beach, watch

BODEGA DUNES LOOP:

DISTANCE: 3¾-mile loop.

TIME: Two or three hours.

TERRAIN: Along the beach, then into rolling dunes, climbing to the precipitation ridge before circling back to trailhead.

ELEVATION GAIN/LOSS: 180 feet+/180 feet-.

BEST TIME: Spring and summer for wildflowers.

WARNINGS: Blowing sand makes this hike unpleasant in high winds; light winds OK. Just as walking beach sand is more strenuous than walking a firm path, walking in loose dunes is even more strenuous; pace yourself accordingly. Watch for and yield to horses on the trail.

DIRECTIONS TO TRAILHEAD: Turn west off Highway 1 at M.11.70 into Bodega Dunes Campground. Go .4 mile to entrance kiosk, then take first right, going .8 mile to picnic area and trailhead.

FEES: Day use: $3/vehicle. Car camping: $10/night.

FURTHER INFO: Sonoma Coast State Beach (707)875-3483.

OTHER SUGGESTION: You can also HIKE NORTH ALONG THE BEACH from the parking area. It is 1¾ miles round trip to the mouth of Salmon Creek.

for harbor seals fishing in the surf. From November through April you may see the breathing spouts of California gray whales beyond the breakers. Sanderlings and sandpipers feed along the wet sand at water line.

At ¼ mile you pass two trails leading east over the top of the foredune, the first ridge of the dunes running parallel to the shore. Continue south along the beach. At ⅜ mile the foredune is lower than it was up the beach. Continue south, passing several more trails leading east into the dunes.

The beach broadens at ⅝ mile, where much driftwood lies along the high-tide line. You are crossing the San Andreas Fault here, as it heads northwest into the Pacific (returning to land just south of Fort Ross). Looking east through gaps in the foredune, you can see high dunes rising to 120 feet ⅜ mile inland. Bodega Dunes Campground lies east of the high ridge.

Continue south along the beach, passing many more paths into the dunes. You may pass several rough driftwood forts built by happy beachcombers. The structures wash away after occasional peak high tides. At ⅞ mile a broad path leads east over a low point in the foredune. At one mile the beach narrows. Around 1⅛ miles you pass several large driftwood logs. The shore begins to angle west of south toward the green rise of Mussel Point.

At 1¼ miles you pass a sturdy driftwood fort with an immense pine log foundation. The beach ahead is very broad. In 250 feet, a path signed "Bodega Head Trail" leads southeast into the dunes, the route of the described loop. (You can continue along the beach to the granite shelf at the base of Mussel Point, but the point, a research area for the University of California Marine Laboratory, is closed to the public. Add ⅝ mile to walk to the point and back.)

As you leave the beach and approach the dunes, notice the salt-tolerant plant called sea rocket growing along the base of the foredune. Foredunes form only where vegetation grows that traps blowing sand. Pass a nearly buried trail mileage sign, then head southeast through a gap in the foredune. Your trail soon bends left.

At 1⅜ miles you reach a junction beside a Bishop pine snag. Five trails radiate like spokes from this hub: clockwise from the one you came up, they include 1) a return to the beach, 2) the lowest and shortest route back to the parking lot and campground, 3) the main route, marked with green posts with an angled top, 4) the equestrian loop, which you will join at the next junction.

Take choice #3, following the green posts east. At first the dune vegetation consists of European beach grass with scattered pockets of ice plant, both species introduced after the original vegetation (of rye grass, bromegrass and bush lupine) was overgrazed. Your winding trail gradually climbs. Around 1½ miles you pass the first clumps of bush lupine, the most hardy survivor of the original plants. Coyote brush, beach primrose, beach morning glory and sand verbena also grow along the trail of soft sand.

Before 1⅞ miles you climb to a saddle between high dunes, then descend to another junction at 2 miles. The equestrian trail enters from the right. The trail straight ahead leads to Bodega Head in 1¾ miles, described in reverse direction as Trail #22.

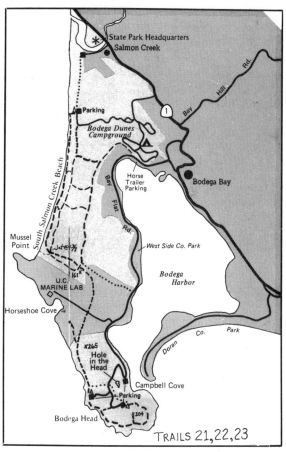

TRAILS 21, 22, 23

You turn left to climb northeast on a trail open to equestrians. You quickly reach the top of a dune. Just before the top, another trail branches right, heading east to Westside Regional Park on the shore of Bodega Harbor. From the top of the dune, look east to Bodega Harbor and south to the highest of the Bodega Dunes, one of the highest in the state at 161 feet.

Your trail heads north along the crest of the dunes, passing purple seaside daisy, yarrow, coyote brush, bush lupine and beach grass. The trail levels, winding through the dunes. At 2⅛ miles your path turns east briefly. A dune on your right is shrouded in dense vegetation dominated by bush lupine. Growing in the shade of the other plants are lush miners lettuce and mosses.

Turn north again, following the ridge of the dune. Your route stays level to 2¼ miles, then climbs to top another dune. You pass ice plant and other dense vegetation mixed with the ubiquitous beach grass. You descend briefly at 2½ miles, then climb to another top. You are on the west face of a high dune with a view to the breakers.

Your trail winds along a high ridge of the dunes, heading generally north. Beyond 2¾ miles you descend between two dunes, then bend left to wind through a canyon. At 2⅞ miles you climb in deep, loose sand to pass through a lupine-filled gap, then climb to another dune top.

After a second lupine-choked gap you reach the 3-mile point and descend, swinging right to approach houses sheltered by trees. The trees form a precipitation ridge, a place where wind carrying sand is deflected upward by the trees, causing the wind to drop its sand, creating a ridge.

Swing parallel to a weathered fence and descend briefly to an unmarked junction. To reach Bodega Dunes Campground, continue northeast for ⅜ mile on the high trail that follows the eastern park boundary. But to return to the trailhead, go left, descending gradually northwest along a swale in the dunes.

Young cypresses form a hedge row on your right. At 3¼ miles the cypress are short and windblown. Stay right at a fork and continue along the windrow. At 3⅜ miles your trail forks again. The left fork leads to the beach. You go right, heading north, climbing gradually in loose sand, a cypress windrow now on your left. You cross two paths that bisect your northward route. After the second one, a shell midden lies beneath cypresses on your left.

You meet the paved road at 3⅝ miles. Follow the road north for ⅛ mile to the parking lot and trailhead.

22.

BODEGA HEAD NORTH to DUNES
THROUGH A RESTRICTED RESERVE

This trail starts on state park land, then enters the 326-acre Bodega Marine Reserve, an area otherwise off-limits to the public. Please stay on the trail to protect the Reserve. You will pass from rocky shoreline, over the highest point on Bodega Head, through coastal prairie and into rolling vegetated sand dunes, with options of continuing to the beach or further exploring the extensive dunes. The Marine Laboratory, accessible by the paved road near Gaffney Point, is open to the public on Fridays from 2 to 4 p.m.

From the west parking lot, your trail heads north along the west shore of Bodega Head. In 200 feet cross the top of a gully, where a spur descends west to a small pocket beach.

Your trail continues north, climbing steeply through fields of ice plant with magenta and yellow flowers. The ice plant is from South Africa, pernicious to the native species here.

As you continue a steady climb, ignore the well-trod left forks that lead out to the eroded headlands along the shore. Soon a carpet of purple seaside daisies line your path. Buttercups, lupine and coast buckwheat mix with the daisies. At ⅛ mile your climb levels briefly, then resumes. Fine views of this rocky shoreline unfold. Beyond ¼ mile the climb eases. Large bush lupine dominate the vegetation.

You soon come to a fork where the through trail veers right. Go left for a short side trip to Horseshoe Cove Overlook. The broad spur climbs steadily, passing several granite outcrops. Your path levels, passing an antenna, then comes to the rock-studded overlook at ½ mile.

You have a bird's-eye view of U-shaped Horseshoe Cove, the University of California Marine Laboratory on its north shore, the green arm of Mussel Point stretching seaward and Bodega Dunes beyond. Your height provides an excellent vantage for whale watching. The picturesque granitic rocks at the overlook shelter hen and chicks, leather ferns and an assortment of colorful lichens. The area to the north is closed for research purposes. The staff of the Marine Lab ask that you go no farther.

Return to the junction, having walked ¾ mile from your starting point. Turn left for the trail north through the Marine Reserve to the dunes. Head east, then northeast through dense ice plant, soon replaced by bush lupine.

At ⅞ mile a dense grove of eucalyptus thrives in a protected canyon downhill on your right. You begin a gradual descent north, the sights and sounds of busy Bodega Harbor rising from the right.

At one mile your descent increases. You quickly come to the boundary sign for the U.C. Reserve. Please stay on the trail within the Reserve. In 300 feet your trail leaves the road, branching left to head north on a narrow track. You pass through grasslands with scattered bush lupine.

Beyond 1⅛ miles, cross the paved road to the Marine Lab and continue northeast. In spring and summer, hardy coastal manroot vines climb on the bush lupine. Descend toward the transition zone between the coastal scrub/grasslands and the vegetated dunes ahead. The differences in vegetation form a nearly straight boundary line.

Soon your trail turns left and meanders along the boundary of the two habitats. At 1¼ miles you veer right, entering the dunes. Round green posts with an angled top mark your path from here to the beach. You soon turn

DISTANCE: 4 miles round trip to junction with Trail #21, 5 miles round trip to beach.

TIME: Two or three hours.

TERRAIN: Climb along bluff to Horseshoe Cove Overlook, then through coastal scrub to Bodega Dunes and return.

ELEVATION GAIN/LOSS: 440 feet+/440 feet- round trip to dunes junction; 560 feet+/560 feet- round trip to beach.

BEST TIME: Spring and summer for wildflowers. A clear day for outstanding views.

WARNINGS: Stay on trail and off adjacent property of U.C. Marine Reserve, where experiments are in progress.

DIRECTIONS TO TRAILHEAD: Turn west off Highway 1 in the town of Bodega Bay at M.11.05 onto Bay Flat Road. Go 4 miles, then take the right fork to the west Bodega Head parking lot.

FURTHER INFO: Sonoma Coast State Beach (707)875-3483.

OTHER SUGGESTION: This trail combines nicely with either Trail #21 or #23 for a longer hike.

north and head toward high dunes ahead. European beach grass, coyote brush and bush lupine grow along the path. A deflation plain, or water catch basin, is on the right.

At 1⅜ miles your trail bends right and dips, wrapping around the base of a high dune. A Krummholzy Douglas fir struggles to survive on the leeward side of the dune. You wind north through the dunes. At 1½ miles you start a gradual climb. Beyond 1⅝ mile you head toward the tallest dunes on the peninsula. They rise on your left at 1¾ miles, the tallest 161 feet above sea level.

At 1⅞ miles you pass through a stile and enter state park land. Descend to the base of a dune, then head north along its base. At 2 miles you meet a junction with Trail #21 (at its 2-mile point). You can go right to follow that trail for a longer, more arduous hike.

The shortest route to the beach lies straight ahead, still marked by the green posts. It tops a saddle at 2⅛ miles where you overlook the meeting of the dunes and the

Pacific (assuming it is not too foggy, a slightly risky proposition in this part of Sonoma County). Then your trail makes a gradual winding descent over varying dune terrain to a junction beside an old pine snag at 2½ miles. Another ⅛ mile brings you to South Salmon Creek Beach.

Return by the same trail. Bypassing the side trip to Horseshoe Cove Overlook, you will return to the trailhead at just over 5 miles.

23.

BODEGA HEAD LOOP
GRANITE IMMIGRANT FROM THE SOUTH

Bodega Head sprawls seaward from the Sonoma Coast, its sandy arm like a giant crab's claw reaching out to sea. On this hike you will see the granitic underpinnings of this peninsula. The Head is composed of quartz diorite, a light, coarse-grained igneous rock similar to granite. The rocks of Bodega Head are thought to have originated near the Tehachapi Mountains at the southern end of the Sierra Nevada. For the past 40 million years, Bodega Head has been riding the Pacific Plate north along the coast, traveling 350 miles in relation to the Coast Range to the east. Tagging along on this cataclysmic yet snail's-pace ride are Point Reyes and the Farallon Islands to the south and Point Arena to the north. The San Andreas Fault bisects the Head just south of Bodega Dunes Campground.

It is best to save this hike for a clear day when you can see all the rugged convolutions of this dramatic coastline. For a longer excursion, you can combine this loop with the trail north along the west side of the Head (Trail #22).

Just north of the trailhead for this hike is the world's most expensive duck pond, site of one of California's first environmental struggles. Now called "Hole in the Head," the name aptly describes the states of mind of the people who planned to build a large nuclear power plant virtually atop

DISTANCE: 1⅝-mile loop.

TIME: One hour.

TERRAIN: Circle the high headlands of Bodega Head, with views to Tomales and Point Reyes, following a rugged, convoluted shore.

ELEVATION GAIN/LOSS: 280 feet+/280 feet-.

BEST TIME: Any clear day. Spring or summer for wildflowers.

WARNINGS: Stay back from steep cliffs.

DIRECTIONS TO TRAILHEAD: Turn west off Highway 1 in the town of Bodega Bay at M.11.05 onto Bay Flat Road. Go 4 miles, then take the left fork to east parking lot.

FURTHER INFO: Sonoma Coast State Beach (707)875-3483.

the San Andreas Fault. The "Hole" that was to become the foundation for the facility was dug without public hearings, creating a great clamor of frightened and outraged citizens who effectively organized to scuttle the project.

Your trail starts from the east parking lot overlooking Bodega Harbor. Take the path that heads east, passing to the left of the restrooms. The level trail winds through coastal scrub of bush lupine, coyote brush and cow parsnip. A spur soon forks left, descending to the mouth of Bodega Harbor below you. The sand spit of Doran Beach stretches east of the mouth for nearly two miles. You take the level right fork, heading southeast.

At ⅛ mile the gentle green rise of Tomales Bluff lies straight ahead, five miles across Bodega Bay. The San Andreas Fault underlies Tomales Bay, to the left of the bluff. Your trail turns south and descends slightly. Another spur forks left, descending toward the shore. You wind through head-high bush lupine, some with stalks three inches in diameter.

At ¼ mile you pass the top of a lush gulch. Continue south, soon coming to the steep bluff's edge above the sea. Poppies, coast buckwheat and yarrow join the lupine here. Less than ½ mile offshore lies Bodega Rock, a breeding site for Brandt's cormorants and western gulls. You may hear

the barking of California sea lions on the rock.

Your trail climbs southwest following the rim of the Head. Sea fig grows on the steep slopes below the trail. At ½ mile you pass the Bodega Head Beacon and your trail levels. To the east the mainland coast is cut by Pinnacle Gulch (see Trail #24), Shorttail Gulch and the deep canyon of the Estero Americano, the Sonoma-Marin County line. Due south lies the rugged outcrop of Point Reyes.

Your trail climbs west through sparse vegetation, buttercups and coast buckwheat scattered in the grass. You climb to the highest point on the rim at ⅝ mile, nearly 160 feet above the sea. A side trail branches right, climbing gently in less than ⅛ mile to the 204-foot summit of Bodega Head. Rounded granite rocks protrude from the grasslands at the summit, where you have a 360 degree view.

Returning to the main trail, you descend along the Head's rim with breathtaking views of the jagged cliff and an inaccessible pocket beach below. At ¾ mile your descent ends at a grassy promontory just 100 feet above the shore. You will get no closer to Point Reyes on foot today. Notice that sandstone from old marine deposits overlays the granite bedrock of Bodega Head here, though the granite is visible at tideline.

Climb north, then northwest along the bluff's edge. As you climb, you draw parallel to a broader path. Before ⅞ mile your grassy path levels atop a sculpted granite outcrop with a convoluted shore. In 200 feet a spur branches right, providing the shortest return to the trailhead.

The described route continues along the rim, paralleling the broad path (better with young children and for those who dislike heights). You descend gradually, heading northwest. At one mile a granite ridge juts south, providing fine views. On a very clear day you can see 18 miles up the coast to Northwest Cape beyond Fort Ross. Continue along the rim, passing highly eroded sandstone. Soon fields of purple seaside daisies line the trail.

At 1⅛ miles you overlook the blond sand of a tiny, pristine pocket beach between you and the west parking lot. Your trail wraps inland, heading for the cypress trees at the head of the small cove.

Just before you reach the shapely cypresses, a trail branches right. From this junction you can continue straight for ⅛ mile to the west parking lot if you want to combine this hike with Trail #22. Otherwise take the right fork, heading east over level grasslands with clumps of sticky monkeyflowers and Douglas iris. At 1¼ miles you climb gradually to merge with a trail from the right as you come to a gate, then the paved road.

It is ¼ mile up the road to your starting point. Or you can pick up a faint trail across the road and pick your way through grasslands to the parking lot. Either way you return to your starting point at 1⅝ miles.

24.

PINNACLE GULCH
FOLLOW A CREEK TO A SECLUDED BEACH

The dirt trail starts across the street from the paved parking area. Your trail descends southeast, passing bush lupine, coyote brush, yarrow and iris. As the trail descends, the coastal scrub vegetation becomes more dense. Berry vines and sticky monkeyflower join the tangle of plants.

You soon reach the head of Pinnacle Gulch where grasslands offer a view of the Pacific Ocean. Your trail descends five switchbacks into the gulch. Before ⅛ mile you are beside the creek in the scrub-choked canyon. Willows grow along the stream where your path levels briefly. Plantain, black sage, poison oak, cow parsnip and sword fern mix with other coastal scrub plants.

Your path descends gradually along the stream, passing poppy, paintbrush and beach strawberry. Native grasses grow on the steep hillside across the creek. The trail climbs briefly, then levels, with a glimpse of the ocean at the end of the gulch. Birds sing from the coastal scrub. You resume a gradual descent passing hen and chicks, coast buckwheat, buttercup and vetch.

At ¼ mile you see several houses perched high above on

DISTANCE: 1⅛ miles round trip to beach (at low tide
   you can walk south ⅜ mile or more).

TERRAIN: Down a steep coastal-scrub-filled canyon to an
   isolated beach.

ELEVATION GAIN/LOSS: 200 feet+/200 feet-.

BEST TIME: Nice anytime. Low tide best for beach
   exploring, spring and summer best for wildflowers.

WARNINGS: Stay off adjacent private property.
   Watch for poison oak. Watch for rogue waves on the
   beach.

DIRECTIONS TO TRAILHEAD: Just south of Bodega
   Bay on Highway 1 at M.8.76, turn west onto South
   Harbor Way, then left on Heron Drive. In .9 mile,
   turn left onto Mockingbird and come to trailhead
   parking area.

FEES: Day use: $2/vehicle.

FURTHER INFO: Sonoma County Regional Parks
   (707)527-2450.

the rim of the canyon. You continue a gradual descent, soon coming to more luxuriant vegetation, with thimbleberry joining the mix. You pass under the limbs of wildly sprawling willows, where their dense vegetation hides the creek. The sound of running water rises from below.

You climb briefly to ⅜ mile as the vegetation thins, then resume a gradual descent. Soon a coffeeberry bush on the left has foliage stressed and salt-burned by its proximity to the ocean. Salmonberries crowd the creek.

You climb briefly to ½ mile, then descend past paint-brush, gum plant and poison oak to the beach on the shore of Bodega Bay. Pinnacle Rock stands just offshore to the west. The long ridge of Bodega Head reaches seaward beyond the rock. To the northwest the long low arm of Doran Beach stretches to the mouth of Bodega Harbor. A rugged and rocky, cliff-backed shoreline stretches southeast. About five miles down the coast, the shore meets the mouth of Tomales Bay, with Tomales Bluff jutting seaward on its west shore. Much closer, about 1¼ miles down the coast, you can see Estero Americano. The broad, deep canyon serves as the Sonoma-Marin County line.

The dark sand beach at Pinnacle Gulch is less than ¼ mile long at high tide. The isolation of this wild, rugged

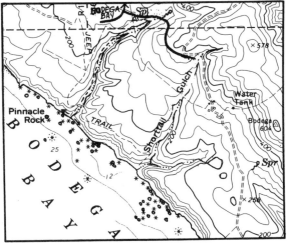

coast so close to the town of Bodega Bay merits a visit during most any tide or weather. Beware, however, that the ocean can be ferocious and unforgiving here despite being on a bay. Stay out of the water, where rip currents could carry you out to sea. Watch for oversize killer waves and stay back from the surf.

If the ocean is calm and you know the tide is ebbing, with caution you can explore up and down the coast. You can walk ¼ mile north along the sand before you come to a rocky promontory which blocks the way to Doran Beach.

You can walk south from Pinnacle Gulch Beach whenever the seas are calm and the tide is moderate and ebbing, but the lower the tide the farther you can go. From the mouth of the gulch you walk southeast on sand for almost ⅛ mile. You then come to a rocky point that requires a tide lower than +4.5 feet to pass. If tide and surf are low enough, rock hop around the point to reach a second sandy beach that extends to ¼ mile.

You then reach another pile of rocks that provide a passage more rugged than the last, but easily traversable. After 200 feet of rock hopping, a third sandy beach provides easy walking. You reach the mouth of Shorttail Gulch at ⅜ mile.

To proceed farther along the rugged coast you need to do some rock climbing. Most people will want to turn back here. At a tide lower than +2 feet, experienced hikers can proceed by scrambling up and down a 30-foot-high rock ledge. You reach a sandy, low-tide beach littered with big rocks. At ⅝ mile, another jumble of rocks makes passage difficult. During a minus tide on a calm day, you might pick your way all the way to Estero Americano. Be sure to start your return before the rising tide, to make certain you will not be stranded.

BETWEEN HIGHWAYS 1 & 101

LAKE SONOMA
INCLUDES NEXT THREE TRAILS

Lake Sonoma provides Sonoma County's largest public recreation area. The 2700-acre lake behind Warm Springs Dam nestles in 18,000 acres of steeply rolling coastal hills that remain mostly in a natural state, offering redwood, fir and oak forests and steep grasslands. One of the best wildflower displays in this flower-rich county occurs every spring around Lake Sonoma. An 8000-acre wildlife area in the north half of the park is off limits to hikers, but fosters an abundant variety of mammal and bird species that spill over into the areas reached by 40 miles of trails.

The three trails described here offer distinctly different choices. Woodland Ridge is an easy day hike. The second trail provides the only mountain-bike loop at Lake Sonoma, with chances for fishing and primitive camping. The third and most difficult trail offers several choices of secluded backcountry camps along the wooded south shore of Warm Springs Arm.

Altogether, the area offers 103 quiet, pretty primitive camps, mostly on the lake shore, in 15 separate areas. These can be reached only by hiking or boating, but are open year-round, unless closed following major rains. A large campground for vehicles, open May through September, overlooks the lake. Lake Sonoma offers great fishing for bass and channel catfish, and many quiet, out-of-the-way inlets ideal for canoeing. Ask the Corps of Engineers for more information.

25.

WOODLAND RIDGE LOOP
SHORT, INVIGORATING NATURE LOOP

This pleasant loop provides an introduction to the varied habitats of the Lake Sonoma area. While the longer Lake Sonoma trails may be more rewarding, this hike is ideal for families and people not inclined to explore the longer trails.

From the gravel parking lot south of the Visitor Center, you cross a wooden bridge over a concrete culvert and come to

WOODLAND RIDGE LOOP:

DISTANCE: 1½-mile loop.

TIME: One hour.

TERRAIN: Climb from grasslands through redwood forest into oak forest, then to scenic overlook.

ELEVATION GAIN/LOSS: 150 feet+/150 feet-.

BEST TIME: Spring for wildflowers. Nice anytime.

WARNINGS: Watch for poison oak. Take your time on the steep first section of trail. Trails close after major rains in winter.

DIRECTIONS TO TRAILHEAD: Exit Highway 101 onto Canyon Road (M.43.6 from the north, M.43.05 from south). Go west on Canyon Road for 2.1 miles. Then go right 3.2 miles on Dry Creek Road to Lake Sonoma Visitor Center. Trail starts at small gravel parking lot south of main parking area.

FURTHER INFO: Lake Sonoma Corps of Engineers (707)433-9483.

OTHER SUGGESTION: A short, wheelchair-accessible walk leads through the Visitor Center (open weekdays 9:30-4, weekends 10-5, closed Tuesday and Wednesday) to the FISH HATCHERY, where an exhibit shows local birds including hawks, owls, ducks, loons, pheasants and many smaller birds. (¼ mile round trip).

a picnic area. Turn left and parallel the culvert and Stewart's Point Road.

You soon enter a small grove of redwoods where your trail turns right. Climb 63 wooden steps, leaving the redwoods for a forest of large bay laurel trees. Their pungent leaves and nuts had many uses for the Southern Pomo, who called these lands home long before white settlers arrived.

At the top of the steps, you enter a forest of young redwoods growing beside weathered stumps. Your trail turns left as the climb eases. You descend briefly, then contour the hillside through mixed forest of oak, bay, madrone, redwood and Douglas fir.

Beyond ⅛ mile more steps signal the resumption of a steady climb. You switchback right, then left, then right again through mixed forest. At ¼ mile your climb steepens, passing Douglas firs to four feet in diameter. Poison oak vines climb some of the trunks. After you switchback left, your climb eases and the forest thins.

The trail swings right, climbing along a bald ridge lined with oak and manzanita. In spring many wildflowers grow in the grassy clearings, including California poppy, Indian warrior, Indian pink, blue dicks and grass nut.

Around ⅜ mile you have an excellent view of the Mayacmas Mountains to the east. The prominent peak on the left is Geyser Peak. On cool days you may see white plumes of steam rising from its geysers. Rocky Mt. St. Helena rises on the right, at the head of the Napa Valley 20 miles away.

Ascend along the open ridge. Four kinds of oak grow here: evergreen coast live oak, canyon live oak, interior live oak and deciduous black oak. They all produce acorns, a staple of the Pomo diet. At ½ mile madrones shade your otherwise sunny climb. After another short climb, you reach the summit of this hike, where you have more views of the Mayacmas Range and Alexander and Dry Creek Valleys.

You descend to parallel Stewarts Point Road briefly, then swing right and continue a winding descent through mixed hardwood forest. Near ⅝ mile you get a glimpse of Lake Sonoma to the northwest.

Before ¾ mile you descend steps to a fork. Go left on a side trail through a steep, brushy canyon. You wind, dip, rise, descend steps, then climb steeply to a vista point at ⅞ mile. You overlook the Visitor Center and fish hatchery below, Warm Springs Dam and Lake Sonoma on your left.

Retrace your steps to the junction, where you go straight to complete the loop. Descend gradually through oak forest with scattered young Douglas firs. At 1⅛ miles your trail turns right and descends into a dark. dense madrone forest, a twisting tangle of shiny-barked branches. Descend along a steep gully that feeds Dry Creek after rains. Sticky monkeyflowers grow beside the trail.

Your descent steepens. In fall the path is littered with slippery black oak leaves. At 1¼ miles your trail bends left, coming to a view of the parking lot and Visitor Center below. You wind down through the oak woodlands, passing native bunch grasses.

Descend four dozen steps, then pass a large water tank at 1⅜ miles. A few more steps bring you to the bottom of the hill. Turn right and wind through a cleared area and over a bridge to return to the picnic grounds and parking area.

26

HALF-A-CANOE LOOP
ROLLER COASTER TRAIL OVERLOOKING LAKE

Your trail descends from No Name Flat parking area into oak woodlands, crossing a bridge in 150 feet. Make a winding climb through grasslands with scattered oaks and buckeyes. At ⅛ mile you can glimpse a corner of Lake Sonoma. Your climb soon eases, then levels heading west.

At ¼ mile you climb gently through oak-studded grasslands. The climb steepens and winds at ⅜ mile, then turns west and descends. At ½ mile you meet the broad Half-a-Canoe Trail.

Turn left and descend southeast along the dirt road to ⅝ mile. The path levels, then climbs east onto a ridge top with grand views of the surrounding countryside and a picture of the elevation changes that lie ahead. On the left, alternating canyons, ridges and valleys stretch all the way to Mt. St. Helena, 23 miles east. To the northeast, you may see the plumes of the Geysers on a cool day. On your right, an immense, steep grassland plunges to the shore of the Warm Springs Arm 700 feet below. If you complete this loop, you will descend to that shore.

The next section of trail climbs up and down roller coaster hills along the ridge top, a great run for mountain bikers. (Bikers: please slow and watch at blind corners for horse and foot traffic; if you speed, you are responsible for accidents!)

At one mile you descend to a junction with Little Flat Trail on the left (1⅝ miles, mostly down, to Little Flat Trailhead). From the junction, you continue the roller coaster run, a short up followed by a long descent.

At 1¼ miles you leave oak woodlands for grasslands with golden fairy lanterns. Digger pines and toyons are scattered along the dry ridge. You pass outcrops of serpentine rock as the road climbs, dips and climbs along the ridge top, with more grand views of steep canyon country.

Around 1½ miles you enter a grove of large black oaks. At 1⅝ miles you meet the Bummer Peak spur on your left. The faint spur climbs ⅛ mile to the top of the 1150-foot peak, where blue-eyed grass, star lily and Douglas iris sparkle in grasslands. The views from the summit are limited by trees. They open up on the south face, which plunges steeply to a narrow spot on the Warm Springs Arm.

From the Bummer Peak saddle, the fire road descends

HALF-A-CANOE LOOP:

DISTANCE: 5-mile loop; or 3⅜ miles round trip to Bummer Peak Camp.

TIME: Three hour hike, one hour bike.

TERRAIN: Roller coaster descent along rolling ridge to Bummer Peak Camp. Then steep descent to lake and Lone Pine Camp. Along shore to Madrone Point Spur, then climb up creek canyon.

ELEVATION GAIN/LOSS: Loop: 1120 feet+/1120 feet-; 920 feet+/920 feet- round trip to Bummer Peak Camp.

BEST TIME: Spring

WARNINGS: Ticks, rattlesnakes and scorpions live in the area. Steep trail; take it easy. Mountain bikes must slow for blind corners. Trail may be closed in winter when slippery and muddy.

DIRECTIONS TO TRAILHEAD: Exit Highway 101 at M.36.1 and go northwest on Dry Creek Road for 10½ miles to Lake Sonoma Visitor Center. Go west from there 1.8 miles to junction with Stewarts Point Road. Go straight at junction (on Rockpile Road) for 2.4 miles, then left into No Name Flat parking lot.

FURTHER INFO: Lake Sonoma (707)433-9483.

OTHER SUGGESTION: Although this is the only trail at Lake Sonoma open to mountain bikes, there are many more miles of hiking and equestrian trails.

300 feet to Bummer Peak Camp, then turns south through the heart of the pretty camp where the glassy lake shimmers through the leaves of live oaks and madrones.

At 1¾ miles your trail descends, swinging right to return to steep glades overlooking the sparkling waters of the lake. You make a winding descent west, looking toward wooded Picnic Creek and mossy Buzzard Rock across the lake. You level briefly then continue your winding descent.

At 2 miles your descent steepens into a twisting plunge, passing buttercup, tarweed and iris. You make a big bend left and continue your steep descent. Beside the trail in spring and early summer grows a dense carpet of tiny star-shaped flowers with a pleasant, piny fragrance. False baby stars, of the phlox family, range in color from deep pink or lilac to white to yellow, often all in one patch. Here it occurs with rattlesnake grass and woodland star. As you descend, you pass black sage and golden fairy lanterns.

At 2¼ miles your trail levels and meets a spur 100 feet from the shore. The spur goes left for ⅛ mile to Lone Pine Camp, along the shore beneath black and live oaks.

The main trail turns north, paralleling the shore. Vine maple twines in the trees near the junction. At 2⅜ miles cross a gulch where a seasonal stream may provide water into late spring. The trail turns west along the shore. You soon pass elegant brodiaea growing at the base of an oak.

At 2½ miles your trail turns northwest. You soon climb gradually away from the shore. At 2¾ miles you wind along the contours of the shore, considerably higher above the water now. You come to a muddy creek crossing where mimulus grow, then wind west to cross two smaller creeks. After the third creek at 2⅞ miles, you climb west. Your trail soon levels in a large glade.

At 3 miles you meet a junction. The spur on the left goes ½ mile to Madrone Point Camp. The bike loop goes right, climbing to parallel a singing creek on your left. You descend briefly beyond 3⅛ miles, then resume a steady climb up the creek canyon, winding through glades and oak woodlands. Around 3½ miles you pass the inspiration for the trail name on the right.

At 3⅝ miles you level briefly, with a glade on your left where thousands of wildflowers grow in spring. False baby stars and blue-eyed grass are the most abundant. You may hear the gobble-gobble of wild turkeys in this area or see the big birds if you are lucky. Grouse and quail also live nearby. Your climb continues, winding through another glade, then through a gully.

The climb eases, then bends right, climbing to a junction at 3⅞ miles. The left fork climbs ¼ mile to the Liberty Glen Campground kiosk. Go right, making a winding ascent through grasslands. At 4¼ miles, meet Rockpile Road at the Lone Rock Trailhead (no parking allowed).

From Lone Rock your dirt road climbs south into oak forest. The road soon levels beside an immense coast live oak, with blue dicks and poppies in the surrounding grasslands. You descend briefly, then level, traversing steeply rolling grasslands with scattered oaks and madrones. The flannel leaves of wooly mullein line the path.

You pass a large manzanita on the left at 4½ miles, then descend to meet the spur from No Name Flat Trailhead. Go left, retracing your route to reach the trailhead at 5 miles.

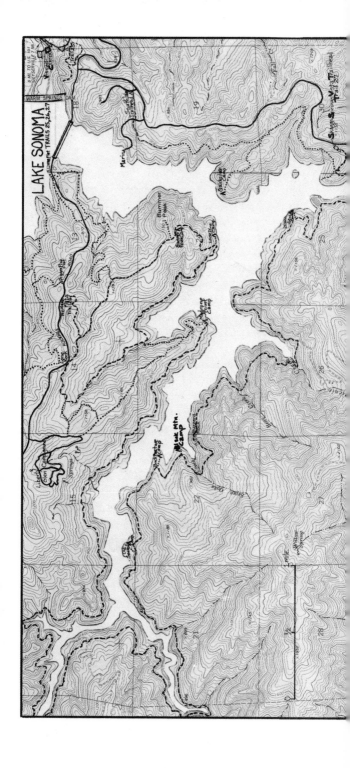

LAKE SONOMA
Also see Hot TRAILS 25, 26, 27

WARM SPRINGS DAM

27

SOUTH SHORE BACKPACK

DOWN, UP AND AROUND TO OLD SAWMILL CAMP

*As Lake Sonoma increases in popularity, you can find
solitude and wilderness by backpacking (also by boating or
day hike) into the beautiful backcountry camps along the
lake's steep, wooded south shore. Every spring the steep
forests and grasslands of the north-facing terrain burst
into color with one of Sonoma County's finest wildflower
displays. After the flowers have faded in summer, the sparkling waters of the lake warm to swimming temperature.*

*The campsites offer shade, seclusion and fine views of
steep, rugged country. The camps provide a touch of
civilization with tables, fire pits with adjustable grills and
trash cans. Wildlife abounds, so with a little luck you will
see hawks, ospreys, wild turkeys, coyotes and perhaps even
a bear. Though the trail never climbs more than 400 feet
in one stretch, the continuous ups and downs following the
convoluted shore add up, making this one of the more
difficult trails in the book, especially for backpacking.*

*From Skaggs Springs Trailhead, you overlook the Warm
Springs Arm of Lake Sonoma. The confluence of Warm
Springs Creek and Little Warm Springs Creek now lies 100
feet below the lake surface, buried with its rich history. A
band of the Southern Pomo called this valley home. The
village of Kahowani was located near the confluence.
Another village, Takoton, was on Dry Creek about a mile
upstream from where the dam is today. Cawako, the prin-
cipal village, was three miles downstream from Takoton.*

*Near Kahowani, hot springs bubbled from the ground at
135 degrees. In the late 1800s Skaggs Springs Resort
tapped the springs, becoming a popular destination. When
the waters began to fill behind the dam in 1982, nothing remained of the resort, but the hot springs were still used.*

Your broad trail descends gradually south through hardwood forest alternating with grasslands. In spring the trail
is lined with buttercups (most common flower on this hike),
blue dicks, blue-eyed grass, lupine, bedstraw, poppies and
vetch. Lake Sonoma's blue waters shimmer below.

Before ¼ mile you leave the broad path, veering right to
descend steeply through grasslands with iris. You switchback three times, descending along a grassy ridge. At ⅜
mile you switchback right and descend into forest where
soap plants, shooting stars, milkmaids and poison oak grow

SOUTH SHORE to OLD SAWMILL CAMP:

DISTANCE: 16 miles round trip to Old Sawmill Camp (difficult); 4 miles round trip to Island View Camp, 8 miles round trip to Picnic Creek (moderate).

TIME: Overnight to Old Sawmill Camp, any portion as day hike.

TERRAIN: Descend to lake's south shore, then many short up and down stretches, crossing creek canyons and rounding points to camp near head of Warm Springs Arm of Lake Sonoma.

ELEVATION GAIN/LOSS: 720 feet+/720 feet- to Island View Camp; 1700 feet+/1700 feet- to Picnic Creek; 3160 feet+/3160 feet- to Black Mountain Camp; 3360 feet+/3360 feet- to Old Sawmill Camp. All round trip.

BEST TIME: Spring for wildflowers, early summer and fall for swimming.

WARNINGS: Watch for rattlesnakes, ticks, scorpions and poison oak. Stay away from wild pigs. Steep country, take it easy, especially in hot weather. Purify water before drinking. Camping permits required. Trails may be slippery or impassable after major storms. Hunting sometimes allowed; check before going.

DIRECTIONS TO TRAILHEAD: See directions for Trail #25. From Visitor Center (permits available), go south on Stewarts Point Road for 1.8 miles to junction. Go left for another 2.8 miles, then turn right to unmarked Skaggs Springs Vista Trailhead.

FEES: No fee for backcountry camps. Car camping at Liberty Glen: $6/night.

FURTHER INFO: Lake Sonoma (707)433-9483.

OTHER SUGGESTION: If you prefer a longer backpack, you can start at SOUTHLAKE TRAILHEAD, ½ mile beyond the left turn, adding 5.2 miles to total distance. Quicksilver Camp is on that trail segment.

beneath oaks, bay laurels and California buckeyes. Forget-me-nots and maidenhair ferns grow in shady spots.

At ⅝ mile you reach a junction. The trail on the right leads to Quicksilver Camp and Southlake Trailhead.

Straight ahead a spur descends to the lake. You go left, climbing and descending with the contour of the land.

Beyond ¾ mile you descend moderately to cross Little Warm Springs Creek, then climb steeply by switchbacks to gain a ridge at 1⅛ miles. Then climb more switchbacks through oak woodlands. At 1⅜ miles you cross a small gully where native bunch grass grows beside tiny white flowers called woodland star. Descend gradually to 1½ miles, where you cross a deep gulch.

Your trail makes a winding climb, then descends gradually, following the shore. At 1¾ miles an unmarked spur descends to the shore. Continue your descent to another spur at 1⅞ miles. This side trail, marked "Island View Camp" descends ¼ mile to a pleasant camp beside the lake.

The main trail climbs northwest, then west. At 2 miles you switchback left and climb into a large meadow, where a few young redwoods mix with oaks and buckeyes. You soon return to oak forest, then pick up an old road at 2¼ miles. Climb gradually through steep terrain, passing maidenhair ferns, lupine and flowering currant. In a steep, rocky spot, star-shaped cream fawn lilies grow in profusion.

You climb southwest to cross a tiny creek in a deep canyon at 2½ miles, where bay laurel, big leaf maple and redwood grow. Your trail climbs briefly, then descends across sunny slopes dappled with wildflowers. At 2⅝ miles a large live oak overhangs the steep slope on the right.

You descend to a glade bordered by madrones, with grand views of the lake. Watch the tops of snags along the shore for ospreys. The fish-eating, hawklike birds perch atop a snag, then dive to catch fish, carrying them in powerful talons. In winter they migrate to South America.

At 2¾ miles your trail makes a winding descent, then levels, near the lake. After your trail turns west, you start a gradual climb through black oak forest. Beyond 3 miles you wind around the Picnic Creek inlet of the lake. The trail rolls with the terrain, passing baby blue eyes and shooting stars as you cross several dry gullies.

At 3⅜ miles you climb to a meadow. Descend briefly to an old road, then follow it on a winding ascent into rugged Picnic Creek Canyon. The rocky terrain supports redwoods, oaks and ferns. Beyond 3¾ miles, the road levels, then descends across more gullies.

At 3⅞ miles you leave the old road for a winding descent to the creek, passing trail plant and star lily . Toyon, wood rose, honeysuckle, poison oak, baby blue eyes, hound's tongue and hazel grow in the moist habitat between trail and creek. At 4 miles you come to redwood-lined Picnic

Creek, a pleasant place for a break.

Second-growth redwoods grow along the creek. The big stumps with springboard cuts were logged by hand before the advent of chainsaws. Shade-loving plants carpet the forest floor. Ferns include woodwardia, sword, coastal wood, leather, maidenhair, and the bird's foot. Tiny Pacific starflowers grow abundantly. You may also find alum root, miners lettuce, fairy bell, fat and slim solomon's seals, twisted stalk, calypso orchid and wood strawberry.

Your trail winds steeply out of the canyon bottom, a view of a small waterfall upstream. At 4⅛ miles you enter drier habitat where large bays and oaks grow. A rocky, sunny slope on the left supports paintbrush, sticky monkeyflower, chamise, blue dick, and a carpet of low-growing, tiny white to lilac flowers with a delightful fragrance, false baby stars. Traverse the steep wall of Picnic Creek Canyon, climbing across a shady slope overlooking the lake.

At 4¾ miles you crest a steep ridge and descend west, leaving Picnic Creek behind. The trail levels along a shady slope, passing beneath gracefully arching madrones. Soon a fern and moss covered cliff is on your left, while the spiny needles of young California nutmeg grow on your right. Then a sunnier rocky slope supports the deep red flowers of Indian warriors. You climb an easy grade.

At 5 miles your trail veers left around the Bear Creek inlet. Descend steep switchbacks to ford fern-lined Bear Creek, which cascades along a series of rocky pools. Then climb sunny slopes where poppies grow. At 5¼ miles you climb steeply through chamise, toyon and manzanita. Your trail bends left to a grassy hill with a view of the lake.

You climb west to 5⅜ miles, returning to hardwood forest, then contour a steep, shady slope. At 5½ miles your level trail winds through a cool gully, then climbs west to traverse a steep gulch. Your path soon levels again.

At 5¾ miles a clearing affords a grand view of the upper Warm Springs Arm,. Make a winding descent to a cool seep with big woodwardia ferns. At 5⅞ miles you climb steeply away from the lake, soon coming to a view of the moss-covered outcrop called Buzzard Rock. Descend to the base of the rock at 6 miles. Red larkspur and monkeyflower grow beside seeps. The trees here are draped with lichen.

You climb steadily to 6¼ miles, then veer left around the inlet of Seven Oaks Creek. Descend to a pleasant creek crossing at 6⅜ miles, then climb north to overlook the lake. A spur on the right descends to Black Mountain Camp. The main trail turns left through a large glade. You climb gradually, passing through an old fence line at 6¾ miles, then into a large meadow. Your trail becomes vague as it winds, then descends to ford a small creek where pioneer eucalyptus grow beside native bays and black oaks.

Cross another big meadow as your trail heads northeast, then picks up an old ranch road to descend through the largest meadow yet, Buck Pasture. At 7 miles your trail turns left as the spur to Buck Pasture Camp descends 300 feet to the prettiest camp along the trail, nestled among rocks and large oaks overlooking the lake.

Continuing to Old Sawmill Camp, your trail contours through the meadow. At 7¼ miles climb moderately through hardwood forest for ⅛ mile. Then cross a small gully before climbing through grasslands. Pass through another fence before 7½ miles, then climb a ridge.

Where the trail descends southwest, I flushed a wild turkey. The twenty-pound tom burst from the chaparral, frantically beating its four-foot wingspan, taking off like an cargo plane on a bee line toward the lake. Quite a thrill!

The trail soon levels in grasslands, a popular rooting spot for wild or feral pigs. They do considerable damage to native plants, feeding on bulbs, corms and tubers that would otherwise produce wildflowers.

Beyond 7¾ miles your trail makes a gradual, winding descent. Then you descend steeply, passing an old spring-house beneath immense black oaks. After a dry gully at 7⅞ miles you climb gradually through grasslands alternating with oak woodlands.

Around 8 miles from your trailhead, descend briefly to the spur to Old Sawmill Camp. It descends north for ⅛ mile to five pleasant sites in a rolling grassland surrounded by immense black oaks, healthy Bishop pines and a few young redwoods. Old fig, apple and plum trees remain from a small community once supported by the sawmill by the creek (now underwater). The old Skaggs Springs Road is between the camp and the lake. Periwinkle, cultivated Oregon grape, blackberry vines and other escaped domestic plants sprinkle the hillside above the winding arm of the lake. A spring box southeast of the outhouses provides drinking water and watercress if it has not dried up. Be sure to purify the water whether from there or the lake.

Many birds visit the clearing at Old Sawmill Camp. You may see quail, jays, hawks, ospreys, golden eagles, wood ducks and woodpeckers. Before sunset we heard the distinct gobble-gobble of wild tom turkeys calling back and forth across the canyon. At night, alternating silence and the symphonic croaking of frogs were pierced by the calls of great horned, barn and screech owls. The howl of a

distant coyote wafted down the canyon from the west.

At dawn the turkeys were at it again. The gobbling came closer, nature's alarm clock for the decadent backpackers trying to sleep past dawn. When we finally awoke, unable to ignore the incredible racket any longer, tom and hen were strolling along the road below our camp, turkeys on parade. His bright red wattles sparkled in the rising sun. Their body feathers shimmered in bronze iridescence.

The trail continues west from the camp turn-off, ascending and descending for short stretches, following the lake shore to the inlet of Warm Springs Creek. The trail fords the large creek at 9⅛ miles, then climbs ⅛ mile to a junction. To continue around the lake go right, trekking through more ups and downs along the rugged shore.

At 11 miles you come to Rancheria Creek where a maze of trails may be confusing (map and compass handy here). You head east to follow the Warm Springs Arm's dry north shore staying high above the shore. Madrone Point Camp is 16 miles from the Skaggs Springs Vista Trailhead, a reasonable hike from Old Sawmill Camp.

If you wish to return the shortest way from Old Sawmill or one of the other south shore camps, you head east along the shore, retracing your steps. Do remember that the final ¾ mile entails a long uphill pull. If the day is hot, it is best to climb out either early or very late in the day.

28

ARMSTRONG WOODS LOOP
THROUGH THE DEEP, DARK VIRGIN FOREST

The Southern Pomo had dozens of villages along the Russian River east and north of the present park. They hunted and foraged in the rolling hills to the west of their settlements. But they referred to the grove of giant redwoods along Fife Creek as "the dark hole." They stayed out of this dark, cool forest, believing it was inhabited by evil spirits.

In 1874 Colonel James Armstrong came to California to invest. Working in the logging industry, he became fascinated by the redwoods and sought to save the ancient grove along Fife Creek near Guerneville (then known as Stumptown). After his death in 1900, his family continued the effort for preservation. Armstrong Woods became a county park in 1917, then joined the State Park system in 1934.

This hike starts at the main parking area, just outside the park entrance. Walk north past the entrance kiosk and continue cautiously along the road for ⅛ mile. Veer left as the road forks, coming to the Parson Jones Tree. At 310 feet, this giant is the tallest tree in the park.

In 75 feet the Pioneer Trail goes right as the service road continues northwest. Walk the level trail north through redwood forest with trees of mixed sizes. Scattered Douglas firs, bay laurels, tanoaks and big leaf maples also grow in the forest. In fall the maples add bright splashes of color, catching sunlight filtering through the dark forest. Plants in the understory include hazel, redwood sorrel, trillium, sword ferns and poison oak. You pass numbered posts keyed to the nature trail (brochures available at kiosk).

At ¼ mile you come to an upended redwood root on the left, worn smooth by many hands over time. Your trail winds around a gnarled giant, then crosses a paved road.

Veer left on the trail to the Armstrong Tree. The path parallels the road. Many hazels here radiate a lovely green glow as they catch the filtered light. Redwoods along the path are larger than most of the trees you have passed. On the left a new platform protects the roots of a giant beside the trail. The deck allows you to get close to the ancient tree without hurting its shallow root system. Wood rose and bracken fern join the understory.

As your path curves right, look up for a good perspective on the immense Armstrong Tree 150 feet ahead. Estimated to be 1400 years old, it is only two feet shorter than the

ARMSTRONG WOODS LOOP:

DISTANCE: 1¼-mile loop or 2¾-mile loop.

TIME: One or two hours.

TERRAIN: Level flood plain filled with virgin redwoods, with optional climb to ridge.

ELEVATION GAIN/LOSS: Negligible for short loop, 440 feet+/440 feet- for longer loop.

BEST TIME: Spring for wildflowers. Nice anytime.

WARNINGS: Watch for poison oak. May be muddy after rains.

DIRECTIONS TO TRAILHEAD: The town of Guerneville (silent E's) is on Highway 116, 13 miles east of Jenner on the coast, about 20 miles west of Santa Rosa. At the four-way stop in Guerneville, turn north onto Armstrong Woods Road and go 2.2 miles to main parking area and park entrance.

FEES: Day use: $3/vehicle.

FURTHER INFO: Armstrong Redwoods State Reserve (707)869-2015 or 865-2391.

OTHER SUGGESTIONS: A ridge loop of about 5 miles climbs to overlook the virgin forest on the POOL RIDGE and EAST RIDGE TRAILS, linking with trails to the campground and trail system at Austin Creek (see Trail #29). You can arrange HORSEBACK TRAIL RIDES by calling (707)579-1520.

Parson Jones Tree. With its 14.6-foot diameter, the Armstrong Tree is the most massive tree in the grove.

Your trail forks at ½ mile as you come to the base of the colossus. The left fork connects with the Pool Ridge Trail, which climbs steeply north to meet the trails in Austin Creek State Recreation Area (see Trail #29). Take the right fork, descending briefly, then curving left along the base of a hillside. Moist ground supports clintonia, trillium and slim solomon's seal. You climb slightly along the base of the hillside, overlooking seasonal Fife Creek.

At ⅝ mile you descend into a tangle of trails. Stay to the left on the quieter side of the nature loop. You immediately pass a big redwood on the left with large knobby burls. The path hugs the base of the slope. You soon encounter several fire-toppled redwood giants leaning against the hill. Redwood slash stacked tipi-fashion against a stump mimics the way that the Pomos built their shelters. The stump is crowned with redwood sorrel.

Your trail winds around more large redwoods, then crosses a bridge across the creek at ¾ mile. You quickly meet a circle around a gnarled, burl-encrusted giant, the Icicle Tree. Its burls have grown stalactite-like formations that reach toward the ground, a very uncommon growth form. After the circle, salmonberry (magenta blossoms in spring, tart berries in summer) grows on the left.

The path soon ends as you meet the Pioneer Trail. For the easiest loop of 1¼ miles, go right on the broad path, heading south paralleling the road. (See next paragraph for a longer option). Redwood violets grow abundantly along the trail. Soon a triple-topped giant on the right is 11 feet in diameter. At ⅞ mile a carpet of trillium, inside-out flower and redwood sorrel cover the forest floor. Continue south, passing the Burbank Circle to complete the loop and cross the paved road before one mile. Another ¼ mile brings you back to the parking lot.

For a longer, more arduous loop, go left on the broad path at ¾ mile. Soon a 100-year-old redwood grows atop an old stump on the left, beside two virgin trees. Notice how the roots of the young tree reached six feet to find soil after sprouting atop the stump. Beyond ⅞ mile you parallel the creek, then cross two small bridges to reach the picnic area at one mile from the trailhead.

Veer right and walk the paved road briefly, then veer right again onto a paved fork. At 1⅛ miles a restroom is on your left, the top of the picnic area on your right. You promptly come to a parking lot on the edge of a large clearing. Veer right to the east end of the lot and head up the East Ridge Trail.

You cross a bridge over the east fork of Fife Creek and climb northeast. At 1¼ miles your climb steepens in a mixed forest of redwoods, firs and hardwoods. At 1⅜ miles you wind around two venerable old giants, then pass a huge, hollow stump. Climb switchbacks through hardwood forest to a junction on the ridge at 1½ miles. The left fork climbs north to Bullfrog Pond in 3 miles.

You take the right fork and climb along the ridge. The thin soil here is very different from the canyon floor, supporting a variety of hardwoods with scattered Douglas firs. Climb to a top at 1⅝ miles, then dip and rise to a higher knob at 1¾ miles, where you have views over the

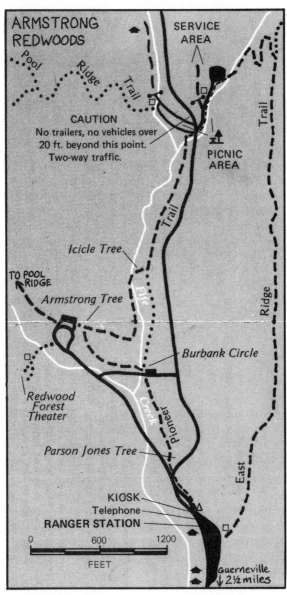

ARMSTRONG REDWOODS

SERVICE AREA

Pool Ridge Trail

CAUTION
No trailers, no vehicles over
20 ft. beyond this point.
Two-way traffic.

PICNIC AREA

Trail

Icicle Tree

TO POOL RIDGE

Armstrong Tree

Fife

Ridge

Burbank Circle

Redwood Forest Theater

Creek

Pioneer

Parson Jones Tree

East

KIOSK
Telephone
RANGER STATION

0   600   1200

FEET

Guerneville
↓ 2½ miles

surrounding forest.

Descend south in a roller coaster manner, climbing to two more wooded hilltops by 2 miles. Birds and small mammals frequent the ridge. Descend, then climb moderately steeply to 2⅛ miles, passing firs to five feet diameter.

You leave the ridge to descend its west slope. Descend steeply at 2¼ miles, then make a gradual winding descent to return to redwood forest with dense huckleberry understory at 2½ miles. You get occasional glimpses of the dense grove of giants on the canyon floor. Descend to the parking lot at 2¾ miles.

117

29

AUSTIN CREEK

GENTLE, SECLUDED WILDERNESS

Austin Creek State Recreation Area offers 4200 acres of steep, gentle wilderness nestled in the remote canyons of East Austin Creek. Three fine backcountry camps allow hikers and equestrians to camp in this placid hill country, where immense glades alternate with dark green forests. Elevations range from 150 feet along the creek to 1940 feet at McCray Mountain on the park's eastern boundary.

Spring offers the best exploring here. Oregon ash, red alder, big leaf maple, western azalea and oaks display verdant new foliage in the canyons, while wildflowers sparkle among the fresh green grass. Winter can be pleasant between storms, when mild, sunny days of solitude accentuate the rushing, brimming creeks. If you go in summer, be forewarned that it gets very hot. Dry conditions may ban fires or close the camps for a while. You can generally drink safely from the creeks in winter and spring, but in summer, low flows make it advisable to purify water.

The Gilliam Creek Trail descends north into the headwaters of Schoolhouse Creek. Your trail soon enters mixed forest of canyon live oak, black oak, bay laurel, redwood and Douglas fir. You skirt the bottom of a glade, then level.

At ⅛ mile you traverse the bottom of another glade on your right, with a steep, wooded slope on your left. Descend steeply into the forest, passing madrone and toyon. Your path levels at ¼ mile, then climbs briefly. Descend toward an overhanging rock outcrop, then cross a seasonal brook.

At ⅜ mile you climb into an expansive glade, with grand views west to the many ridges and canyons between you and the coast, 14 miles away. Traverse the lower glade, fording another seasonal creek at ½ mile.

At ⅝ mile you climb into another glade with more views. To the northwest stand the stark serpentine slopes of Red Slide, the ridge called The Cedars rising beyond it. Austin Creek drains virtually all the country before you.

Your trail turns west to descend Gilliam Ridge. At ¾ mile you pass beneath large canyon live and black oaks. Leave the ridge, descending to cross a fork of Schoolhouse Creek at ⅞ mile. The trail descends west through woods and glades to cross another tributary at one mile, then descends through rolling grasslands.

Your descent steepens as you follow the winding creek at

AUSTIN CREEK:

DISTANCE: 10⅜-mile loop, with shorter options of a 4- or 9-mile loop.

TIME: Five hours to overnight.

TERRAIN: Descend through glades and forest, then along Schoolhouse and Gilliam Creeks to East Austin Creek. Climb along creek to trail camps, then return steeply up and down one ridge and up another to trailhead.

ELEVATION GAIN/LOSS: 1720 feet+/1720 feet-.

BEST TIME: Spring for wildflowers, winter for solitude.

WARNINGS: Watch for poison oak, rattlesnakes, ticks and scorpions. Camp only in designated camps. Fires allowed only in fire pits.

DIRECTIONS TO TRAILHEAD: From Guerneville, go north on Armstrong Redwoods Road for 3 miles to the picnic area (parking for equestrians). Hikers drive the steep, narrow winding road (impassable to trailers) climbing 1.7 miles to a fork. Go left to signed Gilliam Creek Trail.

FEES: Day use: $3/vehicle. Car camping: $10/night.

FURTHER INFO: Austin Creek State Recreation Area (707)869-2015 or 865-2391.

OTHER SUGGESTIONS: The road's right fork leads to a wonderful, wooded campground. A trail links the campground with the described loop. McCRAY MOUNTAIN TRAIL climbs from the campground.

1⅛ miles. The descent eases as the quickening waters of the creek drop away on the left. You pass several veins of dark brown, then blue-green serpentine rock.

The descent steepens again at 1¼ miles. Round a big bend left to a crossing of a fork of Schoolhouse Creek, lined with moss-draped rocks. Then descend south along the stream. At 1⅝ miles you ford Schoolhouse Creek at its confluence with the tributary.

Your trail descends northwest along the pretty creek. At 1⅞ miles you ford the creek, then ford it again in 200 feet. At 2 miles you climb to pass a gnarled black oak four feet in diameter, then descend to the creek.

At 2⅛ miles you reach a junction near the confluence with Gilliam Creek. (For the shortest loop, go right, fording

Schoolhouse Creek, then follow Gilliam Creek upstream to meet the fire road where you go right for a 4-mile loop.) Our described trail stays left. You follow larger Gilliam Creek as it flows west.

Pass through a sunny clearing before 2⅜ miles, then return to dense, dark hardwood forest. Wood rose grows along the creek. Beyond 2½ miles you follow Gilliam Creek on a particularly pretty stretch of alternating rapids and still, glassy pools. Woodwardia ferns thrive on the banks.

Descend to an easy ford of Gilliam Creek at 2⅝ miles. Wildflowers grow on the sunny north bank in spring, including baby blue eyes, milkmaids, vetch and bedstraw. In 400 feet the trail fords back to the south side of the creek. You can follow a faint trail along the north bank for 250 feet to avoid another ford just ahead.

At 2¾ miles the trail returns to the north bank. The canyon is steeper and narrower downstream, requiring frequent fords. In the dry season you may be able to keep your feet dry, but in winter and spring the likelihood of dry feet diminishes. In 200 feet the trail returns to the south side of Gilliam Creek. Immense bay laurels sprout leather ferns on their trunks. You pass the first redwoods since near the trailhead.

A ford at 2⅞ miles may be crossed on a dry log if the water is not too high. Continue along the north bank through a lovely glade surrounded by buckeyes, madrones and oaks. Cross a tributary at 3 miles, then ford Gilliam Creek at a bathtub-sized pool. Follow the south bank briefly, then ford the creek three more times in the next ⅛ mile. The last ford is beside a beautiful pool in a steep part of the canyon.

Climb steadily to sunny hillsides above the creek's deep, dark canyon. You pass many fir stumps in an area once heavily logged. At 3⅜ miles you climb through a clearing where manzanita and coffeeberry compete with young firs. Your path levels high above the creek, then descends. Level again after 3½ miles, still 100 feet above Gilliam Creek.

You descend to the creek at 3¾ miles, where a spur goes left to Gilliam Creek Camp. Three tables, two fire rings and an outhouse occupy a pretty clearing in a bend of the creek.

You have no way to go but up from this deep hole near the confluence of Gilliam and East Austin Creeks. Head north to a wet ford of East Austin Creek, where cypress grows along the stream. After the ford you climb steeply to meet a broad fire road. Turn right and climb gradually north following East Austin Creek upstream.

At 4 miles your road dips, descending near the creek, then climbs past the Fox Mountain Trail. Continue up canyon, winding with the creek, with occasional views of its pristine waters. The trail passes through mixed forest of fir, bay, canyon live oak, black oak and madrone with scattered woodwardia ferns, manzanita and toyon.

At 4¼ miles an immense, decaying fir stump stands on your left. The slope beside the stump is covered with milkmaids and leather ferns. At 4⅜ miles you have grand views along the winding creek. I saw a herd of wild pigs here, retreating from human scent. You climb over a rise at 4½ miles, then the grade eases.

At 4¾ miles a gigantic black oak overhangs the road. You climb high above East Austin Creek. Descend through a glade and approach a giant redwood between you and the creek. The canyon of Thompson Creek lies to the east. Your path turns northwest following East Austin Creek. The road stays mostly level through cool forest.

At 5⅛ miles you descend to a wet ford of the creek surrounded by large redwoods. As I forded the icy waters on a warm February day, a brown rock with black spots wriggled and moved out to the center of the creek. Two large steelhead were spawning, migrating to their birthplace upstream. Austin Creek is currently closed to fishing.

Across the creek you meet the East Austin Creek Trail. (If you turn right, deduct 1⅜ miles from the total distance.) Our described route turns left. The road climbs gradually up the broad canyon carved by East Austin Creek. Hardwoods and grasslands dominate the floor, while conifers mix with hardwoods on the slopes. Beyond 5⅜ miles the creek stays in view.

At 5⅝ miles you overlook the creek as creek, canyon and

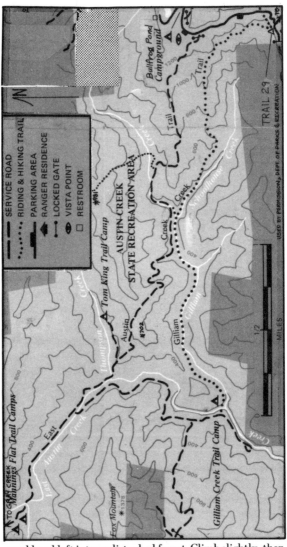

road bend left into undisturbed forest. Climb slightly, then descend to a ford at 5⅞ miles, where cypress, fir, willow, bay laurel and oak grow. Mannings Flat Camp has nice sites nestled in trees on the west bank, overlooking the creek and a beautiful meadow, with wildflowers in spring. Beyond the camp the road continues up the west bank to a junction near the northern park boundary in ½ mile.

Our loop hike retraces your steps down East Austin Creek, returning to the junction at 6½ miles. Go straight on the main trail. At 6⅝ miles you climb a slight hill. Soon the park's largest swimming hole snuggles in a bend of the creek. The waters are slowed by clusters of large, light-colored rocks, great for basking on a warm day.

The road descends to creek level, an 8-foot diameter redwood on the left. Hairy honeysuckle, milkmaid and leather fern grow nearby. At 6⅞ miles you cross a bridge over Thompson Creek, overlooking its confluence with the larger stream. Just before the bridge, a spur on the right descends to another pristine swimming hole.

Your road climbs steeply away from East Austin Creek, overlooking the deep canyon of Thompson Creek. Swing right at 7 miles, then left to meet a spur on the left. The spur heads ¼ mile upstream to Tom King Camp, in a pretty spot beside the creek.

On the main trail, take your time and enjoy the views on a steep climb to the summit at 7½ miles. Then you make a steady, winding descent through a glade to 8 miles. Then descend gradually along a tiny stream.

At 8⅛ miles you come to a glade overlooking Gilliam Creek. An easy ¼ mile brings you to the lateral to the Gilliam Creek Trail. You can turn right to ascend the same trail you came down, returning to the trailhead. Our described route stays on the fire road to climb Panorama Grade, a nice name for a 1000-foot climb with grand views. Backpackers climbing out have been known to call it faintly worse names. Bring on the horses!

Your steady climb starts immediately, following Gilliam Creek as it tumbles and roars on your left. At 8½ miles large twin redwoods stand by the creek. At 8⅝ miles the road bends away from the creek, climbing steeply. Climb to 8⅞ miles, where your ascent eases briefly in a large glade. Quickly resume your steep climb, overlooking Schoolhouse Creek Canyon. Take a break to enjoy the view.

Climb into forest at 9⅜ miles, then return to rolling grasslands. At 9½ miles a footpath forks left, climbing to Bullfrog Pond Campground. Continue steeply up the road to a gate at the Vista Point on the paved road at 9¾ miles.

Turn right and follow the road shoulder for ½ mile. The walk starts out level, then descends to meet a footpath on the right at 10¼ miles. Descend the footpath for less than ⅛ mile to the Gilliam Creek Trailhead and hike's end.

30.

RAGLE RANCH REGIONAL PARK
A COUNTRY FEELING IN A CITY PARK

Ragle Ranch Regional Park has a split personality. The lush green lawns of the eastern portion of the park have softball and soccer fields, a playground, picnic areas and paved jogging and bike paths. But west of the manicured lawns lies the wild beauty of the park's natural side, where oak woodlands, creeks and wetlands support a diverse bird population and provide walker and equestrian with soothing country vistas.

These 156 acres were once the ranch of the pioneer Ragle family, who came to Sebastopol in 1856. When the county parks department acquired the land in 1976, they had the foresight to leave most of the acreage in its natural state. Meanwhile, Sebastopol has grown to encompass the former ranch. A checklist of birds spotted in the park is posted near the entrance.

From the northwest corner of the main parking area at the end of the road, walk north on the paved trail, passing a gazebo on your left. After 200 feet, you turn left on a broad paved path. This trail bends right to head north at ⅛ mile.

You soon reach the end of the pavement, where you continue north on a dirt path. Pass through a gate at ¼ mile and continue north through a second gate. You walk through oak woodlands with a tangle of berry vines and willows on your right.

At ⅜ mile you cross a bridge over a creek. Your trail swings left to follow the slow-moving creek southwest. The big Oregon oaks along the trail support the parasite mistletoe. At ½ mile the creek fans out into wetlands on your left. Your trail skirts a eucalyptus grove, then a vineyard beyond the park boundary.

At ⅝ mile you cross a bridge over Atascadero Creek. The trail forks, the left fork heading south up the creek. (If you take the left fork, you cut ½ mile off the total distance.) Take the right fork, following the creek downstream. Dense willows and berry thickets grow along the creek. Scan the

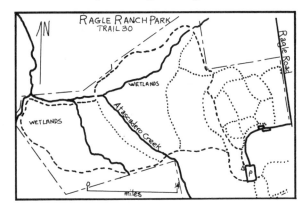

RAGLE RANCH REGIONAL PARK:

DISTANCE: 1⅝-mile loop.

TIME: One hour.

TERRAIN: Through oak woodlands, grasslands and wetlands along several forks of Atascadero Creek.

BEST TIME: Spring for wildflowers, winter for birds.

WARNINGS: Trail will be wet in rainy season; waterproof boots recommended.

DIRECTIONS TO TRAILHEAD: Take Highway 116 or 12 to Sebastopol. From center of town, go west on Bodega Highway for 1.1 miles, then go right on Ragle Road for .5 mile to park entrance on left.

FEES: Day use: $1/vehicle.

FURTHER INFO: Sonoma County Parks (707)527-2041.

OTHER SUGGESTIONS: Many PAVED PATHS wind through the eastern part of the park, ideal for jogging and cycling. SEBASTOPOL-SANTA ROSA RAIL TRAIL, new but already popular, offers three miles of level, paved trail across the Laguna and through farmlands. Eastern trailhead on Petaluma Avenue between Fannan and Abbott Avenues. Western trailhead: turn south off Highway 12 at M.12.2 onto Merced Avenue, meet trail immediately, parking on right.

marshlands on the left for birds.

At ¾ mile, ford a tributary. The crossing can be wet in winter. Your trail bends right, returning to the banks of Atascadero Creek. The creek soon turns to leave the park.

At ⅞ mile your trail turns left to follow the park's western boundary. This section of trail can be very wet in winter and spring. The remains of an old wagon lie in the grasslands on your left. Scattered oaks line the trail until one mile, where you start a gradual climb, still following the boundary. Soon your trail turns east. To the northeast Mount Saint Helena rises above the plain.

You descend slightly at 1⅛ miles, passing a bay laurel. An apple orchard grows beyond the fence on your right. You pass weeping willows at 1¼ miles. In 300 feet the

Atascadero Creek trail merges from the left. You cross a bridge over the creek, then continue east. At 1⅜ miles you enter an area that is very muddy in the rainy season. Redwood timbers span some of the wet area. Then a bridge traverses the worst of the wetlands.

You pass through a gate and climb east through an old pear orchard at 1½ miles, heading toward the gazebo. At the top of the hill, pass through another gate to return to the city side of the park. The gazebo is straight ahead, but veer right to walk through a small community garden. The garden has been designated as a National Peace Site. A post has, written in four languages, "May peace prevail in the world." Your starting/finishing point lies to the east.

31.

HELEN PUTNAM REGIONAL PARK
ROLLING OAK WOODLANDS AND GRASSLANDS

A maze of trails meanders all over the 214 acres of this pastoral park near the Sonoma-Marin County border. The park's steep, rolling grasslands and oak woodlands provide a pristine backdrop for an aerobic workout, whether you are a casual walker or serious runner. One of the best things about these trails is that you can take a different route on the criss-crossing trails every time you visit, yet never fear getting lost. The marvelous views of the surrounding countryside from the steep hills and ridges provide an added bonus.

From the parking lot, follow the paved service road beyond the gate. In 150 feet you come to restrooms and a park map. The first half of the trail is marked by redwood posts. From the map and bulletin board, go left, climbing for 125 feet, then turn right at the first redwood post, marked with an arrow. Your dirt trail descends, ducking under the limb of an oak to cross a gully. You climb moderately into grassy pasture where previous grazing has denuded the land of many of its native plants.

At ⅛ mile your climb eases, overlooking gently rolling, grass-covered coastal hills. The hills, sprinkled with oaks, stretch in all directions—the classic Sonoma County rural landscape. You climb gradually through open grasslands.

At ¼ mile your path levels overlooking a ranch just beyond the park boundary. An old ranch house and its outbuildings are clustered in the shelter of some native oaks. Your trail quickly merges with a broader path on the right, then climbs through a gate, coming to a pond.

Turn right and cross the earthen dam of the pond to meet the paved path along the shore. Go left on the pavement, climbing north. At ⅜ mile daffodils, flannel bush and poppies grow between the trail and the pond. Climb a bit farther to overlook a native oak reforestation project.

You climb away from the pond. Beyond ½ mile the trail angles right. Many oaks grow along the park boundary on

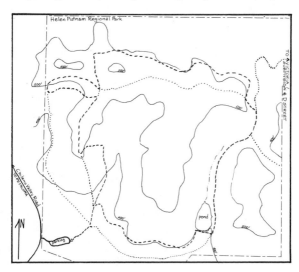

DISTANCE: 1⅞-mile loop.
TIME: One hour.
TERRAIN: Steep, rolling coastal hills.
ELEVATION GAIN/LOSS: 360 feet+/360 feet-.
BEST TIME: Spring for wildflowers. Clear day for views.
WARNINGS: Stay off adjacent private property. Park closes at sunset. Watch for poison oak.
DIRECTIONS TO TRAILHEAD: Exit Highway 101 at Washington Street (M.4.9 from north, M.4.6 from south) and go west to the center of town. Go left on Petaluma Blvd., then take first right. Take Western Avenue for 1.9 miles to Chileno Valley Road. Go left for .8 mile, then left into park.
FEES: Day use: $1/vehicle.
FURTHER INFO: Sonoma County Parks (707)527-2450.

your right. You soon reach the top of the hill. Pass through a fence and meet a maze of trails. (The paved path descends to Victoria Subdivision, connecting with D Street in town.) Look for a redwood post on the left. Follow that trail north, climbing for 200 feet. Then turn right on a faint tread. It soon approaches the paved path, then veers left to follow the edge of oak woodlands. To the east you see sprawling suburbia through the trees, rolling Sonoma hills beyond.

Your trail enters the oak forest, following the contour of a rolling hillside. Soon the view opens up to reveal Mt. St. Helena to the north and Sonoma Mountain to the northeast. In the foreground, residential Petaluma reaches right to the park boundary.

Continue on the trail that contours north. A large California buckeye stands on your left, with fragrant, showy flower spikes in late spring. Its chestnutlike fruit is inedible before leaching (like acorns). The Indians used the toxic nuts to stupefy fish, making them easier to catch.

Your trail rolls into the oak forest. Soap plants, brodiaea, mariposa lily and profuse poison oak border the trail. At ¾ mile you enter a grassy clearing, then return to the forest. Watch out for the low, spreading branches of the live oaks.

At ⅞ mile your trail dips briefly, then climbs. Another view opens to the north. On clear winter days you may see the steam plumes of The Geysers to the left of Mt. St. Helena. Between St. Helena and Sonoma Mountain is Bennett Mountain. All three peaks and the geysers are remnants of this area's ancient volcanic past.

Your trail bends left through a glade surrounded by oak woodlands, where deer graze in the evening. Climb a steep hill at one mile, coming to its top in 300 feet. You come to a steep northeast slope where miners lettuce grows large beside the trail. Then you reach a secluded picnic table with views over the western hills of Sonoma and Marin Counties.

Your level trail turns south, wandering through more beautiful oak woodlands. At 1⅛ miles you climb to a junction of several trails. Take the trail on the far right, which climbs gradually, then levels on the ridge. At 1¼ miles you meet the western park boundary, where your trail bends left and descends south. Just 100 feet after the turn, your path forks. Although you can take the steep boundary trail back to the trailhead, it is easier to take the left fork. It descends east to cross a broad path, then climbs uphill heading southeast, passing godetia and yarrow.

At 1⅜ miles you meet a well-trod path. Turn right and climb gradually southeast. When you start to descend, you have an excellent view west. Your trail descends along the ridge to 1½ miles, where your path splits. The right fork provides the quickest return to the trailhead. Take the left fork, which makes a long bend left, then a gradual descent northeast into an oak-filled canyon.

At 1⅝ miles you meet another path. Turn right and head south down the canyon. While your trail stays in the grasslands, on your left you look down into an oak-jammed gully. Continue your descent to the trailhead at 1⅞ miles.

EAST OF HIGHWAY 101

32.

SHILOH RANCH REGIONAL PARK
LITTLE SLICE OF WILDERNESS IN WINDSOR HILLS

Shiloh Park, dedicated in March 1990, covers 350 acres of steeply rolling oak woodlands. The wild park is home or feeding ground to black-tailed deer, bobcats, gray foxes,

coyotes, wild pigs and rattlesnakes. Many raptors hunt
here, especially red-tailed hawks and kestrels. Please leave
your dog home because of the wildlife. The county hopes to
add 100 acres to the park, extending the boundary
southeast to Mark West Creek before 1991.

Take the Big Leaf Trail opposite the park entrance,
climbing a grassy hill for 250 feet to a fork. The left fork
connects with your return trail. Go right, climbing southeast through oak woodlands, mostly coast live oak with
scattered madrones and manzanitas. The understory is
dense with poison oak and sticky monkeyflower.

You climb gradually through woodlands with scattered
grasslands where many wildflowers grow in spring. You
may see blue dicks, poppies, blue lupines, blue-eyed grass
and buttercups in the first ⅛ mile. After ⅛ mile elegant
brodiaea grows in a shady spot on the left.

Your trail stays mostly level to ¼ mile, then climbs
gradually southeast along the park boundary. On your
right you overlook acres of vineyards that crowd the doors
of a residential neighborhood. At ⅜ mile you pass an
unusual-shaped wooden water tank. Your trail turns away
from the boundary to climb east into woodlands. You are
soon in the shade of young Douglas firs, the understory
dense with soap plants, poison oak, wood strawberries,
hairy honeysuckle vines and young maples. You descend
briefly, then resume a gentle climb paralleling a redwood
split-rail picket fence.

At ⅝ mile your ascent steepens. Pass beneath power lines
and continue climbing, with morning glory vines and
bracken ferns along the trail. At ¾ mile you meet a gulch,
then switchback right to cross it. Then climb through a
glade with more brodiaea, blue-eyed grass and buttercups.

The Big Leaf Trail ends at ⅞ mile as you meet the Ridge
Trail. (With a right turn, you climb briefly, then descend
steeply back to Faught Road.) Go left, climbing northeast
along a grassy ridge with scattered coast live oaks. Soon
ridge and trail descend gradually, passing Douglas iris,
blue-eyed grass, sticky monkeyflower, coyote brush, chamise
and buttercups.

At one mile you resume your climb as the ridge ends,
merging with the larger ridge that towers before you. Large
Douglas firs, both living and snags, grow to four feet in
diameter along the trail. You make a winding ascent
through two lush gullies. Then climb along a sunny cutbank
on your right, where sticky monkeyflowers abound. Indian
paintbrush grow at the top of the cliff. Your trail swings

DISTANCE: 2½-mile Big Leaf Ridge loop, 4 miles with side trips to ponds and east ridge.

TIME: One or two hours.

TERRAIN: Alternating steep and gradual climb to ridge, then descend to ponds. Return down ridge.

ELEVATION GAIN/LOSS:Full hike: 840 feet+/840 feet-. Short loop: 520 feet+/520 feet-.

BEST TIME: Spring for wildflowers. Early or late in day for wildlife.

WARNINGS: Watch for poison oak, ticks and rattle-snakes. Stay off adjacent private property.

DIRECTIONS TO TRAILHEAD: Exit Highway 101 onto Shiloh Road (M.27.9 from north, M.27.4 from south). Go 1.5 miles east to end of Shiloh Road, then go right on Faught Road for .1 mile to park entrance on left.

FEES: Day use: $1/vehicle.

FURTHER INFO: Sonoma County Parks (707)527-2041.

OTHER SUGGESTION: FOOTHILL REGIONAL PARK (opens September 1990), also in Windsor, offers trails on 208 acres. Call County Parks for directions.

right to climb toward a power tower.

You reach the tower and top a ridge in the center of the park at 1¼ miles. Climb a few feet west to a knoll for a view of the entire north county. The Russian River Canyon winds seaward to the west. To the north and northeast you can see the high summits of Sulphur Peak, Geyser Peak and Mount St. Helena.

Return to the main trail and descend, following the power lines briefly. At 1⅜ miles you bend right, continuing your descent. A shady bank on the right shelters wood ferns, star lilies and wood strawberries. After two more bends, you parallel a steep canyon on the left.

You descend to cross the canyon at 1½ miles, then climb steeply to another ridge and a junction at 1⅝ miles. From here you can go left to the trailhead for a 2½-mile loop. Our described hike takes the longer option, going right on the Pond Trail to explore the eastern part of the park.

As you go right, climb steeply to a knob on the ridge, then descend steeply east, passing many iris and blue-eyed grass around 1¾ miles. Then road and ridge climb through a big glade with views northeast to Mount St. Helena, then south over the Santa Rosa plain. Beyond 1⅞ miles you start a gradual winding descent which soon steepens, dropping through another large glade, where the road is lined with crimson clover.

At 2⅛ miles you meet a junction. Go left on the descending road for 400 feet, then veer left on a grassy path that quickly comes to two small ponds. You reach the dam of the second pond at 2⅜ miles. The ponds are somewhat bare except for a few willows along the banks, but in a pretty spot rimmed with grassy hills. In spring it is a little green valley (golden by summer) where blue dicks, blue-eyed grass, yarrow and sun cups sparkle in the grass and hawks and buzzards soar. A future path will descend west along the creek to the trailhead.

Returning to the junction, you can extend your hike by climbing southeast on the road that follows the east ridge of the park. In ⅜ mile from the junction, you climb to a tiny steep knob, the high point of the ridge. It offers views north-northeast to Mt. St. Helena and the rugged country in between, and west toward the coast. The road ends at the southeast corner of the park in another 400 feet. Retrace your steps to the junction of Ridge Trail and Pond Trail.

From the junction your trail climbs northwest under the power line for 200 feet. You pass a level top beside a power tower, then descend west. At first the road is lined with iris, blue-eyed grass and star lilies. But after ⅛ mile you enter chaparral, where chamise and sticky monkeyflower line the way, soon joined by madrone and live oak.

You descend steadily with views west and south to the

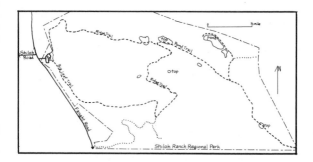

valley that is so quickly filling with new buildings. At ¼ mile the descent eases briefly, then resumes. Mule ears and sticky monkeyflowers line the road. You climb to a small knoll, then resume your descent. Level briefly beyond ⅜ mile, where old man's beard drapes the oaks.

At ½ mile from Ridge/Pond junction your descent steepens. You leave the ridge and wind through forest where woodland star, vetch, buttercup and blue dick grow beneath tall black and live oaks. At ⅝ mile you descend along the edge of a canyon where birds often sing their appreciation of the quiet green forest. You soon come to the bottom of the hill and a fork. Go right, reaching the picnic area and trailhead at ⅞ mile.

33.

MOUNT SAINT HELENA
ROBERT LOUIS STEVENSON'S "SPYGLASS HILL"

Mount Saint Helena towers over the rolling hills and valleys of northern Sonoma County. At 4343 feet, the rugged peak serves as a landmark from the Bay Area to Mendocino County. The mountain was in the territory of the Wappo, a tribe who called themselves "woods people" and resisted attempts by Spanish missionaries to include them in mission life. The natives hallowed the mountain, going to its top for days to fast and pray, waiting for a song from its deity.

Composed of ancient lava, the mountain was formed by folding and uplifting of the earth's crust rather than as a volcanic cone. The peak and the rugged Palisades to the south form an igneous rock island distinct from the surrounding sedimentary rock and the much younger Clear Lake volcanic region to the north.

In 1841 Russians from Fort Ross scaled the summit, planting a cross and naming the peak for the empress of Russia. In 1872 the discovery of a quartz vein rich with

133

silver launched a mining boom here. By 1874 Silverado City, on a flat near the present highway's summit, had 1500 residents. Only a year later boom turned to bust, the rich vein cut off by a fault and never relocated. Most of the buildings were hauled off to other mines in the area.

By 1874 the Lawley Toll Road crossed the flank of the mountain. A stagecoach transported vacationers to Lake County resorts and supplies to quicksilver mines. Black Bart and other highwaymen often robbed the stage of its mining payrolls, escaping into the surrounding wilderness. The Toll House Hotel stood at the road's summit, providing refreshments and shelter for weary travelers.

In May of 1880 Robert Louis Stevenson, on tour from his native Scotland, came to the ghost town of Silverado with his new bride, seeking a dry, healthy climate to recuperate from tuberculosis. They spent two idyllic months in an abandoned bunkhouse on the flank of the mountain. After leaving, Stevenson wrote numerous articles about the region, including The Silverado Squatters. *The mountain made a lasting impression on Stevenson during his brief stay. He called it Spyglass Hill in his most famous work* Treasure Island.

> *Her great bald summit, clear of trees and pasture, a cairn of quartz and cinnabar, rejected kinship with the dark and shaggy wilderness of lesser hilltops.*

Robert Louis Stevenson State Park today consists of 3300 acres on all sides of the mountain. Other than the trail, the park is undeveloped. It is open during daylight hours.

From the parking area on the west side of the summit of Highway 29, the unmarked trail climbs twelve steps, then turns northwest. After 200 feet, you reach a level clearing, the site of the Toll House Hotel. Picnic tables mark the spot today. You can see the old stage road descending north.

Just west of the flat, a sign marks the mountain trail. You climb into a forest of Douglas fir, tanoak, canyon live oak, black oak, bay laurel, madrone and big leaf maple. In spring you may see the white flowers of dogwood trees near the start of your climb. Other understory plants include hazel, wood rose, California nutmeg and hairy honeysuckle.

Beyond ⅛ mile your trail bends left, the first of many switchbacks. You reach the next switchback at ¼ mile. Then your climb eases a bit. Two more switchbacks bring you to ⅜ mile, where the trail gets rockier.

You switch left, then right to ½ mile, then climb north

as the forest thins to reveal views of the rugged countryside. The habitat becomes drier as manzanita and knobcone
pine appear along the trail. Now you switchback more frequently, climbing steadily. Soon the trail bends right and
descends briefly, passing left of a rock outcrop.

At ¾ mile you come to the Robert Louis Stevenson
Memorial. The plaque sits in a shady flat between two
rocky ridges, marking the site of the three-story bunkhouse where the Stevensons sojourned in June and July of
1880. Although little sunlight reaches the spot today,
Stevenson's writings indicate that it was sunnier then. A
spur on the left climbs toward the old mine.

The main trail climbs briefly, then switchbacks right and
climbs steeply. You soon gain a ridge with views north into
Lake County and west toward the bulk of the mountain.
Your trail climbs steeply to a broad gravel road at ⅞ mile.
Turn left onto the road, your route to the summit.

From here it is 4⅛ miles to the North (main) Peak, about
3 miles to South Peak. The nature of the hike changes
radically. You exchange the intimacy and the steepness of

the trail for the broad views and easy grade of the road. The road climbs west, then south. At one mile you overlook the deep, shady canyon that holds the Silverado mine and the site of the Stevenson cabin. In 400 feet you round a big bend, revealing views south into the Napa Valley.

The road turns right and climbs southwest through chaparral with scattered knobcone pines. As you climb gradually along the peak's south face, notice that bay laurel is a prominent member of the chaparral plant community.

At 1½ miles you approach the first big switchback to the right. A few digger pines tower above the road and surrounding brush. These pines with long, gray-green needles, have large cones that produce delicious nuts. The road switchbacks below a large igneous rock outcrop and climbs east. Knobcone pine and manzanita dominate the chaparral, which also includes blueblossom, whitethorn and creeping ceanothus, canyon live oak and Douglas fir.

At 1⅞ miles your route turns northwest. Your steady, easy climb rounds a big switchback left at 2¼ miles, where you can see 7056-foot Snow Mountain to the north. You head south for ⅛ mile before switchbacking right and heading north, a large rock outcrop above on your left.

At 2⅞ miles your road passes under power lines and continues its winding path. Beyond 3 miles, the road bends left and climbs ½ mile to meet the South Peak Trail. The spur climbs ⅜ mile to the 4003-foot lesser summit.

The route to the top heads north. At 3⅝ miles the chaparral consists of dense chinquapin and scattered coffeeberry bushes. Descend slightly for ¼ mile, then climb.

At 4 miles you round a switchback where the road gains the main ridge of the mountain. You are in Napa County, climbing northeast with the Sonoma County line on the ridge to your left. Beyond 4⅛ miles you make the steepest climb yet.

Pass under the power lines again at 4⅜ miles as your climb eases. Fir and nutmeg are the dominant species here. You soon gain a ridge where your route turns sharply left to enter Sonoma County. You head west, the main peak visible ahead. Sugar pines appear along the route.

The road passes through a forest of large Douglas firs and sugar pines. At 4⅝ miles you leave the forest and begin the final climb to the peak. The generator of a television station on your right makes a terrible racket. You reach the top of the world just short of 5 miles from the trailhead.

Although the generator detracts from the wilderness feeling at the summit, you can escape it by walking a few paces down the rock shelves on the north face. You overlook many miles of wild Coast Ranges. To the north, Anthony Peak and Snow Mountain rise prominently in the Yolla Bollies. To their left, Mt. Konocti hides Clear Lake from view, Cobb Mountain and the Geysers mark the north end of the Mayacmas Range, and Lake Sonoma nestles in

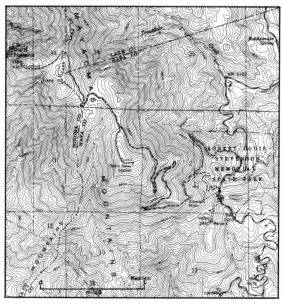

hills beyond Alexander Valley, the Pacific Ocean near Gualala beyond. If the day is clear enough, you see Mt. Shasta nearly 200 miles north-northeast, with Lassen Peak to its right. Pyramid Peak in Desolation Wilderness and the high country north of Yosemite are to the east.

As you retrace your steps south on the trail from the summit, the whole North Bay Area sprawls before you. Santa Rosa is due south, with Sonoma Mountain, San Francisco and the Bay, Carquinez Straits and Mt. Diablo to the left. Point Reyes and the Farallon Islands are south-southwest. You may see these landmarks even more clearly if you take the side trip to South Peak. You will find that the descent takes about half as long as your trip up.

34.

RITCHEY CANYON
REDWOOD CREEK CANYON TO OLD HOMESTEAD

Bothe-Napa Valley State Park lies in a side canyon at the northern end of the Napa Valley. The park's 1900 acres reach west up the canyons of Ritchey and Mill Creeks, sheltering some cool stands of coast redwoods. The park's attractive campground rambles through mixed conifer forest and blue oak woodland overlooking the second growth redwoods of Ritchey Creek.

This area was originally home to the Wappo tribe. In the early 1870s, the socially prominent Hitchcock family of San Francisco acquired these lands as a country retreat. They dubbed it "Lonely." Their daughter, Lillie Hitchcock Coit, came here to rest when she wasn't stirring controversy. An early feminist, Lillie challenged social standards by riding horses astride and forcing her way into an exclusive San Francisco men's club.

From the Horse Trailer parking area just beyond the campground turnoff, take the dirt path heading west beneath oaks, madrones, big leaf maples and Douglas firs. In 200 feet your trail crosses a paved path and parallels the road. Before ⅛ mile the trail veers left to follow Ritchey Creek behind a park residence. You merge with a broad path and continue up the creek, passing redwoods and firs to four feet in diameter. Hazel, wood rose, snowberry, trail plant, ferns, bay laurel, poison oak and wild grape tangle in the understory.

At ¼ mile pass a drinking fountain and climb gradually

RITCHEY CANYON:

DISTANCE: 3½ miles round trip to cascade, 6½ miles to homestead. Add ¾ mile to climb Coyote Peak.

TIME: Two hours for cascade, four for homestead.

TERRAIN: Lush, gentle lower canyon leading to steeper upper canyon, homestead site and views of Napa Valley.

ELEVATION GAIN/LOSS: Cascade: 450 feet+/450 feet-. Homestead site: 1200 feet+/1200 feet-. Coyote Peak: add 500 feet+/500 feet-.

BEST TIME: Spring. Late summer or early fall next best.

WARNINGS: Poison oak is prevalent in the park. Rattlesnakes, ticks, scorpions live here.

DIRECTIONS TO TRAILHEAD: Park is west of Highway 29, 4 miles north of St. Helena, 5 miles south of Calistoga. Turn west at M.33.47 (Napa). Go past entrance station and Visitor Center, then continue straight .2 mile to trailhead.

FEES: Day use: $3/vehicle. Camping: $10/night.

FURTHER INFO: Bothe-Napa State Park (707)942-4575.

OTHER SUGGESTION: The HISTORY TRAIL starts at the end of the park road, passes a pioneer cemetery and climbs over a ridge to Bale Grist Mill, a partially restored 1846 flour mill (2.4 miles round trip).

along the creek. Soon a small waterfall tumbles over a concrete dam. A large California buckeye grows on your right at ⅜ mile. At ½ mile a fork on the right leads to the campground and a trail on the north side of the creek. Continue straight on the Redwood Trail, climbing southwest.

Your trail levels briefly beside a five-foot-diameter Douglas fir on the left. Examine its trunk to see conks, the fruiting bodies of a parasitic fungus that decays the tree from within. Resume your climb through the forest.

Redwoods become sparse at ⅝ mile, where you pass a fire-scarred fir. At the top of a moderately steep hill at ¾ mile, the forest thins as annual grasses and manzanitas intrude. Before ⅞ mile you top another hill and meet the Coyote Peak Trail on the left.

Your trail continues on the right, descending briefly before climbing into dense mixed forest. You pass a lateral (seasonal bridge) to the Ritchey Trail north of the creek. (Equestrians must turn right.) Hikers continue up canyon on the Redwood Trail. At one mile dogwoods grow on the left, presenting flowers in spring and red leaves in fall.

Descend briefly, passing a circle of redwoods with two of the biggest trees to this point along the trail. A six-foot-diameter fir grows just beyond. You pass more big redwoods and firs to 1⅛ mile. Then the forest thins as you climb along the creek. Near 1¼ miles a grove of young redwoods grows between trail and creek, a nice blanket-picnic spot on warm days. The canyon narrows as your trail steepens, hugging the hillside above the creek.

You return to creek side at 1⅜ miles, where woodwardia ferns grow. In 300 feet you reach a ford where you may be turned back at high water (winter and early spring). The ford is usually easy, so let's assume you made it. On the north side of the creek you meet the Spring and Upper Ritchey Canyon Trails at 1½ miles. You can turn right to return down the north side of the creek for the easiest loop (3 miles). The greatest rewards lie ahead. Equestrians must go left to recross the creek, then right on the Spring Trail.

Hikers go right, then quickly left on the footpath to the cascade. It climbs moderately to 1⅝ miles, where you are 100 feet above the creek (on your left). Thimbleberry mixes with the other understory plants. Your trail soon levels, then descends to the creek at 1¾ miles. Ford the creek again, then climb across a side stream cascading over mossy rocks. You switchback up a steep hill and pass an unmarked junction. Continue south to 1⅞ miles where your climb eases. In 200 more feet you meet the Upper Ritchey Canyon Trail.

Turn right to climb to the homestead (left to return downstream for a 3½-mile loop). The trail up canyon climbs gently west, then steepens, passing a large, upended fir. Its demise has cleared a view north to the steep, brushy south-facing slope of the canyon.

At 2 miles from the trailhead, you pass through a cut, fallen redwood, then climb steeply. Your trail levels briefly at 2⅛ miles, then meets the narrow Spring Trail branching left. You continue climbing southwest.

In 500 feet you level again, having climbed above the mixed forest into chaparral. Manzanita, chamise, ceanothus and scrub oak line the trail as you descend steeply, then gradually, returning to redwoods near the creek. At 2⅜ miles you cross a rock-choked side stream. Big white alders

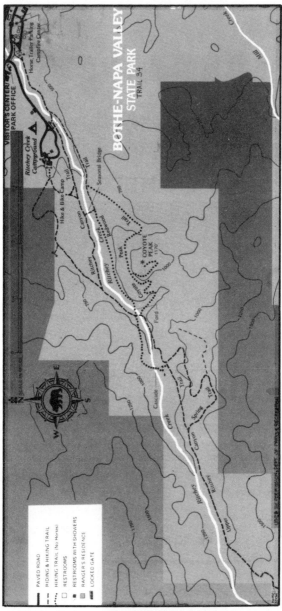

BOTHE-NAPA VALLEY
STATE PARK
TRAIL 34

PAVED ROAD
RIDING & HIKING TRAIL
HIKING TRAIL (No Horses)
☐ RESTROOMS
■ RESTROOMS WITH SHOWERS
▓ RANGER'S RESIDENCE
▰ LOCKED GATE

VISITOR'S CENTER/
PARK OFFICE

Horse Trailer Parking
Campfire Center

Ritchey Creek
Campground

Hiking Trail
Hike & Bike Camp

Canyon Trail

Seasonal Bridge

Ritchey Canyon Redwood Trail

Coyote Peak Trail

*COYOTE
PEAK
1170

Ford

Cascade Creek Trail

Canyon Spring Trail

Ritchey Canyon
Ritchey
Upper Ritchey

and lush elk clover grow in the creek bed.

Your path climbs, then levels and winds through mixed scrub and redwood forest. Around 2½ miles redwoods grow to four feet in diameter. You ford another tributary and climb gradually. At 2⅝ miles a redwood grove beside the creek provides another good picnic spot.

Then climb steeply for 300 feet to cross another side stream where woodwardia ferns and heart-shaped wild ginger grow. Your trail turns southwest, continuing to

141

climb. Beyond 2¾ miles the path levels, then fords another tributary. You climb to drier habitat at 2⅞ miles, where you have a clear view of volcanic cliffs across the canyon to the northwest.

Continue a winding ascent, conifer forest alternating with oak woodlands. You begin a long climb on eroded tread at 3⅛ miles. You descend briefly, then climb again.

Just beyond 3¼ miles, the main trail veers left and climbs south. Take the path that forks right. It descends to cross a dilapidated bridge near a grassy clearing. In 100 feet you pass a memorial stone beneath large redwoods. In another 75 feet you reach a homestead site, a beautiful grassy clearing on an east-facing slope, overlooking the redwood-filled canyon of Ritchey Creek. Although no trace of a house remains, many fruit trees grow in the clearing, as well as rose bushes, grapevines and a walnut tree. Among the fruit trees are pear, plum, fig, peach and at least three varieties of apple. Rocky volcanic cliffs rise above the brushy slope to the north.

Take a break to enjoy this idyllic spot, homesteaded by the Traverso family in 1885. If the fruits are ripe, pick yourself a snack. Otherwise leave the place as you find it. If you sit quietly listening to the birds singing, you may see deer, fox, coyote or other mammals crossing the clearing.

The main trail continues south for ¾ mile to the park boundary. I prefer to return from the homestead, perhaps taking a side trip on the Spring Trail or to the top of Coyote Peak, each of which adds about ¾ mile to the total distance of 6½ miles. Or take the Ritchey Canyon Trail east from the junction below the cascade, following the north side of the creek for a different perspective.

35.

SPRING LAKE/
LAKE RALPHINE LOOPS

GENTLE TRIPLE LOOP IN POPULAR PARKS

The 358 acres of Spring Lake Regional Park are bordered on three sides by city. On weekends and holidays these trails bustle with users young and old, with every kind of human-powered locomotion. But if you travel the park's trails during a quiet time, or camp there at night, you will find an expansive natural area snuggling in green hills where city noise intrudes very little. Spring Lake Park is bordered on the southwest by 152-acre Howarth City Park and on the northeast by 5000-acre Annadel State Park, forming an eight-mile-long natural refuge encircled by city. Spring Lake also offers non-motorized boating, fishing, and a swimming lagoon fed by warm springs.

The hike described here begins at the parking lot near the group picnic area, near the Newanga Avenue entrance. You can walk into the park and join the loop at a dozen other locations. The described hike follows the mostly un-paved equestrian loop around Spring Lake, but you can just as easily follow the paved bike/joggers path or mix portions of the two intertwining trails.

From the parking lot, go east across the Spring Creek overflow channel to join the dirt trail heading northeast. Buttercups and sun cups grow in the grasslands. In 250 feet your trail forks. Take the right fork (no bikes) northeast to another junction and go right again.

You climb a short hill into oak woodlands. At ⅛ mile your footpath parallels a broad path on your left. The forest is mostly coast live oak with bay laurel and buckeye. Soap plant and poison oak grow abundantly in the understory.

At ¼ mile your trail starts a series of short ups and downs, passing hairy honeysuckle and toyon. A spur on the left descends to the lower trail, but you continue on the high path, overlooking the swimming lagoon and the lake.

When your path forks again, take the left fork (right fork to Shady Oak Picnic Area) and descend to cross a road, then head north toward the dam, passing fennel, coyote brush, vetch and berry vines. At ½ mile a cottonwood tree grows on the left. You soon join the paved path, following it across an inlet of the lake at ⅝ mile. Then go left on a dirt path along the shore beside cottonwoods, alders and willows. The paved path runs atop the dam on your right. Continue along the shore passing tules, horsetail ferns and yellow water iris. Before one mile, near the end of the dam, your trail forks. Stay left along the shore.

In 500 feet a faint trail forks right to cross the paved path and climb into woodlands. Go right to take the Howarth Park loop (continue straight to finish the loop around Spring Lake, as described at the end of this report). Beyond 1⅛ miles your dirt path descends to join a broader trail, then climbs west up a rocky hill.

At 1¼ miles your trail levels, then descends through oak woodlands. Beyond 1⅜ miles you pass houses on your right. At 1½ miles you climb a short hill, then level heading west.

Climb another short hill at 1⅝ miles, then wind through

SPRING LAKE/LAKE RALPHINE LOOPS:

DISTANCE: 2¼-mile loop, 4-mile double loop or 6¼-mile triple loop.

TIME: One to three hours.

TERRAIN: Mostly level around Spring Lake, easy climb to Lake Ralphine.

BEST TIME: Spring for wildflowers, but nice anytime.

WARNINGS: You must yield to horses. Watch for poison oak.

DIRECTIONS TO TRAILHEAD: Exit Highway 101 onto Highway 12 West (M.20.05 from north, M.19.35 from south). In 2 miles go right on Hoen Avenue for 1.5 miles, then left on Newanga Avenue for .6 mile to park entrance. Then go right to parking.

FEES: Day use: $2/vehicle (free to walk in). Car camping: $11/night (hot showers for campers!).

FURTHER INFO: Spring Lake Park (707)539-8092.

OTHER SUGGESTION: You can join the loop from the campground on a short trail from campsite #5, meeting the loop ¼ mile west of the trailhead.

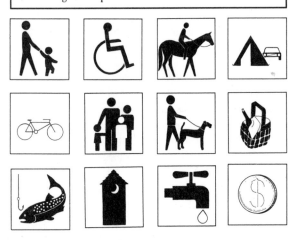

the woods. Another easy grade brings you to 1¾ miles, where you overlook Lake Ralphine through the trees on your left. As you descend gradually, the traffic noises increase. Descend along a redwood fence to a junction. Take the left fork, descending east on a narrow path to the dam of Lake Ralphine at 2 miles. You pass a toilet, then cross the dam, a popular fishing spot. Pass the boat house and come to the parking and picnic area at 2⅛ miles. Continue around the lake to a paved path with a park map beside it.

Take the paved trail northeast around Lake Ralphine, watching for ducks, geese and egrets that frequent the shore. At 2¼ miles go left on a dirt path paralleling the

144

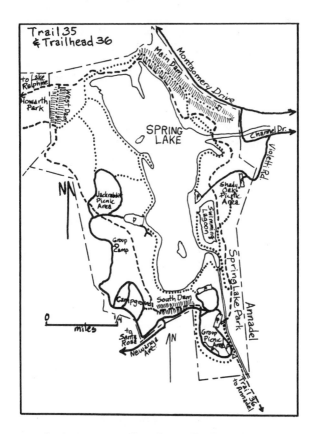

paved route, passing through woodlands with scattered willows, manzanitas, bays and madrones. Snowberry, honeysuckle, toyon and Scotch broom grow in the understory. Beyond 2⅜ miles firs and pines mix with the hardwoods.

At 2½ miles you reach the end of the lake. A trail forks left around the east and north shores. Our described route climbs east to meet the paved path, but stay on the dirt trail on the left. You pass lush vegetation with poison oak, elderberry, vetch and mule ears. Soon the habitat is drier, with coyote brush, buttercup, soap plant and Douglas iris. You pass poppies and yarrow, then meet the west dam of Spring Lake. Climb to the top of the dam at 2¾ miles, where you meet the Spring Lake dirt trail. (The junction where you left that trail is ¼ mile to the left.)

From the south end of the west dam, head south on the gravel horse path. At 2⅞ miles veer right, wrapping around giant water tanks. You soon veer away from the tanks, following the signed horse trail on a gradual climb.

At 3 miles your trail becomes vague as you pass a cinder block building and meet a gravel road. Veer right on the gravel for 200 feet to find the signed horse trail heading south. You parallel a chain link fence briefly, then wind southeast among oaks with sun cups, buttercups, blue dicks and soap plants in the grass.

At 3⅛ miles you cross a paved road and continue southeast on the dirt path through a rocky area. Your trail turns east briefly, then descends to merge with another path near Jackrabbit Picnic Area. At 3¼ miles you head east, paralleling the paved road. You pass the boat ramp parking, then veer right to head southeast, then south.

Around 3½ miles several paths fork right into the Group Camping Area. You continue on the horse loop passing poppies and lupine. In 250 feet you reach the South Dam, where a fork on the right leads to Sonoma County Campground. Go left across the dam to complete your loop at 3¾ miles. You can extend your hike by walking the paved loop for another trip around Spring Lake. Or you can go south from the parking area to connect with Trail #36.

ANNADEL STATE PARK
INCLUDES THE NEXT THREE TRAILS

Annadel is a wilderness refuge surrounded by city. The park offers 5000 acres of hills, creeks, woodlands and meadows reached by nearly 40 miles of trails. You can fish at 26-acre Lake Ilsanjo and go birding at Ledson Marsh. More than 130 bird species have been seen in the park. Threatened with subdivision, Annadel became a state park in 1971 after Sonoma County residents raised over a million dollars to match state and federal funding.

The Southern Pomo and Southern Wappo tribes lived in the area around today's park. They and the Coast Miwoks, who lived just south, gathered obsidian and food in these rolling hills, observing a sometimes uneasy truce.

In 1837 the Mexican government gave sea captain John Wilson a land grant of 19,000 acres including these hills. Wilson, captain of the Ayacucho, the ship made famous by the book Two Years Before the Mast, built a home at his Rancho Los Guilicos but seldom stayed there. William Hood owned the land from 1849 to the 1870s. Samuel Hutchinson acquired the land in the late 1870s. He established a home, farm and cobblestone quarry. He may have named the place "Annie's Dell" for his first daughter. In 1888 Southern Pacific named the railroad station near the Hutchinson home Annadel Station.

In the 1930s Hutchinson's son sold the land to young entrepreneur Joe Coney, who used the land for ranching, farming and hunting until the late 1960s. In 1956 Coney dammed Spring Creek, naming the lake he created for his wife Ilsa and himself—Ilsanjo. He and his friends built many of the trails in use today. Coney often invited the public, including Boy Scouts and Girl Scouts from Sonoma County and the Bay Area, to use his Annadel property.

The dozens of trails in the park interconnect, offering a maze of choices. The next three loops explore most of the trails and mention the others. Do not feel bound to limit your explorations to the described hikes. All the park's trails offer abundant diversity of native plants and wilderness within the populated heart of Sonoma County.

36.

ROUGH GO/CANYON/ SPRING CREEK LOOP

VIEW-LINED ROUTE TO LAKE ILSANJO

From the Horse Trailer parking area at the southeast corner of Spring Lake Park, head south on Spring Creek Trail, a broad gravel road behind the gate at the south end of the lot. Your road winds along channelized Spring Creek through grasslands. In ¼ mile the Stonehedge spur enters on the right. Continue along the road with city on the right, Spring Creek and the green hills of Annadel on the left.

At ½ mile cross a bridge and meet a fork. Go left, climbing the Rough Go Trail. Climb steadily on the road's

ROUGH GO/CANYON/SPRING CREEK LOOP:

DISTANCE: 5½-mile loop.

TIME: Two or three hours.

TERRAIN: Level trail along creek, then climb to large
meadows. Descend to Lake Ilsanjo, then climb and
descend Canyon Trail to complete loop.

ELEVATION GAIN/LOSS: 700 feet+/700 feet-.

BEST TIME: Spring for wildflowers.

WARNINGS: Mountain bikers must yield to hikers and
horses and announce presence when passing. Stay on
marked trails. Watch for poison oak and rattlesnakes.

DIRECTIONS TO TRAILHEAD: Same as Trail #35.

FEES: Day use at Spring Lake: $2/vehicle.

FURTHER INFO: Annadel State Park (707)539-3911.

OTHER SUGGESTION: You can join the loop at the ¼-
mile-point from a no fee access off Stonehedge Road.

rocky tread. Coast live, black and Oregon oaks are scattered
in the grasslands beside the path. Chinese houses, buttercups, blue-eyed grass and vetch grow on the shoulders. Pass
several unmarked spurs. Please stay on named trails.

At ¾ mile your climbing road bends left, then right. At
one mile you pass big rocks on your steady climb. At 1⅜
miles, as the road makes a big bend left, you have views on
the right of wooded Spring Creek Canyon. Your steady
climb continues, passing the Cobblestone Trail on the left.
At 1½ miles you crest a hill and meet the Orchard Trail
on the left. (Both side trails descend to Channel Drive at the
northwest corner of the park.)

Continue on the mostly level Rough Go Trail. Beyond 1⅝
miles you overlook immense False Lake Meadow on your
left. Soon Mt. St. Helena rises beyond the meadow. Poppies,
dwarf lupine and blue-eyed grass add color in spring.

At 1⅞ miles you meet a junction of six trails, three of
them unmarked. On the left, the Live Oak Trail descends
to link with the North Burma Trail. Also on the left, the
W.P. Richardson Trail heads east, descending to the north
shore of Lake Ilsanjo. Continue on the Rough Go Trail,

148

which climbs south, then levels with views over a big meadow to Hood Mountain.

At 2 miles you start a gradual descent toward hidden Lake Ilsanjo. At 2⅜ miles you bend left and the 26-acre lake is suddenly before you. You may see ducks in the tules along the shore. Lake Ilsanjo is one of the most popular places in the park, offering picnic tables, toilets and fishing.

Walk 200 feet to find a picnic table overlooking the lake beside the dam across Spring Creek. The Spring Creek Trail is on the right. It offers the shortest return, 2⅛ miles to the trailhead. Shadier than the Rough Go or Canyon Trails, Spring Creek Trail is a good choice on a hot day.

Our description follows the Rough Go Trail across the dam, meeting the Canyon Trail at 2⅝ miles. You can go left to connect with Trail #37, but the described hike turns right on the Canyon Trail, climbing away from the lake and through a meadow.

At 2¾ miles your trail climbs gradually through grasslands and scattered oak woodlands with blue dicks, buttercups and blue-eyed grass. At 2⅞ miles the dirt road bends left and makes a winding descent into mixed forest with firs, oaks and bays. At 3 miles Hunter Spring is on the left. A sign says the water is unsafe to drink, but the flowing water feels cool and fresh on your face on a hot day. In the forest understory near the spring grow woodwardia ferns, hazel and coffeeberry. Your trail descends to meet the Marsh Trail before 3⅛ miles. Marsh Trail climbs east, then heads southeast to Ledson Marsh in 3 miles.

The Canyon Trail descends gradually with grand views, first north to Mt. St. Helena beyond the rolling hills of Annadel, then west to the Santa Rosa plain, the Russian

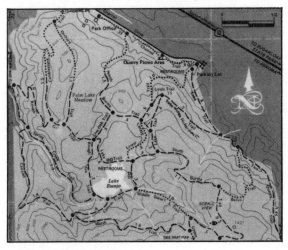

River and the hills toward the coast. Around 3½ miles you can see Spring Lake to the north. Poppies and dwarf lupine grow along the road.

At 3⅝ miles your descent steepens, then makes a big bend right, where elegant brodiaeas grow in spring. The descent eases around 4 miles, where you look east into Spring Creek Canyon. Then resume a steady descent through woodlands, crossing a small creek at 4¼ miles.

Your fire road climbs briefly, passing yarrow, soap plant, blue dick and blue-eyed grass. You soon descend again, the trail cooler now under oaks. At 4½ miles cross a bridge over the creek and meet the Spring Creek Trail. Go left and descend gradually down the canyon. At 5 miles you close the loop, meeting the Rough Go Trail on your right. Continue down the Spring Creek Trail to the trailhead at 5½ miles.

37.

STEVE'S S/SOUTH BURMA/ BASALT LOOP

VARIED, WILDFLOWER-RICH LOOP FOR HIKERS ONLY

Take the W.P. Richardson Trail, a broad road that climbs southeast through forest of Douglas firs and oaks. In 500 feet the narrow Lower Steve's S Trail offers hikers solitude and a more direct (and steeper) route to Lake Ilsanjo. (Bikers and equestrians should use the Richardson Trail.)

Hikers ascend steps and climb southwest through tall fir forest, with scattered spindly bay laurels. Understory plants include soap plant, hedge nettle and poison oak.

By ⅛ mile obsidian chips litter the ground. The Southern Pomo gathered obsidian here for arrowheads and spear points. It is illegal to take obsidian or plants from state park lands.

Climb steadily through the forest, bending left, then right at ¼ mile. Pass bracken, maidenhair and wood ferns. At ⅜ mile snowberry (inedible white berries in summer), miners lettuce and sword ferns join the understory, soon ollowed by lady ferns, fat solomon's seal and wood rose.

At ½ mile you approach a ridge where many large firs grow. The tiny white flowers of woodland stars grow from the duff. Your path soon levels, passing firs to five feet in diameter. At ⅝ mile many oaks and bays grow with the firs in mixed forest. The trail winds, then resumes its climb.

At ¾ mile you meet the broad Louis Trail. (Go left to

STEVE'S S/SOUTH BURMA/BASALT LOOP:

DISTANCE: 5¾-mile loop or 3⅞-mile Lower Steve's S/
W.P. Richardson loop.

TIME: Two or three hours.

TERRAIN: Climb through forest, then level through
meadows, before descent to Lake Ilsanjo. Climb then
mostly level on Marsh Trail. Ascend flower-studded
ridge and descend to views, meadows and quarries.

ELEVATION GAIN/LOSS: Full loop: 1080 feet+/1080
feet-. Short loop: 480 feet+/480 feet-.

BEST TIME: Spring for wildflowers.

WARNINGS: Watch for rattlesnakes, especially in warm
weather. Extensive poison oak along trail. No fires or
camping. Carry drinking water. No bikes or horses
allowed on Lower Steve's S or Basalt Trails. Park
closes at sunset.

DIRECTIONS TO TRAILHEAD: Turn south off Highway
12 at M.18.9 (3.9 miles from Highway 101) onto
Mission Blvd. Go left at stoplight onto Montgomery
Drive. Follow Montgomery for 1.5 miles, then turn
right onto Channel Drive and follow it for 2.3 miles to
end. Trail is on right as you enter parking lot.

FURTHER INFO: Annadel State Park (707)539-3911.

OTHER SUGGESTIONS: Many more trails traverse the
wild, rolling hills of Annadel. Channel Drive offers
three other choices. COBBLESTONE TRAIL, near park
entrance, climbs 2 miles, meeting Orchard and Rough
Go Trails. NORTH BURMA TRAIL, just east of park
office, climbs 2 miles to link with Live Oak, Steve's S,
W.P. Richardson and South Burma Trails. W.P.
RICHARDSON TRAIL (bikes, horses OK) climbs 2½
miles to Lake Ilsanjo, then climbs ½ mile to Rough Go
and Live Oak Trails.

connect with the Richardson Trail.) Steve's S Trail goes
right (open to bikes and horses next ¼ mile). You enter a
large meadow surrounded by oaks, bays, madrones and firs.
Climb through the meadow where blue-eyed grass, lupine
and carpets of goldfields grow in spring.

Continue straight as you meet the North Burma Trail on
the right. You quickly meet another fork, where you go
right on Steve's S Trail (no bikes, no horses in winter). At
one mile you descend toward Lake Ilsanjo. The verdant face

151

of 1887-foot Bennett Mountain shimmers in the sun before you. You descend through grasslands overlooking the lake and the immense meadow on its north shore. Manzanitas grow with coast live and Oregon oaks along the trail. In spring you may see tiny blue larkspur, tarweed, blue dicks, buttercups and prickly bedstraw.

At 1¼ miles your trail levels, entering the large meadow around the lake. Beyond 1⅜ miles you cross the broad Richardson Trail (you can go left for a 3⅞-mile loop) and head south in the shade of mixed forest on Steve's S Trail. You skirt the east side of Lake Ilsanjo, passing mule ears and blue-eyed grass. Around 1⅝ miles two spurs on the right lead to picnic spots and toilets along the shore.

Your trail soon bends left, crossing seasonal Spring Creek. You immediately turn left on Middle Steve's S Trail. (Canyon Trail begins on the right.) Poison oak, iris and wood strawberry grow at the junction. You climb gradually southeast. At 1¾ miles, as your trail starts a winding climb, wood rats have built a pile-of-twigs home under a live oak on the right.

At 1⅞ miles your steep, rocky climb is lined with blue dicks, blue-eyed grass and native bunch grass beneath oaks. You dip through a cool gully at 2 miles, then climb through fir forest. At 2⅛ miles your climb steepens for ¼ mile.

You meet the broad Marsh Trail, a popular mountain bike route. Our described route goes left. (You can go right for ⅛ mile, then left on Upper Steve's S Trail to climb the flanks of Bennett Mountain.) Descend southeast on the Marsh Trail, passing through a grove of young redwoods where your path levels. Continue through fir forest. Beyond 2½ miles oaks dominate the forest. Coyote brush,

Douglas iris, star lily and blue dicks line the road.

At 2¾ miles the road begins an easy climb to beautiful Buick Meadow, where you come to a fork and a rest bench. The right fork leads to Ledson Marsh in one mile (see next trail). You go left on the South Burma Trail, following the left edge of the big meadow. Around 3 miles your broad trail bends left to climb west. You soon overlook Buick Meadow, Sonoma Mountain and Bennett Peak.

At 3¼ miles your trail levels. Star lilies, blue dicks and elegant brodiaeas grow beneath manzanitas. Soon a dense carpet of fragrant Sonoma sage grows along the trail. The sage has delicate purple flowers in spring. It grows in patches, this one covering about an acre. Amidst the sage is narrowleaf buckbrush, chamise and blueblossom, and hairy star tulips and scarlet frittilaries in spring.

Before you leave the sage patch, a picnic table is on the right. A spur on the left leads 250 feet to another table surrounded by chaparral, where you have a view of Santa Rosa plain and Bennett Peak.

The main trail winds, levels, then descends rocky tread to 3½ miles, where another picnic table sits beside the junction with the Basalt Trail. The South Burma Trail continues, meeting the Richardson Trail in one mile. Our described route descends the Basalt Trail (no bikes or horses), winding through forest.

Beyond 3⅝ miles you descend steeply east (watch for loose rocks!) through a clearing in the forest with more Sonoma sage. The trail is mostly steep to 3⅞ miles. Cross a tiny creek twice and descend gently. Your trail wraps around an immense Douglas fir with many large limbs.

At 4 miles your trail levels at a quarry site where the quarriers dug to take rocks of dark basalt. Resume your gentle descent through mixed forest of firs and black oaks. At 4⅛ miles your path bends left into Manzanita Meadow where goldfields and low-growing dwarf brodiaea thrive.

You climb briefly through rocky terrain, then come to a magnificent view of Hood Mountain and Sugarloaf across Valley of the Moon. Your trail descends steeply through blueblossom, with fragrant electric-blue flowers in spring. At 4¼ miles you are at the top of another quarry on the left. Descend to the base of the immense quarry, overgrown with ceanothus and coyote brush, at 4⅜ miles. This quarry was worked in the 1950s.

Then descend north through forest. Your descent steepens at 4⅝ miles. At 4¾ miles your steep descent continues over solid rock until you meet the Two Quarry Trail. Go left on the broad road (open to bikes and horses), following the park boundary northwest.

In ¼ mile you come to a confusing junction with several unmarked paths and the Richardson Trail as it makes a big bend. Bear right, then swing left on the broad dirt road of Richardson Trail. As you begin a gradual descent northeast, city noises intrude on the quiet forest. But soon a gracefully rolling glade on the right provides solace and perhaps browsing deer. Descend along the glade to 5½ miles, then through the forest to the trailhead at 5¾ miles.

38.

SCHULTZ/MARSH/RIDGE/ UPPER STEVE'S S LOOP

EXPLORING THE QUIET SIDE OF ANNADEL

It seems that the number of people you will see on an excursion in Annadel State Park diminishes proportionate to the distance of the trailhead from Santa Rosa. So the Schultz and Lawndale Trailheads on the park's eastern edge provide seclusion as well as the shortest routes to Ledson Marsh, where dozens of bird species have been sighted. The eastern trails are also very close to Sugarloaf Ridge State Park, where you may camp.

The Schultz Trail climbs northwest, quickly entering mixed forest of Douglas fir, coast live oak and madrone. Your trail levels and heads southwest. The lush understory includes coyote brush, toyon, manzanita, sticky monkeyflower, wood strawberry and soap plant. You may see redwood lilies blooming in June and July if deer have not eaten them. You climb gradually to ⅛ mile, then begin a gradual descent through dense Scotch broom.

Your trail descends along the edge of Schultz Canyon, where Douglas firs grow to three feet in diameter beside big leaf maples and bay laurels. Wood rose, blue dicks and blue-eyed grass join the understory. Beyond ¼ mile you cross a seasonal tributary of Sonoma Creek. Ferns, wild grape, snowberry, fat solomon's seal, poison oak and starflower tangle along the creek.

You climb gradually northwest on a rocky tread with the creek on your right, passing tarweed, hazel, hedge nettle, golden fairy lantern and mule ear. At ⅜ mile a stand of redwoods is on your right as your trail switchbacks left to

154

SCHULTZ/MARSH/RIDGE/UPPER STEVE'S S LOOP:

DISTANCE: 4¼ miles round trip to marsh, 7½ miles round trip to Trail #37, 7¼-mile mountain bike loop, or 8⅝-mile Upper Steve's S Loop (hikers, equestrians).

TIME: Two to four hours.

TERRAIN: Easy climb through forest and meadows to Ledson Marsh. Easy climb on Marsh Trail. Moderate climb along ridge to flank of Bennett Mountain, then descend through forest.

ELEVATION GAIN/LOSS: Full loop: 1020 feet+/1200 feet-, 550 feet+/550 feet- round trip to Marsh.

BEST TIME: Spring for wildflowers. Winter for best birding at marsh.

WARNINGS: Watch for poison oak and rattlesnakes. Carry water. Mountain bikers must slow to walking speed at blind corners, yield to horses. No bikes on Upper Steve's S Trail, no horses in winter.

DIRECTIONS TO TRAILHEAD: Take Highway 12 east of Santa Rosa to M.25.6, where you turn south on Lawndale Road. Go 1.2 miles to Lawndale Trailhead, then .6 mile to Schultz Road. Go right on Schultz for .8 mile to Schultz Trailhead, where six cars can park.

FURTHER INFO: Annadel State Park (707)539-3911.

OTHER SUGGESTION: You can also climb to Ledson Marsh from TRAILS #36 or 37 VIA THE MARSH TRAIL, or take the LAWNDALE TRAIL 1¾ miles to marsh.

climb southeast. Black oaks and maples mix with the conifer forest as Hooker's fairy bell, hairy honeysuckle and wood fern join the understory.

At ½ mile your trail bends right to climb through grasslands with scattered black and coast live oaks and manzanita. Mule ears, sticky monkeyflowers and mariposa lilies add color in spring and summer.

At ¾ mile your steady climb offers views south to Sonoma Mountain, southeast to Valley of the Moon and Sonoma Valley beyond. Sugarloaf Ridge State Park is northeast, topped by the peaks of Bald and Red Mountains.

At ⅞ mile your rocky, climbing path turns west. You pass blue dicks, dwarf brodiaea, yarrow and mule ears. Your climb eases at one mile, where you parallel an old stone wall built in the 1800s to mark the boundary of Rancho Los Guilicos (it now marks the park boundary). Your climb resumes, heading toward some power lines.

At 1⅛ miles your rocky road bends right, leaving the stone wall and passing a few firs. You swing right again to climb northeast at 1¼ miles. Ascend a rocky hill where chaparral of chamise, coyote brush, chaparral pea and sticky monkeyflower dominates.

Your climb turns west at 1½ miles. You soon level, then descend through forest and under the power lines at 1⅝ miles, where you meet a broad trail. Go right and head northwest on the Pig Flat Trail. In 100 feet you enter a meadow where the Ridge Trail branches left. A dead-end spur is on the right.

The Pig Flat Trail continues northwest, climbing into fir forest. At 1⅞ miles you dip through a rocky meadow, then resume your climb. Beyond 2 miles your trail levels, then descends to overlook Ledson Marsh. At 2⅛ miles your trail ends at the Marsh Trail. Picnic tables left of the junction have an excellent view of the marsh.

If you go right at the junction (see below for left turn option), the broad Marsh Trail circles the shore of the marsh. You pass the yellow flowers of sweet clover, tarweed and mule ears and the blue flowers of blue dicks and blue-eyed grass. Manzanita, madrone, fir and laurel grow tall along the trail. Take one of the side trails on the left to sneak quietly to the marsh shore, where you may see ducks, grebes and other water-loving birds. Quail inhabit the surrounding forest and grasslands.

The Marsh Trail crosses the marsh's outlet at the head of Schultz Canyon. Continue around the tule-filled marsh to meet the Lawndale Trail at 2½ miles. Veer left to continue around the marsh. By 2⅝ miles you return to the edge of the marsh, where wood duck nesting boxes are mounted on trees. In another 300 feet the Rhyolite Trail

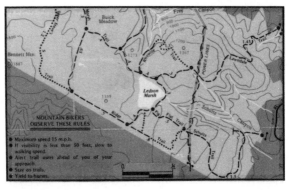

(no bikes) forks right. The state parks people are removing eucalyptus from the land around the marsh to preserve and restore the native vegetation. Narrow-leaved mule ears, poppies and yarrow grow in the grasslands.

At 2¾ miles you leave the marsh, climbing into mixed forest. You climb to 2⅞ miles where you pass an old quarry on the left. Many blue dicks and coastal manroot vines grow here in spring and summer. You descend gradually to 3 miles, where the Two Quarry Trail forks right. Picnic tables and a toilet are located there at the lower end of a large meadow. From the junction the Marsh Trail winds northwest through the meadow. At 3⅜ miles you pass the Ridge Trail on the left. At 3¾ miles you meet the South Burma Trail and the hike described in Trail #37.

If you go left at the end of the Pig Flat Trail, the Marsh Trail circles the marsh's west side, then veers left away from the marsh. At 2¼ miles you climb through forest.

Beyond 2⅜ miles you meet the Ridge Trail that runs along the old stone wall on the park boundary. (You can turn left here to return to the trailhead at 4¾ miles.) Our described hike turns right to climb west-northwest. Houses line the southern, private side of the ridge.

At 2½ miles your trail bends away from the wall, descending briefly. By 2⅝ miles you are again climbing beside the stone wall. You climb steadily on uneven, rocky tread with views of Ledson Marsh, which looks bigger from above than when you first saw it. Across Valley of the Moon, rocky Hood Mountain and grassy Bald Mountain rise to 2700 feet. To their right is Sugarloaf Ridge.

Beyond 2¾ miles you climb to a top, then descend to an

unmarked junction. Do not confuse the trail on the right with the Ridge Trail, which forks right at 3⅛ miles, after another steady climb. From the upper junction, Upper Steve's S Trail (no bikes, no horses in rainy season) continues to climb, following the stone wall up the ridge.

Around 3⅜ miles your climb steepens, then levels. Just before you reach the flat, turn around for a fantastic view of San Pablo Bay, the Berkeley Hills and Mt. Diablo. As the trail levels, a short spur climbs a knoll on the left, with views south to Cotati Valley and Mt. Tamalpais.

Upper Steve's S Trail stays mostly level along the ridge to 3½ miles. You then enter forest and swing right to leave the boundary and ridge, ¼ mile from the 1887-foot summit of Bennett Mountain. Immense black oaks grow along the trail, then Douglas firs to four feet in diameter. Your trail soon descends steeply northeast through the forest, dropping to meet the Marsh Trail at 4¼ miles. You turn right to complete the 8⅝-mile loop, following the Marsh Trail to the junction with Pig Flat Trail, where you turn left to retrace your steps to Schultz Trailhead.

39.

SANTA ROSA CREEK HEADWATERS

HOOD MOUNTAIN REGIONAL PARK

When you turn off Highway 12 onto Los Alamos Road, suburbia surrounds you. But as Los Alamos winds up the steep walls of Santa Rosa Creek Canyon, you quickly leave subdivisions for steep grazing lands with scattered homes. Then the road loses its stripe and narrows enough to give even the most confident driver a case of white-knuckle-itis. It is time to slow to a crawl, even to pull into a turnout to give the countryside a good look. As you wind around the flank of towering Castle Rock, you gain a ridge surrounded by steep, untrammeled mountainsides. As the ridge leads you to the parking area for Hood Mountain Regional Park, congratulate yourself for making a quick escape from the urban blight below.

From the parking area, take the gravel road on the left. You descend east through steep grasslands scattered with oaks toward the headwaters of Santa Rosa Creek. After ⅛ mile your road narrows, turns to dirt and steepens. (Be sure to

SANTA ROSA CREEK HEADWATERS:

DISTANCE: 3½ miles round trip (or more).

TIME: One or two hours.

TERRAIN: From ridge down into deep canyon at headwaters of Santa Rosa Creek, then back up.

ELEVATION GAIN/LOSS: 650 feet+/650 feet-.

BEST TIME: Spring.

WARNINGS: Open weekends only. May be closed during fire season in summer or fall. **Call first.** Be sure you are fit enough to climb back up the steep hill. Watch for poison oak.

DIRECTIONS TO TRAILHEAD: On Highway 12, 6.3 miles east of Highway 101, turn north onto Los Alamos Road and go 4.75 steep, winding miles to park.

FEES: Day use: $1/vehicle.

FURTHER INFO: Sonoma County Parks (707)527-2041.

OTHER SUGGESTIONS: THIS TRAIL CONTINUES SOUTH to the summit of Hood Mountain, then to Sugarloaf Ridge State Park. For the easier ascent of Hood Mountain from the south, see Trail #40. In town, the SANTA ROSA CREEK TRAIL on the north side of the creek between Brush Creek Road and Farmers Lane will be completed fall 1990, providing walkers access to ¾ mile of creek.

save energy to climb this steep hill at the end of your hike.) Coyote brush lines the road.

At ¼ mile two old apple trees overhang the right side of the road with a bushy fig on the left, marking the site of an old homestead. Continue your steady plunge into the canyon, passing madrone, bay laurel, young Douglas fir and oak on the right. Beyond ⅜ mile the forest becomes dense, with interior live oaks and deciduous black oaks. Native bunch grasses grow on the steep cut bank. Ferns and mosses cover the rocky ground.

At ½ mile your road makes a big bend right and steepens as you enter Hood Mountain Regional Park. Several canyons ahead shelter various forks of Santa Rosa Creek. Sticky monkeyflowers grow along the shoulder.

After a side trail branches right (no horses), you reach the park's old parking area at ⅝ mile, with several picnic tables. Take the next trail on the right (OK for horses). You descend through a big S curve bending left, then right. You

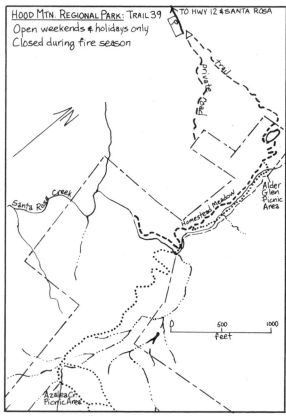

HOOD MTN. REGIONAL PARK: TRAIL 39
Open weekends & holidays only
Closed during fire season
TO HWY 12 & SANTA ROSA

private road

trail

Santa Rosa Creek

Homestead Meadow

Alder Glen Picnic Area

0   500   1000
feet

Azalea Cr. Picnic Area

pass a water faucet and horse trough, then more picnic tables. These overlook a grassy glade sloping down to Santa Rosa Creek within a mile of its source.

Just beyond, at ¾ mile, a footpath forks left, descending to Alder Glen Picnic Area on the creek. California hazel grows beside the junction. The main trail continues its winding descent south, accompanied by the burbling of the creek. You cross a small tributary, climb briefly, then descend again, with wild rose on the right.

The trail climbs to ⅞ mile, then draws near the creek. Your trail levels as a side trail descends on the left. Cimb gradually, then descend again following the twists of the canyon. You pass California buckeye. Local Indians used its chestnutlike fruits to stupefy fish, making them easier to catch.

At 1⅛ miles you enter Homestead Meadow, where deer often graze. The trail makes a gradual descent to 1¼ miles, where it joins a broad road. The ruins of a small shed stand beside a rock outcrop nearby. Go left around the rock and come to Santa Rosa Creek, where moss-draped alders and bays grow. The trail to Azalea Creek and Hood Mountain

160

fords the creek (wet crossing in winter and spring) and climbs south, 1⅛ miles to Azalea Creek, 4⅛ miles to the top of Hood Mountain.

The described hike takes the trail on the right before the ford. Follow the trail west alongside the beautiful creek. Before 1½ miles dense woodwardia ferns drape over the opposite bank. In another ⅛ mile your trail veers left and descends briefly, crossing a bridge over a tributary. Soon your path narrows and cuts alongside a rock outcrop where leather ferns grow from the stone. At 1¾ miles your trail descends to the creek and ends. This shady spot provides a pleasant resting place on a warm day. Santa Rosa Creek tumbles west, plunging 400 feet in the next two miles only to be channeled through suburban sprawl. But from trail's end, the creek appears much as it has for centuries, showing no signs of human tampering with its joyously gurgling, meandering course.

From here, unlike the creek, you have nowhere to go but up, retracing your steps toward the headwaters. If you have time, take the Alder Glen spur to examine more of these pristine headwaters. Remember: the park closes at sunset.

SUGARLOAF RIDGE STATE PARK
INCLUDES THE NEXT THREE TRAILS

Only a half hour from Santa Rosa or Sonoma, you can escape to a gentle wilderness in the heart of the Mayacmas Range, nestled amidst some of the range's highest peaks. At night in the park's splendid campground, coyotes howl and owls hoot, punctuating the soft murmur of Sonoma Creek, while infinite stars glimmer in the dark sky. It is difficult to believe that cities lurk so near.

Sugarloaf Ridge State Park encompasses 2700 acres of steep, rolling hills along the headwaters of Sonoma Creek. The hills shelter various habitats, including oak and conifer forests, chaparral and grasslands. About 25 miles of trails explore the park, with some of the best described in the next three routes.

The Southern Wappo village of Wilikos was located here long before the first Spanish settlers came to California. The Wappos lived in dome-shaped huts up to 40 feet long, made of poles and grass thatch. About 100 residents occupied roughly 40 dwellings. A large sweathouse in the village center was used exclusively by the men for smoking, steam baths and ceremonies. Members of the tribe would travel to

the coast and Clear Lake to fish and trade with other tribes,
but hunted for game locally. Resistant to exploitation by
theSpanish, many of the Wappos were killed in cholera and
smallpox epidemics in the 1830s. Most of the survivors were
moved to the Mendocino Indian Reservation around 1860.

Because these lands were marginal for farming, not until
the 1860s did white Americans settle around Sugarloaf
Ridge. The state bought the property in 1920, planning to
dam the creek to provide water to Sonoma State Hospital.
But the objections of surrounding property owners kept the
plan in limbo. In 1964 the area became part of the State
Park System.

40.

HOOD MOUNTAIN
from SUGARLOAF

GOOD CLIMB ON THE GOODSPEED TRAIL

From the parking area just inside the park boundary, the
Goodspeed Trail immediately fords Sonoma Creek (wet
crossing in winter and spring), then turns north, heading
upstream along Bear Creek. Bay laurel, hazel, madrone and
ash trees grow beneath redwoods and firs along the stream.

At ⅛ mile you cross a bridge over Bear Creek. Follow the
west bank briefly, then switchback left to start a long,
steady climb. The forest soon thins and chaparral species
dominate. Coyote brush, manzanita, bay laurel, chamise,
sticky monkeyflower and oaks compete for space on the dry
south slope.

Around ¼ mile you switchback right, then left, gaining
the first views of the parklands up canyon. Climb steadily
on rocky tread with occasional switchbacks. Beyond ½ mile
coffeeberry and creeping ceanothus join the tangle of
brush. You overlook wooded Bear Creek Canyon to the
east. Continue a steady, well-graded climb.

As your trail levels, then descends at ¾ mile, you have
views southwest to the creeping suburbs in Valley of the
Moon. You cross a dirt road and descend gradually. Hairy
honeysuckle and toyon mix with the chaparral here.
Descend four switchbacks to cross a seasonal creek at one
mile. At the boulder-strewn crossing of the heavily eroded
creek, the blue-green rocks indicate serpentine soils. White
alders grow along the creek.

You switchback up the slope of the creek and climb
generally west. Whitethorn mixes with the other chaparral.

At 1⅛ miles pass under power lines and leave chaparral for Douglas fir forest. Trees to four feet in diameter provide welcome shade on a warm day. Soon an understory of manzanita is dying as the taller oaks and firs steal the sunlight.

You switchback right and climb through the forest. At 1½ miles you pass "stay on trail" signs at a spot where you might be confused by a side trail. At 1⅝ mile the trail bends left, then right, climbing a brushy, rocky ridge.

You swing left, leaving the ridge at 1¾ miles, then cross a seasonal (usually dry) creek crowded with hardwoods. You might stop for a shady rest because the next section of trail crosses open, south-facing slopes.

Leaving the creek, you climb into grasslands. At 1⅞ miles you traverse a brushy south slope. But you soon return to a steep grassy slope as you leave the state park for Hood Mountain Regional Park at 2 miles. Dark green Sugarloaf Ridge rises across wooded Adobe Canyon.

You climb steadily through the large glade, a prime spot for wildflowers in spring. At 2⅛ miles a big, lone bay laurel grows above the trail. You return to chaparral briefly, but by 2¼ miles your trail steepens, traversing a steep grassy hillside. At 2⅜ miles you begin a steep, hot, slow climb, an indication of the arduous climb to the summit. The vegetation varies frequently now, from grasslands to chaparral to oak woodlands and back again.

At 2½ miles you switchback right and climb steeply through a rocky area, traversing the top of the same steep slope. At 2⅝ miles you approach the ridge of Hood Mountain, passing through an area where little grows but gnarled chamise. Top the ridge, swing left and descend.

At 2¾ miles you climb through dwarf hardwood forest

DISTANCE: 7¾ miles round trip.

TIME: Four hours.

TERRAIN: Climb across three creek canyons and up the ridge to great views.

ELEVATION GAIN/LOSS: 2400 feet+/2400 feet-.

BEST TIME: Any cool, clear day. Best flowers in spring.

WARNINGS: Watch for poison oak, rattlesnakes and ticks. Steep trail, often hot, usually dry: use caution. **Closed during fire season.**

DIRECTIONS TO TRAILHEAD: On Highway 12 between Santa Rosa and Kenwood, turn north at M.26.2 onto Adobe Canyon Road (11 miles from Highway 101). Go 2.3 miles to parking area on left.

FEES: Day use: $3/vehicle.

FURTHER INFO: Sugarloaf Ridge State Park (707)833-5712.

OTHER SUGGESTION: See Trail #39.

barely tall enough to provide welcome shade. This preposterous forest grows on the cool north slope below the wind-pummeled ridgetop. At 2⅞ miles you climb into a forest of moderately large live oaks. Then climb steeply through a brushy area to 3 miles where you near the rocky ridgetop and merge with a better trail. (Remember this spot on your way back down the mountain; if you do not turn left onto the narrow trail, the broad trail will lead you down the other side of the ridge on a different, somewhat confusing route to rejoin the main trail around the 2½-mile-point.)

Your trail climbs beneath large manzanitas, then into mixed forest. At 3⅛ miles the climb turns gradual beneath wind-stunted firs. You soon leave the forest for grassy ridgetop with birdseye views of Valley of the Moon. Gunsight Rock appears to the northwest. Continue your climb through more oak forest. As the steep climb eases, you see Bishop pines. Before long they dominate the forest.

At 3½ miles, take the side trail on the left. You climb over the ridge top, winding west for ⅛ mile to Gunsight Rock, 2600 feet above sea level. Although the summit of Hood Mountain is only ¼ mile farther, Gunsight provides the best views west and south.

From the notch of Gunsight Rock, you overlook most of

Sonoma County. Valley of the Moon sprawls below you, the long top of Sonoma Mountain rising beyond it. On a clear day Mt. Tamalpais juts skyward beyond Sonoma Mountain. To the south, tidal flats extend to San Francisco Bay. Mt. Diablo is the high peak southeast. To the west lies Santa Rosa. Beyond it, green hills roll gently toward the sea. To the north stands Sulphur Peak near the Geysers and Mt. St. Helena. To the east, Bald Mountain, Red Mountain (with microwave towers) and pointed Brushy Peak lie within Sugarloaf Ridge State Park. To the southeast are Little Bald Mountain, Sugarloaf Ridge and Mount Veeder. Enjoy the view from this hawk's perch where red-tailed hawks and hummingbirds soar on the wind.

Return to the main trail and turn left. You climb north, then steeply east, passing Altar Rock, 3⅞ miles from your trailhead. You briefly continue the steep climb before descending past a trail sign. You then climb along bleached sandstone, in and out of forest and chaparral. You finally climb steeply north along a hot, south-facing ridge to reach the top of Hood Mountain (elevation 2730 feet) at 4 miles.

Its flat top is cleared of brush. Although the views are not as spectacular as Gunsight Rock's, if the day is clear, look east to Bald Mountain and scan the horizon northward. You may see the snowy peaks of the Sierra Nevada glistening on the skyline. From the summit two trails head north to explore the rest of Hood Mountain Regional Park, the horse and mountain bike trail on the left (service road) and a footpath on the right.

Return on the same trail you ascended. Passing through the clearings on the ridge, look for native California fuchsia. It grows in nondescript gray-green clumps when not flowering. But in late summer and fall, its bright scarlet, trumpet-shaped flowers provide one of the few native foods for hummingbirds on their southern migration.

41.

SONOMA CANYON/ PONY GATE LOOP

WATERFALL AND WILDFLOWERS

This hike excels in early spring, when the waterfall and creeks roar with the replenishment of recent rains. Then the deciduous trees show their new growth and wildflowers burst brightly from the meadows. The trail is also pleasant in light rain, when everything glistens with revitalizing mois-

ture. Although you can also start the loop from the entrance kiosk, I prefer the way it unfolds from the lower end.

Park in the wide turnout just east of the trailhead. Cautiously walk downhill along the road shoulder for 300 feet to the signed Canyon Loop Trailhead. Your trail descends southeast into a forest of big Douglas firs and medium redwoods with scattered oaks and madrones. The trail soon levels 50 feet above Sonoma Creek. The lush understory includes wood rose, bay laurel, snowberry, columbine and native bunch grasses.

Descend again, leveling briefly at ⅛ mile where leather-leaf and lady ferns grow. Continue your descent across a bridge over Pony Gate Creek, overlooking its confluence with Sonoma Creek as it tumbles down the rocky canyon. The south bank rises steeply toward Sugarloaf Ridge, the summit of which is only a mile away, 1200 feet above.

Continue upstream on the trail. In 250 feet you get your first glimpse of the waterfall beyond cascades upstream. The trail passes under a leaning black oak, then a bay laurel. Alders and sycamores also grow along the creek.

166

SONOMA CANYON/PONY GATE LOOP:

DISTANCE: 1¾-mile loop.

TIME: One hour.

TERRAIN: Up canyon along creek to waterfall, then up and down hillside with views of canyon to return to starting point.

ELEVATION GAIN/LOSS: 560 feet+/560 feet-.

BEST TIME: Early spring when the waterfall roars. Canyon Trail nice anytime; Pony Gate can be hot on sunny days in summer.

WARNINGS: Watch for poison oak, ticks and stinging nettles. Stay off slippery rocks near waterfall. Use caution crossing road.

DIRECTIONS TO TRAILHEAD: See Trail #40 for general directions. The trailhead for this hike is 2.6 miles from Highway 12.

FEES: Day use: $3/vehicle. Car camping: $10/night.

FURTHER INFO: Sugarloaf Ridge State Park (707)833-5712.

At ¼ mile meet steps climbing through a moss- and fern-draped rock garden left of the falls. Before climbing the steps, take the short spur on the right to the base of the waterfall. The falls tumble over boulders strewn along a mossy precipice, sending up spray to wet the surrounding greenery. A tiny side stream cascades down the opposite bank. The pungent smell of bay laurel permeates the air.

The main trail climbs steps up a rocky side gully. You switchback right, passing maidenhair and leather ferns. You climb steeply, then moderately to ⅜ mile, where the trail broadens and bends left as you continue to climb, surrounded by mossy boulders. Oaks dominate the forest, with scattered madrones and young firs.

The trail levels as it leads away from the creek, then resumes a gradual ascent, passing sticky monkeyflower. At ½ mile you cross a seasonal side stream at a small clearing. Then the trail bends right and climbs. Soon the forest canopy parts, allowing toyon and other brush species to thrive. You cross another tributary, then swing left to climb alongside it, passing vines of dutchman's pipe.

Just beyond ⅝ mile, you climb to the paved road just below the entrance kiosk. Cross the road cautiously and start along the Pony Gate Trail (horses OK). Pony Gate climbs east into a grassy clearing surrounded by oak woodlands. Then your trail winds out of the clearing, climbing through hardwood forest.

At ¾ mile your trail bends left to skirt one of the large glades that are a hallmark of Sugarloaf Ridge State Park. The trail stays in the trees here, but keep your eyes on the glade for possible sightings of wildlife. The trail contours the steep hillside, then climbs briefly to enter a small clearing that overlooks the deep, wooded canyon of Sonoma Creek. Bush lupine and bracken fern cluster along the trail.

Continue through oak forest, then pass between two gnarled oaks into a glade at ⅞ mile. Climb to meet a trail on your right. Take the left fork, continuing beneath oaks. After a clearing cross a rocky (and usually dry) creek bed. The trail bends left and descends to cross another brook.

At one mile you meet the Ridge View Trail on your right. It climbs east to join the Bald Mountain Trail in ½ mile. You descend moderately over clay soil that may be slippery after rain. At 1⅛ miles your trail bends right, then left, continuing a steady descent through oak woodlands. After a big bend right, descend across a gully and contour along the bottom of a rolling glade. At 1¼ mile you pass a stand of young Douglas firs encroaching on the glade.

You leave the glade to descend steps into a dark forest. Cross another rocky gully, then descend steeply toward the cascades of Pony Gate Creek. You ford the creek at 1⅜ miles, then climb steeply for 100 feet. Climb moderately to join an old road, then resume a moderate descent. Limbs of bay and oak arch gracefully over your path.

At 1½ miles you can see the paved road far down the steep slope on your left. Your trail bends right and descends southwest. At 1⅝ miles the forest thins to allow views of the big conifers along Sonoma Creek. Chaparral grows above the trail: manzanita, chamise, scrub oak and sticky monkeyflower. You continue to descend as the trail bends right, then left to reach the paved road at 1¾ miles. Your starting point is just uphill along the road.

42.

BALD MOUNTAIN LOOP
THROUGH THE HEART OF SUGARLOAF

From the parking lot, you climb gradually through grass-lands on the Bald Mountain Trail. At ⅛ mile you pass a weathered phone pole, then switchback left into mixed chaparral and oak woodland. Interior live oak dominates, with bay laurel, manzanita, coffeeberry and chamise. You switchback right, passing toyon, with bright red berries in winter. Then switchback left, past creeping ceanothus.

As your trail bends right, a view of Hood Mountain opens to the northwest. You return to grasslands at ¼ mile and quickly reach a junction. You will return by the Bald Mountain Trail on the left. Take the Meadow Trail on the right and descend to the Group Camp at ⅜ mile.

Cross the paved parking lot and join the gravel trail to cross a tributary of Sonoma Creek and head east. A big meadow, with a large solitary oak in its center, stretches between you and Sonoma Creek. I spotted a coyote retreating up the hill one winter morning. At ⅝ mile you cross another tributary. The road levels and heads toward Little Bald Mountain.Coyote brush and bay laurel line the path.

At ¾ mile you descend slightly and approach tree-lined Sonoma Creek. Your road winds along the creek, passing oak, bay laurel, willow, madrone and alder trees. By ⅞ mile a big meadow is on the far side of the creek. You start a gradual climb. California rose beside the path can be distinguished from wood rose by its long curved thorns.

At one mile the creek meanders away from the road. Your road winds through a meadow where a riot of wildflowers grow in spring. Cross a seasonal creek and enter forest of oaks and young maples. Cross a bridge over Sonoma Creek, where an immense maple towers.

Your path then forks. The right fork leads to Malm Flat and Hillside Trails. You go left on the Digger Pine Trail. This narrow dirt road quickly crosses Sonoma Creek again, a ford that can be wet in winter.

Before 1⅜ miles the Vista Trail (hikers only) branches left. Stay on Digger Pine Trail, climbing gradually along Sonoma Creek. As you bend toward the creek, a large California buckeye grows on the right. You ford the creek and start a steady climb along a tributary.

At 1½ miles your trail steepens briefly, crosses a culvert on the side stream and winds through mixed forest and chaparral. You climb steeply over loose tread to 1¾ miles. Then the climb eases. You parallel power lines, climbing steadily. Sticky monkeyflower and toyon line your path.

At 1⅞ miles your trail makes a big bend right, passes under the power lines and continues climbing. Before 2 miles the road is covered with loose rock on a steep section that mountain bikers may have to walk. Great views lie behind you. Climb steadily on better tread, winding left.

BALD MOUNTAIN LOOP:

DISTANCE: 6½-mile loop (hike, bike or horse) or 7¼-mile loop (hikers only).

TIME: Three to four hours.

TERRAIN: Through meadows along creek, then climb to and along high ridge to peak with great views, then down paved road or footpath.

ELEVATION GAIN/LOSS: 1630 feet+/1630 feet-.

BEST TIME: Spring for wildflowers. Any clear day.

WARNINGS: Carry water. Mountain bikers use caution: slow on blind corners, yield to equestrians and hikers. Watch for poison oak, ticks and rattlesnakes.

DIRECTIONS TO TRAILHEAD: On Highway 12 between Santa Rosa and Kenwood, turn north onto Adobe Canyon Road at M.26.2. Go 3.5 miles to Day Use Parking Area (.1 mile beyond kiosk).

FEES: Day use: $3/vehicle. Car camping: $10/night.

FURTHER INFO: Sugarloaf Ridge State Park (707)833-5712.

OTHER SUGGESTION: The CREEKSIDE NATURE TRAIL is a short (¾ mile), easy walk providing an introduction to habitats and plant species in the park. It leaves from the picnic area opposite the parking lot.

Climb steeply from 2¼ to 2⅜ miles, passing your first digger pines amidst a manzanita thicket.

You reach 2000 feet elevation as you pass back under the power lines and climb along the ridge. The terrain on your left drops steeply into a brushy canyon with many digger pines. A short, steep climb brings you to 2½ miles, where the road levels for the best view yet. Then climb gradually through dense chaparral with buckbrush and chamise.

Beyond 2⅝ miles the road reaches the main ridge, where Brushy Peak Trail forks right. You continue straight on the Digger Pine Trail, climbing a steep hill with glimpses of Napa Valley to the east. At 2¾ miles a gated road on the right leads onto private property.

Your route promptly reaches a top, then descends west,

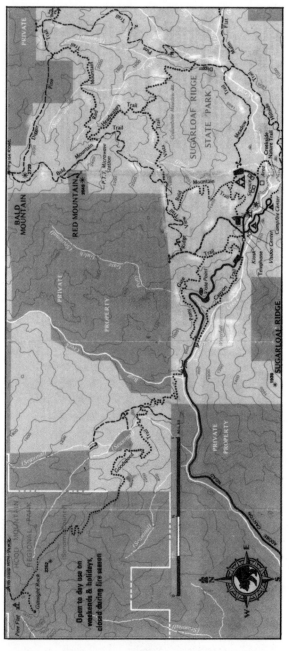

with Bald Mountain dead ahead. At 2⅞ miles the road levels as brush gives way to forest of oak, bay and madrone. You descend again, then climb steeply to 3 miles, where Red Mountain Trail (hikers only) forks left. Continue to climb, with another view into the lush Napa Valley. Beyond 3⅛ miles you climb steeply again, then dip briefly, only to climb again. At 3¼ miles a level respite soon leads to an easy climb lined with whitethorn and bush lupine. Then climb moderately with grasslands on the left and big black oaks on the right. Make another steep climb to 3¾ miles where you approach the summit of Bald Mountain.

As you top the 2729-foot peak, take a rest, confident that it is all downhill from here. The summit is bald grasslands except for clumps of chamise on the south face.

The day I first climbed the peak, I arrived in sunshine and sat beside a knot of chamise for protection from a chilly wind. Soon a dense cloak of fog enveloped the peak, obscuring all views. The view described here presents what one sees on the clearest day.

To the north the Mayacmas Range sprawls northward to its highest point at Mt. St. Helena (4343'), 20 miles away. Fifty miles beyond and to the right of Mt. St. Helena, Snow Mountain (7056') marks the southern end of the Mendocino Range. To the west stands Hood Mountain, one foot higher than Bald. Beyond Hood's left flank, Valley of the Moon snuggles at the base of Sonoma Mountain (2295'). Mt. Tamalpais (2606') peaks over Sonoma's left shoulder. On the clearest day you may be able to spot the Golden Gate Bridge towers about three finger widths left of Mt. Tam (binoculars help). If it is that clear, the Transamerica Pyramid juts skyward from the city skyline. The bay lies directly south, beyond the flank of nearby Red Mountain. Mt. Diablo (3849') is the tallest peak on the southern horizon. Much closer are Little Bald Mountain (2275'), Mt. Veeder (2677') and Brushy Peak (2243'). To the east you see Napa Valley vineyards and the town of St. Helena. On the horizon east-northeast the snowy peaks of the Sierra Nevada near Lake Tahoe glisten.

The trail down heads north, quickly meeting the High Ridge Trail (explores little-traveled northern extreme of Sugarloaf Park). You turn left and head west to a saddle at 3⅞ miles, then start a long descent. Your dirt road bends right and steepens, meeting a paved road at 4¼ miles. On the right the pavement ascends Red Mountain. You go left on the paved road, descending steadily.

At 4⅜ miles the descent steepens. You descend through hardwood forest with an understory of native grasses. At 4½ miles the path levels briefly, passing a picnic table. Pass under power lines and resume your descent.

You meet the Red Mountain Trail on the left at 4⅝ miles. Bikers and equestrians must continue on the paved road, making the steady descent on pavement to 5½ miles, then going left on Bald Mountain Trail to reach the trailhead at 6½ miles. Weary hikers can do the same. But if you are game for more exploration, turn left and descend into beautiful black oak forest. At 4¾ miles Douglas iris line the trail. Then your descent steepens, dropping into the canyon at the headwaters of Sonoma Creek.

Before 4⅞ miles you meet the Headwaters Trail, where you go right. The trail wraps around a big rock and descends near upper Sonoma Creek. The path is intermittently steep and gentle, but most always descending. Before 5 miles the creek steepens as well. It roars down these cascades after a major storm. As the descent eases, lady ferns line the path. Then the first of several very steep sections merits caution.

You climb slightly to 5⅛ miles, then descend through live oak forest with scattered madrones, maples and firs. Around 5¼ miles you climb through a moss-covered rock garden where leather and maidenhair ferns grow, passing an immense big leaf maple on the left, known as the Ceremony Tree. You turn away from the creek, cross a tributary and climb one more short, steep hill. Then descend to the Vista Trail before 5⅜ miles.

Turn right and climb steeply for 200 feet to an immense, beautiful glade, with poppies and other wildflowers in spring. Your trail rolls through these grasslands, grand vistas of the park unfolding with each step. Before 5½ miles the trail bends right, crossing another corner of the glade. Your view includes Sugarloaf Ridge and the hills to the west. Descend a bit to a rock outcrop on the left at 5⅝ miles.

The trail bends right to explore yet another corner of this long glade. Climb briefly to 5¾ miles, then drop through more grasslands into hardwood forest at the head of a tributary. Woodwardia ferns grow along the creek.

At 5⅞ miles you are suddenly in chaparral of twisted manzanita. You level briefly, then descend through another glade. Soon a small seasonal pond lies on your right, where reeds, mint and wildflowers abound. At 6 miles your trail ends at the paved road.

Descend along the pavement for ¼ mile to a bench where the Bald Mountain Trail forks left. The side trail takes the shortest route to the trailhead, although bikers may prefer to continue on pavement. Go left, descending into oak forest. Switchback four times as the path steepens. At 6½ miles you switchback twice more into grasslands.

At 6¾ miles complete your loop, reaching the junction where the trail on the left goes to the Group Camp. You go right, retracing your steps to the trailhead at 7¼ miles.

43

NATURE CONSERVANCY'S FAIRFIELD OSBORN PRESERVE

RICH BIOLOGICAL DIVERSITY IN A SMALL PACKAGE

Fairfield Osborn Preserve, a holding of the Nature Conservancy, nestles on the steep western flank of Sonoma Mountain. The preserve's 210 acres offer a wondrous diversity of habitats supporting over 300 species of plants in oak, riparian and fir forest, grassland, chaparral, freshwater marsh, pond, freshwater seep and vernal pool communities.

Sonoma Mountain, which looms over the Preserve, has volcanic origins. It formed as a low volcanic ridge about 7 million years ago, when Cotati Valley was a saltwater bay. Enormous fissures vented huge quantities of molten lava, and eruptions spread ash and debris for miles. The mountain uplifted to its present height perhaps as recently as one million years ago. This cataclysmic history contributed to the rich diversity found here today.

In relatively recent times, the Coast Miwok tribe reached its northern extremity here, with the village of Lumentakala on the slopes of Sonoma Mountain. European settlers failed in their attempts to work this land, but left graceful stone walls (perhaps built by Chinese laborers) and foreign plants. In 1972 William and Joan Roth donated the site to the Nature Conservancy, naming it to honor Mrs. Roth's father, a pioneering conservationist.

From the parking area, go around the gate and walk 150 feet. Veer left past interpretive signs in an area with many domesticated plants gone wild. Go left on a footpath marked "hikers," register and borrow a trail guide, then go through the gate. (Be sure to close this and other gates behind you.) Cross tiny Courtship Creek, rich in aquatic bugs, and meet a fork. Go left (you will return on the right), climbing gently through Butterfly Meadow, where blue-eyed grass and buttercups grow. Willows grow on your left.

At ⅛ mile the sedge and rush jungle of Rail Marsh is on your left. Secretive Virginia rails and soras live in the dense vegetation. A short spur forks left to the weeping willow at the edge of crescent-shaped Tule Pond, covered with millions of tiny duckweed plants. If you sit quietly beneath the willow, ducks and pond turtles may appear. Aromatic mugwort growing nearby is often found in the habitat of

DISTANCE: ¾-mile loop, 1⅞-mile double loop or
5¾-mile triple loop.

TIME: Short loops: one hour. Full hike: three hours.

TERRAIN: Gentle first loop climbs through grasslands
past two ponds with marshes, then descends through
oak woodlands. Moderate second loop crosses creeks
and climbs ridge with views to coast. Steep third loop
climbs through grasslands and woodlands to vernal
pool, seep and pond on flank of Sonoma Mountain.

ELEVATION GAIN/LOSS: First loop: 80 feet+/80 feet-.
Two loops: 320 feet+/320 feet-. Three loops: 960
feet+/960 feet-.

BEST TIME: Wildflowers nearly year-round, best in
spring. Spring and fall for migrating birds.

WARNINGS: Open weekends and holidays only. No
smoking, dogs, horses, bikes. Watch for poison oak,
ticks and rattlesnakes. You must ask caretaker's
permission to hike upper loop.

DIRECTIONS TO TRAILHEAD: Exit Highway 101 at
Rohnert Park Expressway (M.14.35 from north, M.13.6
from south). Go east 2½ miles, then right on Petaluma
Hill Road. In 1.2 miles go left on Roberts Road. Go 1.3
miles, then right on narrow, winding Lichau Road for
3.5 miles to parking on right.

FURTHER INFO: Fairfield Osborn Preserve
(707)795-5069.

OTHER SUGGESTION: CRANE CREEK REGIONAL
PARK offers 2 miles of easy trails through rolling
grasslands and oak woodlands along Crane Creek. To
reach the park, where Lichau Road goes right, you
continue straight for .5 mile to park on left.

the lazuli bunting, which summers here. Red-breasted
sapsuckers have drilled holes in the willow's trunk.

Continue uphill on the main trail, passing #5 on the
interpretive trail. Small shells and chips of obsidian mark
a midden, where Coast Miwoks once camped. Please leave
these artifacts in place. In 50 feet the upper loop branches
left (described below).

Beyond the junction many cow parsnips grow below the
dam of Cattail Pond. Your trail climbs to overlook the pond
at ¼ mile. You cross a seep where two unusual nonvascu-

lar plants grow: water fern and hornwort. Poplars and mule ears grow in the meadow above the pond.

Cattail Pond attracts diverse wildlife. Red-wing blackbirds and black phoebes live among the cattails. Wood ducks and mallards visit. One sunny day, 86 western pond turtles were seen sunning around the pond. Other amphibians include red-legged frogs, bullfrogs and rough-skinned newts. Damselflies and dragonflies hunt for insects.

Your trail descends along the pond's south edge. At 3/8 mile you descend switchbacks into woodlands along Trillium Creek, where oaks, bays, alders and maples grow. At 1/2 mile a plaque commemorates Fairfield Osborn. Trail plant, soap plant, hedge nettle, hairy honeysuckle and poison oak grow nearby. Descend past coast and canyon live oak to the site of the old swimming hole, where you may see trillium, fairy bells and red-flowering currant.

Soon a spur on the left leads to the south loop. (For the shortest walk, go straight, completing the interpretive loop in 1/4 mile.) Our described hike turns left and descends to ford Copeland Creek.

Boulder-jammed Copeland Creek is unlike any other year-round stream below snow level in California. The Miwoks called it Thunder Creek because during major storms the rocks in its bed crash and clatter downstream, producing a rumble heard all over the mountainside and crushing everything in their path. Thus no fish live here, allowing a vast diversity of invertebrate life, including 150 aquatic insect species. Most unusual is the California eyed asellid, an aquatic sow bug found at only six sites in the world. This diversity supports Pacific giant salamanders and other insect predators. Durable, fast-growing white alders are the dominant tree along the creek, where maple and bay also grow. Wood, shield, sword and leather-leaf ferns crowd the banks.

After the ford your trail climbs south, following tiny Aralia Creek upstream. You ford the creek, then turn right, entering an oak-rimmed meadow at 3/4 mile, where buttercup, miniature lupine and blue-eyed grass grow. Continue to a junction on a ridge at 7/8 mile. Go straight, climbing, then descending the ridge, with views over Cotati Valley and through Petaluma Wind Gap to the Pacific.

Your trail soon forks. Go left through chaparral of chamise, sticky monkeyflower and silktassel. You return to oak woodlands, crossing another tributary at 1 1/8 miles. Climb seven switchbacks and recross the creek where giant scouring rushes and elk clover (a ginseng relative) thrive.

Climb steeply, returning to the ridge junction at 1 1/4

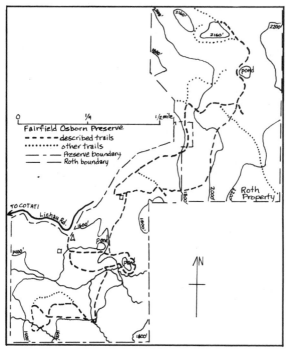

miles, where you go straight, descending to ford tiny
Hidden Creek. Veer right at a junction, climbing gradually
on a faint path along the rim of Copeland Creek Canyon.
On the left you overlook the chaotic, geologically active
creek where a slide has dumped boulders and trees into its
bed. Red penstemon grows nearby.

You ascend the rim, passing hazel, fat solomon's seal and
starflower. Return to the meadow, then retrace your steps
across Aralia and Copeland Creeks to the interpretive loop.

Climb west to #12. An ecotone is the edge between two
plant communities, where more species occur than in either
habitat. You overlook the ecotone between grassland and
oak woodland, a good place to spot raptors. Cooper's, red-
tailed and sharp-shinned hawks, kestrels, screech and great
horned owls and golden eagles have been seen here.

Your trail climbs past trees draped with old man's beard
and other lichens. The path levels through grasslands at 1¾
miles, passing Oregon oaks with galls, apple-sized growths
that serve as nurseries for gall wasp larvae. You soon
complete the loop. You can return to the parking lot at 1⅞
miles or ask the caretaker's permission to hike the upper
loop, mostly on private property owned by the Roths.

If you have permission, follow the first loop to the upper
loop junction near the midden. Go left on the unmarked
trail, overlooking Rail Marsh. You enter the forest and

cross a gully where gooseberry, coffee fern, snowberry and native grasses grow, then climb to a gate. Go through the gate and past the classroom to a junction at 2¼ miles.

Go right on the broad Forest Trail, climbing east under power lines. At 2⅜ miles the road levels briefly and meets a footpath on the left. Go left to another fork in 300 feet (if you reach a gate you went too far). Then go right, climbing to a vernal pool beside a moss-covered stone wall at 2½ miles. The pool holds water from late fall until about May. Then you can see the rare Lobb's buttercup. Its tiny white flowers have a vanilla-like fragrance. The soupy pond teems with copepods and fairy shrimp.

Retrace your steps for 100 feet, then turn right on a faint trail climbing steeply through oak woodlands in rocky soil. At 2¾ miles you wind through Gopher Meadow, then climb steeply to Douglas Fir Road before 3 miles. Cross the road and continue 250 feet on the footpath. You meet Pond Road, but go right on a faint trail that parallels the road, then enters a lush meadow. The faint trail skirts the right edge of the meadow for 300 feet to a vernal-pool-like seep at the base of a big jumble of rocks. More Lobb's buttercup grows here, usually lasting later into the dry season than at the vernal pool. Hazel, and prickly currant grow along the shore beneath arching oaks and bays. You are ½ mile and only 400 feet below the 2463-foot summit of Sonoma Mountain, but the top is on private property. The top of Jack London State Park is one mile east (see Trail #45).

Return to Pond Road and go right, heading north. At 3¼ miles you reach an old gate beside the largest pond on this hike, a favorite stopover for migrating ducks. Willows and rushes line the far shore. Many birds sing in tall oaks around the pond. You may see herons and kingfishers.

On a foggy day you may want to return from here. On a clear day continue on the deteriorating road, curving along the dam, then climbing to the ridge of Sonoma Mountain. At 3⅞ miles the road forks. Turn right for an immediate reward of grand views. Matanzas Creek and Bennett Valley are in the foreground. Bennett Mountain and the hills of Annadel rise beyond. Farther north stand Mt. St. Helena, the Palisades and other peaks of the Mayacmas Range. Sugarloaf Ridge is northeast, with Berryessa Peak and Blue Ridge beyond, 30 miles away. On a clear day you may see the Sierra Nevada near Lake Tahoe to the right of Berryessa Peak.

You can follow the ridge for ⅜ mile to the property boundary, but the views get no better. The described hike returns from 3⅞ miles. Retrace your steps for ¾ mile to the creek from the seep pond. From there (4⅝ miles) descend Pond Trail west. You pass Douglas Fir Road on the left, then your descent steepens.

At 4⅞ miles you approach a gate. Before the gate, go left on a faint path through grasslands. The tread improves, passing through oak woodlands, then a rolling glade. Descend to an old wooden bridge at 5⅛ miles. The trail makes a steep creek crossing, then winds southwest, dropping steeply through oak forest, glades and a rocky area to a creek crossing around 5¼ miles. At a junction 50 feet beyond, take the well-trod trail on the right. Descend through a meadow to a shady bench at the Preserve's bus turnaround. Go south to the trail and classroom at 5½ miles, then retrace your steps to the first loop. Go right, coming to the parking area at 6 miles.

JACK LONDON STATE HISTORIC PARK
INCLUDES NEXT TWO TRAILS

I liked those hills up there. They were beautiful ...and I wanted beauty. So I extended the boundary up to the top of that ridge and all along it ...I bought beauty, and I was content with beauty for a while.

Jack London was a brash and brilliant young Californian who never allowed himself the time to grow old. Born out of wedlock January 12, 1876 in San Francisco, Jack lifted himself from poverty to become one of the most popular and acclaimed writers of his generation, one of the first American authors to make a million dollars from his work. He succeeded with adventure stories, but wrote eloquently of the dilemma of the human condition. He lived for love and beauty, but died at age 40, exhausted and physically spent.

Jack's mother and stepfather frequently moved the family from one bay area town to another, seeking a decent living. As an adolescent Jack worked various jobs, selling newspapers, setting pins in a bowling alley, keeping bees. At fifteen he became an oyster pirate on San Francisco Bay, robbing other people's oyster beds for excitement and easy profit. At seventeen Jack became a seaman on a sealing schooner, taking a seven-month cruise to Japan. These early experiences nourished his love of sailing.

Upon his return Jack worked several jobs of hard physical labor, "inhuman hours on barbarous jobs." Wanderlust soon sent him tramping cross-country. At Niagara Falls he was arrested for vagrancy and served a month in prison, then rode the rails back to Oakland.

The hardships and suffering Jack encountered on his tramping adventures pushed him toward his life-long commitment to socialism and encouraged him to seek an education. He attended Oakland High School for a year and enrolled in the University of California at Berkeley in 1896. But the impatient, restless young man soon dropped college.

When news of the Klondike gold rush reached California, Jack London put together a grubstake and headed for the Yukon. He found little gold during his year in the Northland, but the sojourn was one of the most important events in his life. "It was in the Klondike that I found myself," he said later. London returned to Oakland and began writing. He sold some stories to Overland Monthly and Atlantic Monthly. Within two years of his return from the Klondike, Houghton-Mifflin published Jack's first book, The Son of the Wolf, to favorable reviews, launching his career.

Jack London married Bessie Maddern, and they produced two daughters. It was during this loveless marriage that Jack wrote The Call of the Wild, his great short novel that has been published in 70 languages. Jack and Bessie separated in 1903.

Jack first went to the Sonoma Valley to escape the notoriety caused by his simultaneous best seller and the break up of his marriage. He was immediately drawn to its marvelous natural landscape: peaceful wooded hills and year-round streams interspersed with orchards and vineyards. In Glen Ellen he met and courted the spirited Charmian Kittredge, whose family owned a lodge there. In 1905 Jack spent some of his royalties to buy 127 acres of a rundown farm on the wooded slopes of Sonoma Mountain, the start of his beloved Beauty Ranch.

> All I wanted was a quiet place in the country to write and loaf in and get out of Nature that something which we all need, only the most of us don't know it.

But Jack was too restless and eager for adventure to settle down and spend all his time there. He built a sailboat and set out with Charmian to sail around the world. They got as far as the South Pacific and Australia before Jack's health problems forced him to sell the boat and return to Glen Ellen.

From 1909 to 1914 he expanded his ranch. In 1911 they moved to a small house on the ranch and began work on Wolf House, the mansion where they planned to live out their days. Jack threw himself into scientific agriculture, based upon the principles of his friend Luther Burbank, farming and working the ranch. Jack and Charmian entertained friends here, including other literary giants of their times like novelist Frank Norris and poets George Sterling and Joaquin Miller.

Then in 1913, Wolf House burned, just before the Londons were to move in. They were painfully aware that someone, perhaps a friend, may have deliberately set the fire. The mystery remains unsolved. Jack never fully recovered from this disaster.

Jack wrote prolifically throughout the good and bad times, in fact right to the day he died. He almost never missed his early morning writing stint, consistently producing 1000 words a day. Between 1900 and 1916, he completed more than fifty books, hundreds of short stories and numerous articles on diverse subjects. Add to this his extensive touring, lecturing, socializing and voluminous correspondence, not to mention the operation of the ranch, it is easy to see why Jack tried to limit his "wasted" sleeping time to no more than four or five hours a night.

Suffering from an expanding variety of health problems, Jack ignored the advice of his doctors to relax his work habits, improve his diet, give up alcohol and get more exercise. If anything Jack worked even harder to realize his ambitions and pay off the mounting debts that his grand schemes produced. He generously continued to support friends and relatives.

Jack never grew complacent in his success. A few months before his death, he told Charmian, "I am standing on the edge of a world so new, so terrible, so wonderful, that I am almost afraid to look over into it." But look he did, writing prolifically and daringly up to the day he died, November 22, 1916, of an unintentional overdose of morphine, taken to ease his pain from gastrointestinal poisoning and a kidney condition.

The obituary in the San Francisco Bulletin *summarized the world's loss:*

> *No writer, unless it were Mark Twain, ever had a more romantic life than Jack London. The untimely death of this most popular of American fictionists has profoundly shocked a world that expected him to live and work for many years longer.*

Jack's old friend George Sterling correctly predicted that "[h]is greatness will surge triumphantly above race and time."

44.

JACK LONDON'S WOLF HOUSE RUINS

REMNANTS OF A DREAM NEARLY COME TRUE

From the lower parking area, head east on the paved path. In 350 feet you come to the House of Happy Walls, which serves as the park's Visitor Center. Pay your day-use fee and explore the fine exhibits, so evocative of the Londons' time at Beauty Ranch.

Charmian London had the House of Happy Walls built in 1919-22, after Jack had died. She lived here (when not traveling) until her death in 1955 at age 84. Her will specified that the house be used as a memorial to Jack and a museum.

This house is similar to Wolf House in that it has walls of volcanic stone and a roof of Spanish tiles, but it is more intimate and formal. Much of the furniture was designed by the Londons and built for Wolf House. The library has furnishings from Jack London's study, which was in the cottage (see next trail).

From the Visitor Center, take the gravel path descending east. You pass a display of wagons and farm equipment from Beauty Ranch, although Jack's beloved passenger

wagons are absent.

Your trail turns left, descending through forest of madrones, oaks, bays, buckeyes, toyon and young firs. Beyond ⅛ mile the path bends left again, passing massive live oaks. At ¼ mile your trail levels and skirts the edge of a meadow. In spring you will see Indian warriors, buttercups, hound's tongue, and poppies. Cross a tiny creek at the bottom of the meadow, climb briefly, then descend through forest where you may hear a murmuring creek. You pass a rest bench and a drinking fountain.

At ⅜ mile you cross another creek and meet a broad paved trail. Turn left on the paved path, which levels as the creek drops away on the left. The path swings right and climbs a hill, then descends.

At ½ mile you reach a junction, with another drinking fountain and bench. Go right, descending along the edge of a glade with fruit trees on your right, black and live oaks on the left. Sonoma Mountain rises to the southwest. At ⅝ mile your descent steepens, coming to Wolf House ruins, surrounded by redwood forest above Asbury Creek.

Take the path that wraps left around the ruins. Climb the leather-leaf fern-draped stairs on the south wall to overlook the house. A floor plan there helps you visualize the Londons' dream. Notice the stag party room (for men only), the fireproof manuscript vault and Jack's sleeping tower.

JACK LONDON'S WOLF HOUSE RUINS:

DISTANCE: 1½ miles round trip.

TIME: One hour.

TERRAIN: Easy descent through woodlands and grasslands to ruins of Jack London's house, surrounded by redwoods.

ELEVATION GAIN/LOSS: 160 feet+/160 feet-.

BEST TIME: Spring for wildflowers. Nice anytime.

WARNINGS: Watch for poison oak and rattlesnakes.

DIRECTIONS TO TRAILHEAD: At M.30.7 on Highway 12 east of Santa Rosa, turn south on Arnold Drive. In .9 mile, in the town of Glen Ellen, as Arnold Drive veers left, you go right on London Ranch Road. Go 1.25 miles to entrance, then left to trailhead.

FEES: Day use: $3/vehicle.

FURTHER INFO: Jack London State Historic Park (707)938-5216.

OTHER SUGGESTION: JACK LONDON BOOKSTORE, 14300 Arnold Drive, has a wonderful collection of books by and about the sailor on horseback.

The rough-cut maroon volcanic rock of the interior and exterior walls presents a rugged look. Unpeeled redwood logs framed the front entrance and beautiful redwood paneling graced the inside walls. The double-thick concrete foundation and lower walls were intended to be fireproof. All the modern utilities and appliances then available were installed. The four-story house had 15,000 square feet, 26 rooms and nine fireplaces. The outdoor pool was to be stocked with bass.

With his Wolf House, poverty-born Jack London strove to realize a life-long dream. Construction began in 1911 on the house designed by well-known San Francisco architect Albert Farr with much input from the Londons. By August 1913 London had spent more than $80,000 and the project was nearly complete. On August 22 final cleanup began and plans were made to move the Londons' belongings into the mansion. In the middle of that night Jack received word that the house was burning. By the time the Londons arrived, the roof had collapsed and nothing could be saved. The Londons' grand dream and much of their fortune crumbled into ash. Today moss, lichen and ferns inhabit the space for which Jack and Charmian had such plans.

Continue clockwise around the ruins, returning to the graceful arches of the front entrance at ¾ mile. Perhaps you will see a red-tailed hawk circling overhead, its shrill, mournful cry piercing the silence. How easily our dreams can turn to ruin!

Retrace your steps uphill, returning to the junction at ⅞ mile. Take the side path on the right, climbing through oak woodlands to a knoll before one mile. Jack London knew this place and wrote about it in his novel *Burning Daylight*.

> He came out abruptly upon the cypresses. They were enclosed in a small square of ancient fence; the pickets he could plainly see had been hewn and sharpened by hand. Inside were the mounds of two children's graves. Two wooden headboards, likewise hand-hewn, told the story: Little David, died [November 25, 1876]; and Little Lily, died [August 8, 1877]. "The poor little kids," Daylight muttered.

On the left a large block of red lava marks Jack London's grave. Only three years after the devastating fire, his ashes were buried in a copper urn sealed in concrete. Charmian was buried beside him many years later. Jack chose to have his remains rest beside the two young innocents in this tranquil spot.

Return to the paved trail and go right. When you reach the junction with the dirt path you descended, beyond 1⅛ miles, you can go right to return to the House of Happy Walls or continue on the paved path. Either way you come to the parking area at 1½ miles.

45.

SONOMA MOUNTAIN

"MOST BEAUTIFUL PRIMITIVE LAND TO BE FOUND IN CALIFORNIA"

Jack London wrote eloquently of the wild upper reaches of his Beauty Ranch:

> *On the steep incline above the spring grew tiny maiden-hair ferns, while higher up were larger ferns and breaks. Great, moss-covered trunks of fallen trees lay here and there, slowly sinking back and merging into the level of the forest mould.*

*Beyond it, in a slightly clearer space, wild grape
and honeysuckle hung in green riot from gnarled
old oak trees. A gray Douglas squirrel crept out on
a branch and watched him. From somewhere
came the distant knocking of a woodpecker. This
sound did not disturb the hush and awe of the
place. Quiet woods' noises belonged there and
made the solitude complete. The tiny bubbling
ripple of the spring and the gray flash of tree-
squirrel were as yardsticks with which to measure
the silence and motionless repose. "Might be a
million miles from anywhere."*

From the upper parking area, your trail climbs southwest
into a eucalyptus grove, one of several Jack London planted
on his Beauty Ranch. In 250 feet you reach a trail map and
pleasant picnic ground. Go straight, descending slightly to
the road from the equestrian trailhead signed "Lake Trail."
To the left stand three stone buildings. The Sherry Barn
dates from 1884, the pre-London winery days. Behind it
stand London's Manure Pit and Stallion Barn.

Go right on the dirt road, climbing past the stone
Distillery Building on your left at ⅛ mile. A short spur on
the left leads to the humble cottage where Jack London
worked in his final years. Jack added the small room on the
southwest side of the building after Wolf House burned in
1913. He wrote many of his later works, including *The Star
Rover*, in this study overlooking the vineyards. On November
22, 1916, Jack London died in the glassed porch on the
southeast side.

The main trail soon forks. Bear right and head along the
mustard-dappled vineyard on your left. You can see stone
retaining walls built to terrace the steeper fields, to prevent
erosion and retain moisture. As your road bends left, a spur
on the right leads to London's Pig Palace and silos.

Staying left, you climb gradually around the vineyard at
¼ mile. At ⅜ mile, you top a rise where a rare white eucalyptus stands on the right. Beyond it the view north
encompasses Valley of the Moon and Hood Mountain, a
volcanic outcrop of the Mayacmas Range (see Trail #40).

Your trail bends left at a corner of the vineyard and
climbs, with wild forest (and a smattering of London's
eucalyptus) on your right. As you approach a gate on the
road, a trail branches right, entering the forest. Equestrians
and mountain bikers must continue on the road. Hikers
take the more intimate path that dips, then climbs through
forest of redwood, Douglas fir, bay laurel, big leaf maple,

SONOMA MOUNTAIN:

DISTANCE: 8⅛ miles round trip.

TIME: Four or five hours.

TERRAIN: Past vineyards and historical buildings to small lake, then climb through oak woodlands and grasslands to shoulder of Sonoma Mountain.

ELEVATION GAIN/LOSS: 1800 feet+/1800 feet-.

BEST TIME: Spring for wildflowers. Clear day for views.

WARNINGS: Watch for poison oak, ticks and rattlesnakes. Stay off adjacent private property.

DIRECTIONS TO TRAILHEAD: At M.30.7 on Highway 12 east of Santa Rosa, turn south onto Arnold Drive. In .9 mile, in the town of Glen Ellen, as Arnold veers left, you go right on London Ranch Road. Go 1.25 miles to entrance, then right to trailhead.

FEES: Day use: $3/vehicle.

FURTHER INFO: Jack London State Park (707)938-5216.

madrone and eucalyptus. In the understory you may find toyon, coffeeberry, hazel, hairy honeysuckle, sword fern and assorted wildflowers. Before ⅝ mile your trail bends left, climbing through the forest. The main trail climbs steadily, passing redwoods to three feet in diameter.

At ¾ mile the Lake Trail splits. Take the less traveled right fork, climbing gradually, then steeply through dense forest. At ⅞ mile your trail forks again. Take the left fork for a ⅜ mile side trip to the lake and back.

The side trail reaches the tules at the upper end of the five-acre lake at one mile, then follows the oak-shaded north shore to London's rustic redwood bathhouse and the beach and picnic area. Jack and Charmian London played here, often alone, sometimes with large groups of friends. A curving stone dam forms the east shore. If you come upon the lake quietly when no one is here, hundreds of birds squawk and shrill, producing a joyous symphony of sounds.

Bikers and equestrians will meet the lake at the dam and continue up the road from there. Our described hike returns to the junction north of the lake at 1¼ miles. Go straight at the junction, climbing northwest toward Sonoma Mountain. You soon switchback left and climb gradually through forest above the lake. You can glimpse the lake through the trees.

At 1½ miles you meet the main trail (road) at a big bend where you go right, climbing steadily through mixed forest. Maidenhair and leather-leaf ferns grow on the bank on the right, as does poison oak.

At 1⅝ miles you enter Mays Clearing, where a view unfolds southeast along the flank of Sonoma Mountain and down Valley of the Moon toward the north end of San Francisco Bay. The Fallen Leaf Trail forks left, descending ½ mile to Sonoma State Hospital lands, where the trail system is sometimes open to the public.

The Mountain Trail veers right and climbs into the forest. At 1¾ miles you climb steadily along the north slope of a ridge, where lady and maidenhair ferns grow beneath mixed forest. At 1⅞ miles you meet the upper end of the Fallen Bridge Trail at Woodcutter's Meadow. The spur goes left over a saddle, climbing to North Asbury Creek before descending steeply to the other end of its loop.

Your trail veers right, climbing through the forest. Around 2 miles you skirt several glades, mapped as Pine Tree Meadows although only one pine grows here; large firs dominate the surrounding forest. The trail makes a big bend left as the sound of rushing water rises from Graham Creek. You return to the forest at 2⅛ miles, then meet Lower Treadmill Road, which forks left to climb steeply.

The Mountain Trail climbs steadily, then descends briefly to cross two forks of South Graham Creek, where redwoods and woodwardia ferns grow. You climb steeply through rocky terrain in lush forest, meeting Upper Treadmill Road beyond 2⅝ miles. Your climb eases, continuing through redwood forest to cross Middle Graham Creek and reach London's Deer Camp at 2¾ miles.

Marked as a rest area on the park map, Deer Camp offers a picnic table in a grove of redwoods along a spring-fed creek jammed with woodwardia ferns. The site looks north across a beautiful glade surrounded by oak forest. Jack London would bring his guests to camp and hunt here. An old stone wall rims the east edge of the clearing above the grove. Beyond it sits a knoll with a fine view east to Valley of the Moon and the Mayacmas Range.

Your trail climbs through the glade to a junction at 2⅞ miles. On the right Cowan Meadow Trail climbs north. Your Mountain Trail goes left, climbing steeply through

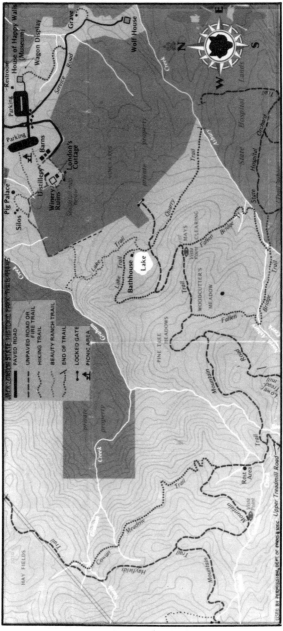

hardwood forest. At 3 miles you round a big bend left, then make the steepest climb yet as your trail passes native bunch grasses beneath black oaks and bay laurels.

Your climb eases at 3⅛ miles where an overlook on the left perches above a steeply rolling glade. Climb steeply again, at 3¼ miles approaching the precipitous canyon of Middle Graham Creek. The rugged climb continues through

189

a beautiful meadow, then returns to oak forest.

At 3½ miles the trail levels and enters a rolling glade studded with mistletoe-draped black oaks. You meet the Hayfields Trail, which branches right, meandering for nearly a mile to the park's north boundary. Go left, contouring through grasslands, then climbing to the largest glade yet at 3¾ miles, stretching west to the summit of Sonoma Mountain.

Your road soon bends left, leaving the grasslands to return to oak forest. Beyond 3⅞ miles, Mountain Trail bends right and draws alongside one of the headwaters of Middle Graham Creek. You climb along the creek, reaching the park boundary before 4 miles.

The park map shows the trail ending here. In fact, a footpath climbs north along the boundary fence to reenter the immense glade. At 4⅛ miles you climb a very steep, short hill to the park's summit, the crest of Sonoma Mountain's east ridge. At 2380 feet you are about 80 feet below the mountain top, visible with its forest of antennae and microwave relays ¼ mile west. Private property stands between you and the summit of the mountain, but the park's summit provides grand views and an aerie more peaceful than the rise to the west.

Jack London scaled Sonoma Mountain many times. He obviously loved it up here:

> There were no houses in the summit of Sonoma Mountain, and, all alone under the azure California sky, he reigned in on the ...edge of the peak. He saw open pasture country, intersected with wooden canyons, descending ... from his feet, crease on crease and roll on roll, from lower level to lower level, to the floor of [the] valley. Swinging his horse, he surveyed the west and north, from Santa Rosa to Mount St. Helena, and on to the east, across Sonoma Valley, to the chaparral-covered range that shut off the view of Napa Valley. ...[H]e continued the circle of his survey to the southeast, where, across the waters of San Pablo Bay, he could see, sharp and distant, the twin peaks of Mount Diablo. To the south was Mount Tamalpais, and, yes, he was right, fifty miles away, where the draughty winds of the Pacific blew in the Golden Gate, the smoke of San Francisco made a low-lying haze against the sky. He was loath to depart, and it was not for an hour that he was able to tear himself away and take the descent of the mountain.

When you are able to tear away, return by the same route

you ascended. If you stay on the main road all the way you will save about ¼ mile, making the total hike 8⅛ miles. If you return late in the day, keep a sharp eye out for the deer, coyote, fox, racoon and other mammals that become active in the evening. Remember that the park closes at the hour posted at the entrance kiosk.

46.

CANYON/RIDGE LOOP

SONOMA VALLEY REGIONAL PARK

In 1880 the San Francisco and North Pacific Railroad completed tracks from the shore of San Pablo Bay, through the bustling town of Sonoma and up Valley of the Moon to sleepy Glen Ellen. Their passenger train soon became a popular excursion for city-weary people fleeing to the country for a weekend or a week. The railroad chugged through what is now Sonoma Valley Regional Park before reaching the end of the line at the Glen Ellen Depot, less than a mile north. The line was extended to Santa Rosa before 1890, then discontinued in 1935 after business dwindled in the depression.

These rolling oak- and wildflower-studded hills served many years as the dairy farm for nearby Sonoma State Hospital. Sonoma County acquired the lush 162 acres in 1973 for a park. Today a growing trail system explores the canyons and ridges tucked among the folds of Valley of the Moon. The paved Canyon Trail is as gentle as the Ridge Trail is angular. You can stay on the former for an easy walk, also accessible to people with handicaps (with some assistance). Or you can climb to the top of the park for expansive views of Glen Ellen, Valley of the Moon and the Mayacmas and Sonoma Ranges. On a clear day the Ridge Trail provides ample reward for its short climb.

From the parking lot, the paved Canyon Trail passes through a gate and heads toward two huge green water tanks. In 250 feet your path turns right and starts a gentle descent, passing grass nut and poppies in spring. At ⅛ mile a fenced area on the right is the first of several graze control study areas to protect the native vegetation. Also on the right is a picnic table beside Oregon oaks. A tiny seasonal creek starts here, burbling beside the picnic spot.

Trail and creek descend gently, following and criss-crossing each other. Your trail winds through Oregon oak

forest draped with the gray-green lichen called old man's beard. At ¼ mile the creek crosses to the left of your path. Mariposa lilies grow on the right. Steep, wooded hills rise beside the trail, but you descend gently.

At ⅜ mile, as the creek returns to the right side of the trail, another picnic table sits beside the stream. Scattered manzanitas, blue dicks and yarrow grow here. Watch out for poison oak twining around oaks along the trail.

At ½ mile a footpath on your left climbs a side canyon. Stay on the paved path, swerving left across the creek. Tiny white flowers called milkmaids grow abundantly here as early as January. As you continue your gentle descent, Sonoma Mountain rises to the west.

You pass another picnic table on the right at ⅝ mile. If you picnic here, stay away from the nearby oak wrapped in poison oak vines. In 75 feet, a massive Oregon oak three feet in diameter is on the right. Buckeye, bay laurel and coast live oak grow nearby.

Soon a tiny gully descends from the left. Beside it grow soap plants, a lily with many uses to Indians and early settlers. The local Wappo tribe used glue from the bulb, a green dye from the leaves for tattooing, and ate leaves and roasted bulbs. Settlers crushed the raw bulbs to make soap and shampoo. Soap plants grow profusely on this walk. Hikers rarely see soap plant's delicate white flowers which

CANYON/RIDGE LOOP:

DISTANCE: 2½-mile loop.

TIME: One or two hours.

TERRAIN: Gentle descent on paved trail down wooded canyon, then along old railroad grade. Return by same trail for easiest walk, or climb footpath to ridge with views, then return to trailhead.

ELEVATION GAIN/LOSS: Loop: 320 feet+/320 feet-. Paved path: 160 feet+/160 feet-.

BEST TIME: Spring for wildflowers.

WARNINGS: Watch for poison oak. Stay off adjacent private property.

DIRECTIONS TO TRAILHEAD: On Highway 12 in Glen Ellen at M.31.08, turn west into Sonoma Valley Regional Park.

FEES: Day use: $1/vehicle.

FURTHER INFO: Sonoma Valley Regional Park (707)539-8092.

only open in the evening or on cloudy days.

Your trail climbs a slight rise as the creek wanders away on the right. At ¾ mile several picnic tables line the creek near an immense fallen oak as you approach the old railroad right-of-way. Your paved trail bends left, then right to join the level railroad bed. (You can turn right to follow the bed to the park boundary, a ⅜-mile side trip.) The main trail passes through a dense grove of madrones as houses appear on your right. As you turn south, Sonoma Creek parallels your path on the right. The road noise comes from busy Arnold Drive on the far side of the creek.

At one mile a dirt trail runs between you and Sonoma Creek. Pass a large manzanita on the left. At 1⅛ miles the hill on your left is crowded with soap plants beneath live and Oregon oaks. In 400 feet your paved path splits into three forks: a dirt footpath climbs the bank on your left, the graveled railroad bed in the center curves left, while your paved path swings right. The latter climbs a slight rise to two last picnic tables at 1¼ miles before coming to a gate

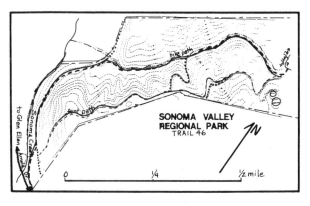

SONOMA VALLEY
REGIONAL PARK
TRAIL 46

0   ¼   ½ mile

and Arnold Drive. For the easiest walk, retrace your steps, returning to the parking lot at 2½ miles.

If you prefer a slightly more challenging hike, take the dirt footpath. It climbs around the end of a fence, then ascends north into oak forest. Many rocks lie beside the trail, some as large as Volkswagen Bugs. You climb steadily to 1⅝ miles, where soap plants and vetch grow beneath Oregon and live oaks. Scattered manzanita, bay laurel, buckeye and toyon grow along the trail.

You pass yarrow as your trail bends right and climbs steeply. At 1¾ miles you reach the ridge and meet the park boundary fence. Milkmaid and sun cup brighten the way in winter, poppy, Indian warrior and paintbrush in spring. Your path bends left, descending along the ridgetop.

The trail soon forks, the left fork descending steeply to the paved path. Bear right, continuing a gradual descent near ridge and fence line. At 1⅞ miles you climb again, continuing along the fence. You soon reach a high top on the ridge. You look out over broken terrain that supports the geological theory that Valley of the Moon is a series of basins rather than a true valley. Over time, Sonoma Creek has carved a channel to connect the separate basins.

Descend gradually along the ridge to 2 miles, where your trail levels. Then you dip and climb near the ridge crest. At 2⅛ miles another trail forks left, descending northwest. Your Ridge Trail goes northeast as views open up to Lake Suttonfield and Sonoma State Hospital. Continue along the contours of the ridge to a broad hilltop at 2¼ miles, where a maze of trails wanders in all directions. The well-trod main path is easy to follow. You descend, winding through a forest of dwarf Oregon oaks. Soon an old road merges with the trail from the right. Follow the obvious path to one last small ridgetop where you have a fine view over pastoral park lands and Valley of the Moon beyond. You can see Sugarloaf Ridge and Hood Mountain to the north.

Your path descends from here. Beyond 2⅜ miles you again meet the boundary fence. Descend toward the big water tanks, then veer left between large oaks and descend toward the parking lot. You join a gravel road that descends to the paved path. You reach the parking lot at 2½ miles.

47.

MAXWELL FARMS REGIONAL PARK

COUNTRY OASIS IN CITY OF SONOMA

Dedicated in 1988, Maxwell Farms Regional Park offers 85 acres of woods and fields bordering Sonoma Creek. Turn-of-the-century conservationist George Maxwell, who fought for the rights of small farmers, developed these lands as a farm. Though the park is small, it provides peace and solitude not far from Sonoma Valley's busiest intersection.

From the southwest end of the paved parking lot, walk northwest into the gravel overflow lot and take the path that veers left toward Sonoma Mountain. In 400 feet you cross a ditch and turn left to parallel Verano Avenue.

Descend into oak woodlands at ⅛ mile, then through a stand of English walnut trees. Himalaya blackberry and native snowberry and bay laurel grow along the path. You cross a gully where periwinkle carpets the ground.

Before ¼ mile you meet a broad path where bikers can go left. I prefer to continue straight on the footpath that descends near Sonoma Creek. In 200 feet the trail bends left. You can see the creek 100 feet west. A spur descends into a jungle of wild grape vining on white alder, cottonwood, willow and bay trees along the creek.

The main footpath parallels the creek, passing periwinkle, snowberry and coyote brush. Climb to meet the broad trail, but immediately veer right on a path lined with poison oak. You can see a meadow through the trees on your left. A bay tree on the right of the trail is eight feet in diameter and 100 feet tall.

Before ⅜ mile a fence on your right blocks a 20-foot plunge to the shallow creek. Your trail skirts the meadow and a plowed fire break on the left. Veer right on the lower path along the top of the creek bank. Bamboo, willows and young cottonwoods grow densely on the right.

Your path climbs back to the meadow, where a main spur

MAXWELL FARMS REGIONAL PARK:

DISTANCE: 1⅛-mile loop.

TIME: Less than one hour.

TERRAIN: Grasslands and woods along Sonoma Creek.

BEST TIME: Spring for wildflowers.

WARNINGS: Watch for poison oak. Stay off adjacent private property.

DIRECTIONS TO TRAILHEAD: Turn west off Highway 12 (at M.36., north end of Sonoma) onto Verano Avenue, then quickly left into park.

FEES: Day use: $1/vehicle.

FURTHER INFO: Maxwell Farms Regional Park (707)938-2794.

OTHER SUGGESTIONS: A BIKE PATH connects Maxwell Farms Park with SONOMA STATE HISTORIC PARK, a must-see for first time visitors. Follow the bike path east to LACHRYMA MONTIS, General Vallejo's home for his last 40 years. The BIKE PATH continues to Fourth Street East, but the main attraction is SONOMA STATE HISTORIC PARK, a cluster of some of Northern California's oldest buildings that encircle large, shady SONOMA PLAZA. (It is 1¼ miles from MAXWELL FARMS to PLAZA.)

goes left. Go straight, returning to woodlands above the creek. At ½ mile a gravel spur on the right descends 150 feet to the creek. The main trail continues straight, then veers left to return to the fire break and meadow. A path goes straight to the parking lot, but veer right on the path along the fire break, heading southeast.

Your trail stays left of a fence. At ⅝ mile turn left as you meet the park boundary. Head east through grasslands lined with oaks, paralleling the boundary. Soon another fire break path forks left. Continue 150 feet to a footpath that veers left into forest at ¾ mile. The trail winds in and out of the woods, a windrow left by farmer Maxwell to create a protected microclimate in the adjacent fields.

At ⅞ mile a horseshoe pit and group picnic area are on your right. Cross a service road, the playground uphill on

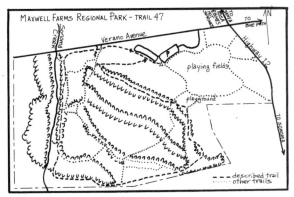

your right. You can cross the road and continue on a footpath along the edge of the wild side of the park.

The path winds through more bay and oak forest with twining wild grapevines. Several paths branch left to cross a gully, but to conclude your walk stay east of the gully. At one mile your trail swings right to meet a fire break. Go northeast on the path through the poppy-filled meadow. You climb a hill and return to the parking lot at 1⅛ miles.

48.

SONOMA'S OTHER SHORE

LOWER TUBBS ISLAND WILDLIFE REFUGE

This trail differs from any other in the book. A level, easy hike passes through farmlands, with views offering an unusual perspective on San Francisco Bay and its surrounding landmarks. After 2¾ miles you reach the marshes of 332-acre Lower Tubbs Island Wildlife Refuge, where over 200 species of resident and migrating birds will be found. The bird population and diversity are highest in fall and winter, but some birds are here year-round. Try to time your visit with a low tide, when birds will be busiest (and most visible) feeding on the mud flats along the bay and in the marshes. If you have a compass, bring it to help pinpoint the landmarks. The hike is less than 20 feet above sea level.

Behind the brown gate, a dirt road heads southeast atop a levee surrounded by level farmlands, a canal on the left, Tolay Creek on the right. Soon a sign confirms that Lower Tubbs Island is ahead. Another sign warns that no firearms are allowed except shotguns for hunting pheasants and waterfowl. (It is best not to take this trail during pheasant-hunting season, mid-October to mid-January.)

At ⅛ mile your road bends left. Wild turnips, fennel, mustard and grasses grow at roadside. Red-winged blackbirds dart across the fields. Quail and pheasants are more reclusive, but you may flush them from cover. At ¼ mile the road bends right to head southeast toward Mt. Diablo. Mt. Tamalpais is southwest. A slough is on your right. Road and levee bend left, then right.

At ½ mile a lone eucalyptus stands on the left, the only shade on the entire hike. If you brought a compass, aim due south. If visibility is good the Bank of America skyscraper and Transamerica Pyramid rise above Point Richmond. You might see part of the Richmond Bridge to their right.

Continue southeast. At ¾ mile your road bends left, then back to the right. The confluence of two sloughs is on your left. Pass a farm road that forks left, as your road bends right to head toward Mt. Tamalpais. You curve right again at one mile. At 1⅜ miles your road makes a gradual bend left. When you tire of walking on the hard-packed road, walk the levee on the right. I flushed a pheasant here that had been hiding in the grasses. The slight elevation gain of the levee enhances the views on this flatland.

At 1½ miles your road bends left to head south. At 1⅝ miles you swing left again, passing a metal pumphouse. From atop the levee here, an east tower of the Richmond Bridge is due south. The tip of the Pyramid is 3 finger-widths (at arm's length) to the left. Two fingers to the right of the east bridge tower, a more easily visible west tower of the bridge rises above the bay. Three fingers to the right of that, a tower of the Golden Gate Bridge rises above Tiburon. Each mile divulges a few more landmarks, which seem to float on the bay and horizon. As the road winds, the landmarks shift their positions relative to each other.

Your trail turns toward Mt. Diablo on the levee road. Coyote brush grows beside the road. At 1⅞ miles a lagoon is on your right. At 2 miles road and levee jog left. At 2¼ miles swing right and head due south. First Angel Island is left of a tower of the Richmond Bridge, then wanders to the right. At one point Sutro Towers are left of Angel Island, then they are on the right. The changing perspectives create a dreamy effect.

Around 2½ miles a sign informs you that you are entering Lower Tubbs Island Wildlife Refuge, no dogs or hunting allowed beyond this point. Ice plant grows densely on the road shoulder. At 2⅝ miles a funky house leans over a canal on the left. Opposite the house a trail called Wingspan Way forks right, passing yucca and narcissus to reach a tidal flat at the edge of bay wetlands by ⅛ mile. You

DISTANCE: 5¾ to 7⅝ miles, round trip.

TIME: Three hours to all day.

TERRAIN: Level road along sloughs to bay shore.

BEST TIME: Low tide in fall or winter for best birding. Spring for wildflowers.

WARNINGS: Use caution in hunting season: mid-October to mid-January, especially opening weekend.

DIRECTIONS TO TRAILHEAD: Trailhead is just east of intersection of Highways 37 and 121. From intersection go east briefly on Highway 37 across railroad tracks and Tolay Creek. Parking area is on right, beside brown gate (do not block gate). FROM NORTH: Exit Highway 101 onto Highway 116 East (M.3.95). Go 12 miles to Highway 121, then south on 121 for 6.5 miles to Highway 37. FROM SOUTH: Exit Highway 101 onto Highway 37 (at M.18.8, Marin County). Go 7.5 miles to intersection with Highway 121.

FURTHER INFO: San Pablo Bay National Wildlife Refuge (415)792-0222.

continue straight. A sign soon informs you that Lower Tubbs Island was acquired for the public by the Nature Conservancy. Another trail forks right, the end of your loop trail in 2½ miles.

The main road continues ¼ mile to the open bay. Farmland is on the left, salt marsh on the right. Pickleweed, saltbush and other salt-tolerant plants cover the marsh.

At 2⅞ miles your road splits as you meet the bay shore. During a plus tide it is all water to the south and east, but at zero or minus tide mud flats line the shore. In fall and winter migrating birds feed here. You may see dowitchers, killdeers, sandpipers, sanderlings, curlews and many more.

Your route turns right, with salt marsh on the right and bay tidelands on the left. The bright blue roof of Marin Civic Center snuggles at the base of Mt. Tamalpais. Pt. Richmond is due south, surrounded by other Bay Area landmarks. The Berkeley Hills are south-southeast. Mt. Diablo rises to the southeast, with Carquinez Straits now visible to its left.

At 3⅛ miles cross a gate where slough and marsh on the right empty into the bay if the tide is ebbing, the opposite

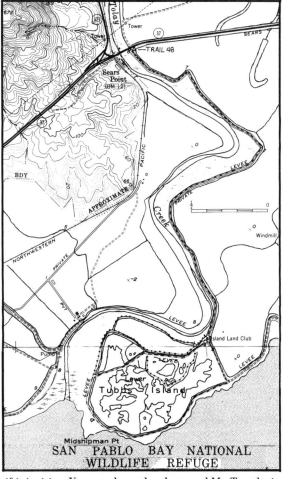

SAN PABLO BAY NATIONAL
WILDLIFE REFUGE

if it is rising. Your road soon bends toward Mt. Tamalpais.
Road and levee wind right and left around 3⅜ miles.

Pass the ruins of an old dock on the left. Until the advent
of railroads in the 1870s, ferries transported most people
from the Bay Area to the Sonoma bay shore. Passengers
and freight were transported by stage to Sonoma.

Continue along the levee road. At 3⅝ miles you cross
another gate where slough and marsh empty into the bay.
In 250 feet you reach the southern extreme of this hike.
The Sonoma-Marin county line is one mile south, the
Richmond city limits, five miles. San Francisco's skyscrap-
ers still rise above Pt. Richmond. Angel Island can be seen
beyond the Richmond Bridge. Your road bends right. Mid-
shipman Point is the green marshy promontory due west.

Beyond 3¾ miles the ruins of another ferry dock settle
into the bay shore. Weathered redwood and iron rest on
rip-rap at the edge of the mud flats. Today the ruins teem

with mussels, barnacles, and lively purple shore crabs. Imagine this site a bustling ferry landing, bringing settlers and commerce to booming Sonoma via this lonesome bay shore. You have a view west to the mouth of the Petaluma River, still navigable to the town of Petaluma, where other ferry landings were in the 1800s.

Continue on the levee road. At the mouth of Tolay Creek it turns northwest. At 4 miles you cross another slough gate. Your road bends right, heading north-northeast.

At 4¼ miles you turn right, taking Mid Marsh Trail across a slough, winding northeast toward the eccentric house. Great and snowy egrets live here. Wind through salt marsh and ponds rich in bird life, with dense pickleweed lining the path. At 4⅜ miles a pond is on your left, bird tracks wander across the mud flat on your right. At 4½ miles red and green algae-covered marshes are on your left.

At 4⅝ miles your road forks. The path on the right makes a loop to explore Mid Marsh Pond in the heart of Lower Tubbs Island. Your described hike continues straight. At 4¾ miles pass a big pond on the right surrounded by dense salt marsh. While it may look as if nothing lives in the marsh, in fact salt marshes are among the most nutrient-rich, productive habitats in the world. They harbor many birds, small mammals, shellfish and the larval stages of many fish and invertebrates that live elsewhere as adults.

Your path gets brushy, then slightly swampy, but quickly climbs to higher ground. At 4⅞ miles your road bends left to head straight for the tower house. Wingspan Way runs parallel on the left.

Before 5 miles you merge with the outer loop path and your tread improves. At 5⅛ miles you complete the loop, returning to the sign and main road just south of the house. Head north, retracing your steps 2½ miles to the trailhead at 7⅝ miles.

CROSS REFERENCE LISTING

TRAILS FOR HANDICAPPED ACCESS

1. Headlands to Beach Loop
10. Salt Point to Stump Beach (first 1/8 mile)
12. Stockhoff Creek (see Other Suggestions)
15. Fort Ross Creek (to the fort)
17. North of Jenner (Black Ranch)
20. Shell to Wrights Beach (at Wrights Beach)
21. Bodega Dunes (first 1/8 mile)
28. Armstrong Woods
30. Ragle Ranch (paved paths)
35. Spring Lake Loop (paved path)
46. Canyon/Ridge (paved path)

TRAILS FOR BACKPACKING

26. Half-a-Canoe Loop
27. South Shore to Old Sawmill Camp
29. Austin Creek

TRAILS FOR MOUNTAIN BIKES

1. Headlands to Beach Loop
9. Pygmy Forest Loop
14. Kolmer Gulch
26. Half-a-Canoe Loop
30. Ragle Ranch (see Other Suggestions)
31. Helen Putnam
33. Mt. St. Helena
35. Spring Lake Loop
36. Rough Go/Canyon/Spring Creek Loop
38. Schultz/Marsh/Ridge/Upper Steve's S Loop
42. Bald Mountain Loop
45. Sonoma Mountain
46. Canyon/Ridge Loop
47. Maxwell Farms
48. Sonoma's Other Shore

TRAILS FOR EQUESTRIANS

9. Pygmy Forest Loop
21. Bodega Dunes Loop
26. Half-a-Canoe Loop
27. South Shore to Old Sawmill Camp
28. Armstrong Woods (see Other Suggestions)
29. Austin Creek
30. Ragle Ranch
32. Shiloh Ranch
34. Ritchey Canyon
35. Spring Lake Loop
36. Rough Go/Canyon/ Spring Creek Loop
38. Schultz/Marsh/Ridge/Upper Steve's S Loop
39. Santa Rosa Creek Headwaters
42. Bald Mountain Loop
45. Sonoma Mountain

BEACH WALKS

1. Headlands to Beach Loop
5. Other Sea Ranch Trails
10. Salt Point to Stump Beach
13. Fort Ross North Headlands
15. Fort Ross Creek
16. Sonoma's Lost Coast
17. North of Jenner
19. Blind Beach to Shell Beach
20. Shell Beach to Wrights Beach
21. Bodega Dunes Loop
22. Bodega Head North to Dunes
24. Pinnacle Gulch

COMMON & SCIENTIFIC NAMES OF
PLANTS ALONG THE TRAILS

*Fine grass covered the slope—spangled with flowers, with
here and there patches of color, orange and purple and
golden.* —Jack London, All Gold Canyon

alum root, *Heuchera micrantha*

* alyssum, *Lobularia maritima*

angelica, *Angelica tomentosa*

azalea, *Rhododendron occidentale*

baby blue eyes, *Nemophila menziesii*

bay laurel (Calif. bay, pepperwood),
    Umbellularia californica

beach morning glory, *Calystegia soldanella*

beach pea, *Lathyrus japonicus var. glaber*

beach primrose, *Oenothera cheiranthifolia*

beach strawberry, *Fragaria chiloensis*

bear grass, *Xerophyllum tenax*

bedstraw, *Galium spp.*

big leaf maple, *Acer macrophyllum*

bird's foot fern, *Pellaea mucronata*

Bishop pine, *Pinus muricata*

bitterroot, *Lewisia rediviva*

black oak (Calif.), *Quercus kelloggi*

black sage, *Salvia mellifera*

bleeding heart (western), *Dicentra formosa*

blueblossom (Calif. lilac), *Ceanothus
    thyrsiflorus*

blue dick, *Dichelostemma pulchellum*

blue elderberry, *Sambucus mexicana*

blue-eyed grass, *Sisyrinchium bellum*

* blue gum eucalyptus, *Eucalyptus globulus*

blue larkspur, *Delphinium decorum*

blue oak, *Quercus douglasii*

bracken fern, *Pteridium aquilinum var.
    pubescens*

broadleaf ceanothus, *Ceanothus griseus*

buckbrush, *Ceanothus cuneatus*

buttercup, *Ranunculus californicus*

California aster, *Aster chilensis*

California blackberry, *Rubus vitifolius*

California buckeye, *Aesculus californica*

California fuchsia, *Zauschneria californica*

California gooseberry, *Ribes californica*

California maidenhair fern, *Adiantum jor-
    dani*

California nutmeg, *Torreya californica*

California poppy, *Eschscholtzia californica*

California rose, *Rosa californica*

California sycamore, *Platanus racemosa*

* calla lily, *Zantedeschia aethiopica*

calypso orchid (redwood orchid), *Calypso
    bulbosa*

canyon live oak, *Quercus chrysolepis*

cattail, *Typha spp.*

chamise, *Adenostoma fasciculatum*

chaparral pea, *Pickeringia montana*

checker lily, *Fritillaria lanceolata*

chinese houses, *Collinsia heterophylla*

chinquapin, *Castanopsis chrysophylla*

clintonia, *Clintonia andrewsiana*

coast buckwheat, *Eriogonum latifolium*

coast lily, *Lilium maritimum*

coast live oak, *Quercus agrifolia*

coast silktassel, *Garrya elliptica*

coastal manroot (wild cucumber), *Marah
    oreganus*

coffee fern, *Pellaea andromedaefolia*

coffeeberry, *Rhamnus californica*

columbine, *Aquilegia formosa*

corn lily, *Veratrum fimbriatum*

cow parsnip, *Heracleum lanatum*

coyote brush, *Baccharis pilularis*

coyote mint, *Monardella villosa*

cream cup, *Platystemon californicus*

cream fawn lily, *Erythronium californicum*

creeping ceanothus, *Ceanothus prostratus*

* creeping myrtle, *Vinca minor*

* crimson clover, *Trifolium incarnatum*

* cypress, *Cupressus spp.*

dandelion, *Taraxacum officinale*

deer fern, *Blechnum spicant*

digger pine, *Pinus sabiniana*

dogwood, *Cornus nuttali*

Douglas fir, *Pseudotsuga menziesii*

Douglas iris, *Iris douglasiana*

dutchman's pipe, *Aristolochia californica*

dwarf brodiaea, *Brodiaea terrestris*

203

elegant brodiaea, *Brodiaea elegans*

elk clover, *Aralia californica*

* European beach grass, *Ammophila arenaria*

evergreen huckleberry, *Vaccinium ovatum*

evergreen violet (redwood violet), *Viola sempervirens*

fairy bells, *Disporum smithii*

false baby stars, *Linanthus androsacea*

false lily of the valley, *Maianthemum dilatum*

fat solomon's seal, *Smilacina racemosa*

* fennel, *Foeniculum vulgare*

five-finger fern, *Adiantum pedatum var. aleuticum*

flannel bush, *Fremontia californica*

forget-me-not, *Hackelia floribunda*

Fort Bragg manzanita, *Arctostaphylos nummularia*

* foxglove, *Digitalis purpurea*

giant horsetail, *Equisetum telmateia*

godetia (farewell to spring), *Clarkia spp.*

gold back fern, *Pityrogramma triangularis*

golden fairy lantern, *Calochortus amabilis*

goldfields, *Lasthenia chrysostoma*

grand fir, *Abies grandis*

grass nut (Ithuriel's spear), *Triteleia laxa*

gum plant, *Grindelia stricta*

hairy cat's ear, *Hypochoeris radicata*

hairy honeysuckle, *Lonicera hispidula*

hairy manzanita, *Arctostaphylos columbiana*

hazel (California), *Corylus cornuta californica*

hedge nettle, *Stachys bullata*

hen and chicks, *Dudleya farinosa*

* Himalayan blackberry, *Rubus procerus*

horsetail, *Equisetum spp.*

hound's tongue, *Cynoglossum grande*

huckleberry, *Vaccinium spp.*

ice plant, *Mesembryanthemum spp.*

Indian paintbrush, *Castilleja spp.*

Indian pink, *Silene californica*

Indian potato, *Wapeto pterideridia*

Indian warrior, *Pedicularis densiflora*

inside-out flower, *Vancouveria spp.*

interior live oak, *Quercus wislizenii*

knobcone pine, *Pinus attenuata*

Labrador tea, *Ledum glandulosum var. columbianum*

ladies' tresses, *Spiranthus romanzoffiana*

lady fern, *Athyrium filix-femina var. sitchenense*

leather fern (leather-leaf fern), *Polypodium scouleri*

licorice fern, *Polypodium glycyrrhiza*

live-forever, *Dudleya spp.*

Lobb's buttercup, *Ranunculus lobbii*

lupine, *Lupinus latifolius, L. littoralis, L. nanus, L. polyphyllus, L. variicolor, L. rivularis, L. bicolor*

madrone, *Arbutus menziesii*

maidenhair fern, *Adiantum jordanii*

manzanita, *Arctostaphylos spp.*

mariposa lily, *Calochortus luteus*

Mendocino cypress, *Cupressus pygmaea*

Mendocino gentian, *Gentiana setigera*

milkmaids, *Dentaria californica*

miners lettuce, *Montia sibirica*

monkeyflower, *Mimulus guttatus*

mountain mahogany, *Cercocarpus betuloides*

mugwort, *Artemisia douglasiana*

mule's ears, *Wyethia spp.*

* narcissus, *Amaryllidaceae spp.*

narrow-leaf mule ears, *Wyethia angustifolia*

Oregon ash, *Fraxinus latifolia*

Oregon grape, *Berberis spp.*

Oregon white oak, *Quercus garryana*

owl's clover, *Orthocarpus attenuatus*

paintbrush, *Castilleja latifolia, C. affinis, C. foliosa, C. hololeuca, C. wightii, C. mendosensis*

* pampas grass, *Cortaderia selloana*

pearly everlasting, *Anaphalis margaritacea*

pennyroyal, *Mentha pulegium*

penstemon, *Penstemon heterophyllus*

pickleweed, *Salicornia subterminalis*

plantain, *Plantago spp.*

* poison hemlock, *Conium maculatum*

poison oak, *Toxicodendron diversiloba*

popcorn flower, *Plagiobothrys nothofulvus*

poppy, *Eschscholtzia californica*

Queen Anne's lace, *Daucus carota*

raspberry, *Rubus leucodermis*

* rattlesnake grass, *Briza maxima*

rattlesnake plantain, *Goodyera oblongiflora*

red alder, *Alnus rubra*

red elderberry, *Sambucus callicarpa*

red flowering currant, *Ribes sanguineum*

* red hot poker, *Kniphofia uvaria*

red huckleberry, *Vaccinium parvifolium*

red larkspur, *Delphinium nudicaule*

redwood, *Sequoia sempervirens*

redwood lily, *Lilium rubescens*

redwood sorrel, *Oxalis oregana*

rein orchid, *Habenaria elegans*

rhododendron, *Rhododendron macrophyllum*

rush, *Juncus spp.*

salal, *Gaultheria shallon*

salmonberry, *Rubus spectabilis*

saltbush, *Atriplex spp.*

sand verbena, yellow, *Abronia latifolia*

sand verbena, pink, *Abronia umbellata*

scarlet fritillary, *Fritillaria recurva*

* scarlet pimpernel, *Anagallis arvensis*

* Scotch broom, *Cytisus scoparius*

scouring rush, *Equisetum hyemale*

sea rocket, *Cakile maritima*

seaside daisy, *Erigeron glaucous*

sea thrift, *Armeria maritima var. californica*

sedge, *Carex spp.*

shield fern, *Polystichum californicum*

shooting star, *Dodecatheon hendersonii*

shore pine, *Pinus contorta ssp. contorta*

silverweed, *Potentilla egedei var. grandis*

skunk cabbage, *Lysichitum americanum*

slink pod (fetid adders tongue), *Scoliopus
bigelovii*

smooth cat's ear, *Hypochoeris glabra*

snowberry, *Symphoricarpos rivularis*

soap plant, *Chlorogalum pomeridianum*

Sonoma sage, *Salvia sonomensis*

* spearmint, *Mentha spicata*

star lily, *Zygadenus fremontii*

star solomon's seal, *Smilacina racemosa*

star tulip, *Calochortus elegans*

starflower, *Trientalis latifolia*

sticky monkeyflower, *Mimulus aurantiacus*

stinging nettle, *Urtica lyalli*

stream violet, *Viola glabella*

sun cup, *Oenothera ovata*

sword fern, *Polystichum munitum*

tanoak, *Lithocarpus densiflorus*

tarweed, *Hemizonia corymbosa*

thimbleberry, *Rubus parviflorus*

* thistle, *Cirsium spp.*

toyon, *Heteromeles arbutifolia*

trail plant, *Adenocaulon bicolor*

trillium, *Trillium chloropetalum, T. ovatum*

twinberry, *Lonicera involucrata*

twisted stalk, *Streptopus amplexifolius*

vetch, *Vicia spp.*

vine maple, *Acer circinatum*

wallflower, *Erysimum menziesii*

water fern, *Azolla filiculoides*

watercress, *Nasturtium officinale*

wax myrtle (bayberry), *Myrica californica*

western coltsfoot, *Petasites palmatus*

western dog violet, *Viola adunca*

western hemlock, *Tsuga heterophylla*

white alder, *Alnus rhombifolia*

* white eucalyptus, *Eucalyptus albens*

white fritillary, *Fritillaria liliacea*

white hyacinth, *Triteleia hyacinthina*

white oak (valley oak), *Quercus lobata*

whitethorn, *Ceanothus incanus*

wild ginger, *Asarum caudatum*

wild mustard, *Brassica campestris*

wild rose, *Rosa spp.*

willow, *Salix spp.*

windflower, *Anemone deltoidea*

wood fern, *Dryopteris arguta*

wood rose, *Rosa gymnocarpa*

wood strawberry, *Fragaria californica*

woodland buttercup, *Ranunculus uncinatus*

woodland star, *Lithophragma heterophylla*

woodwardia fern, *Woodwardia fimbriata*

wooly mullein, *Verbascum thapsus*

yarrow, *Achillea millefolium*

yellow water iris, *Iris pseudacorus*

* Introduced (feral) species

BIBLIOGRAPHY

Adams, Rick and Louise McCorkle, *The California Highway 1 Book*, Ballantine Books, New York, 1985.

Alt, David D. and Donald W. Hyndman, *Roadside Geology of Northern California*, Mountain Press Publishing Co., Missoula, Montana, 1975.

Becking, Rudolph, *Pocket Flora of the Redwood Forest*, Island Press, Covelo, Ca., 1982.

California Coastal Access Guide, University of California Press, Berkeley, 1983.

California Coastal Resource Guide, University of California Press, Berkeley, 1987.

Edwards, Don, *Making the Most of Sonoma County*, Alameda, Ca., 1988.

Hanse, Harvey J., *Wild Oats in Eden, Sonoma County in the Nineteenth Century*, self-published, Santa Rosa, 1962.

Howard, Arthur D., *Geologic History of Middle California*, University of California Press, Berkeley, 1979.

Jenny, Hans, *The Pygmy Forest Ecological Staircase*, Nature Conservancy, 1973.

Keator, Glenn and Ruth Heady, *Pacific Coast Berry Finder*, Nature Study Guild, Berkeley, 1978.

Keator, Glenn and Ruth Heady, *Pacific Coast Fern Finder*, Nature Study Guild, Berkeley, 1978.

Kroeber, A.L., *Handbook of the Indians of California*, Dover Publications, New York, 1976.

Lyons, Kathleen and Mary Beth Cuneo-Lazaneo, *Plants of the Coast Redwood Region*, Looking Press, Los Altos, Ca., 1988.

McConnaughey, Bayard H. and Evelyn McConnaughey, *Pacific Coast*, Audubon Society Nature Guides, Alfred A. Knopf, New York, 1985.

Munz, Philip A., *California Spring Wildflowers*, University of California Press, Berkeley, 1961.

Munz, Philip A., *Shore Wildflowers of California, Oregon and Washington*, University of California Press, Berkeley, 1973.

Niehaus, Theodore F. and Charles L. Ripper, *Field Guide to Pacific States Wildflowers*, (Peterson Field Guide Series), Houghton Mifflin, Boston, 1976.

Randall, Warren R., Robert F. Keniston and Dale N. Bever, *Manual of Oregon Trees and Shrubs*, Oregon State University Bookstores, Corvallis, Or., 1978.

Russo, Ron and Pam Olhausen, *Pacific Intertidal Life*, Nature Study Guild, Berkeley, 1981.

Sholars, Robert, *The Pygmy Forest and Associated Plant Communities of Coastal Mendocino County, California*, self-published, Mendocino, Ca., 1982.

Watts, Phoebe, *Redwood Region Flower Finder*, Nature Study Guild, Berkeley, 1979.

Watts, Tom, *Pacific Coast Tree Finder*, Nature Study Guild, Berkeley, 1973.

Young, Dorothy King, *Redwood Empire Wildflowers*, Third Edition, Naturegraph Publishers, Happy Camp, Ca., 1976.

INDEX

ABOUT BORED FEET

We began Bored Feet Publications in 1986 to publish and distribute *The Hiker's hip pocket Guides*. If you would like to receive updates on trails included in our publications, send us your name and address, specifying your counties of interest.

We provide a retail mail order service specializing in books and maps about Northern California. Your purchases directly from Bored Feet support our independent publishing efforts to bring you more information about Northern California's spectacular natural beauty. Thanks for your support!

SOME PUBLICATIONS YOU CAN ORDER FROM US:

Hiker's hip pocket Guide to Mendocino Highlands $13.95
  (July 1992) *20 day hikes near Highway 101, 30 backpacks in Yolla Bolly & Snow Mountain Wilderness Areas, with pull-out color map of Yolla Bollys.*
Hiker's hip pocket Guide to Mendocino Coast-1992   11.95
Hiker's hip pocket Guide to Humboldt Coast   11.95
Hiker's hip pocket Guide to Sonoma County-1992   12.95
Boxed Gift Set: Mendo. Coast, Humboldt, Sonoma   34.85
A Tour of Mendocino: 32 Historic Buildings   4.95
Coast Walks *McKinney. 100 hikes on the CA coast* 10.95
California Coastal Access Guide, 3rd edition   15.95
CA Coastal Resource Guide *Companion to above*   15.95
Northern California Atlas & Gazetteer *Book of topo maps for entire north half of state (Gilroy north)*   12.95

MAPS

Trails of the Lost Coast *King Range & Sinkyone*   3.95
California's North Coast Recreation Map *North   3.95
  of Arcata*   waterproof   6.95
Trinity Alps Wilderness Hiking Map & Guide   2.95
Lassen Volcanic National Park Hiking Map & Guide   2.95
                                  waterproof   5.95
We have topographic maps. Write for information.

NATURAL HISTORY

Plants of Coast Redwood Region *210 color photos*   14.95
Pocket Flora of the Redwood Forest *Becking*   15.95
Shore Wildflowers of CA, OR and WA *Munz*   10.95
California Spring Wildflowers *Munz*   8.95
Pacific Coast Tree Finder, Bird Finder, Fern Finder, Berry Finder, Pacific Intertidal Life, Redwood Region Flower Finder   2.00ea

HOW TO ORDER: For shipping to CA address, please add 7.25% tax.

Orders under $15, add $1 shipping. Over $15, add $2. Send check or money order:

BORED FEET
P.O. BOX 1832
MENDOCINO, CA 95460
(707)964-6629

PRICES SUBJECT TO CHANGE WITHOUT NOTICE